SCHOOL
RIGHTS

A PARENT'S
LEGAL HANDBOOK
AND ACTION GUIDE

THOMAS CONDON AND PATRICIA WOLFF

Macmillan • USA

To John, Alyssa, and Samantha Wolff, and Clare and Jack Condon, whose experiences and adventures were the motivation for this book.

MACMILLAN
A Simon & Schuster Macmillan Company
1633 Broadway
New York, NY 10019

A catalogue record is available from the Library of Congress
ISBN 0-02-075890-1

10 9 8 7 6 5 4 3 2 1

Printed in the United States of America

Acknowledgments

We couldn't have prepared this book without the help of scores of educators, advocates, parents, lawyers, and public officials across the country. Two of the most important were our spouses. Anne Condon researched the chapter on school buses, and made countless improvements to the text. Rick Wolff contributed greatly to our understanding of coaching and sports issues. Special thanks must go to Attorney Thomas B. Mooney, one of the country's top education lawyers and an instructor in education law at the University of Connecticut School of Law, who generously shared his encyclopedic knowledge, clarity of thought, and genuine enthusiasm for the workings of public schools. Thanks must also go to Attorney Hollace Brooks of the University of Connecticut law school's legal clinic, whose considerable expertise in special education issues was invaluable. Finally, thanks to friend and colleague Robert Frahm, president of the Education Writers Association, for his help in identifying the leading authorities in many educational specialties.

Contents

Introduction

In 1973 a group of educators and other interested citizens looked at a decade-long decline in test scores in America's public schools and decided something was missing from those schools.

Parents.

They formed the National Committee for Citizens in Education (NCCE) in Washington, D.C., to help increase the role of parents in the country's public schools.

"We were looked on as pariahs, or worse," recalled NCCE official Susan Hall. That was the era when parents were cookie machines. They were supposed to stock bake sales, attend basketball games and otherwise butt out.

After 20 years, NCCE merged with the Center for Law and Education in 1994. But the people who started NCCE were right on the mark. As more than a hundred studies now show, parental involvement is the single most important factor in a child's academic success.

Parents provide what University of Chicago sociologist James S. Colemen calls "social capital," that is, "the attention and involvement of adults in children's learning."

The message is getting around; we seem to be at the beginning of a revolution of parental involvement. Across the country, efforts have been undertaken to improve schools from within:

- Hundreds of schools around the country have embraced the "Comer method," developed by renowned Yale University child psychiatrist James P. Comer, in which parents become partners with teachers, principals and counselors in the running of schools. Where necessary, parents are trained to guide their children's education.

- Parents are gaining power as members of school councils in cities such as Cleveland, Chicago and Indianapolis. At nearly every one of Chicago's 600-plus public schools, a half-dozen parents are elected to the local school council, the policy-making board for each school.

- Since 1989 the Home and School Institute has trained thousands of parents in the techniques developed by Dorothy Rich and explained in her book *Megaskills*. Rich offers numerous planned activities, or "recipes," in which parents reinforce what their children are learning in school.

- Also in 1989, a group of two dozen parents banded together to stop middle-class flight from the public schools in Jackson, Mississippi. They restored racial and economic balance to the Jackson schools, and did it so well that the group, called Parents for Public Schools, now has more than 3,500 members across the country.

- The Bailey School in Lowell, Massachusetts, set aside a room in the school building for programs for parents in 1992. The room, called the family center, has been the site of parental programs in stress management, self-esteem, homework and discipline, as well as English classes for minority-language parents. Many other schools around the country are developing similar programs.

- The Memphis Parent Training program, which stresses leadership, advocacy, school governance and personal development for parents, has more than 3,000 parents registered in ongoing classes and 37,000 parents involved in at least one program activity.

The list goes on; the implication is obvious. Parents are making themselves an integral part of the nation's schools. Parents are helping in classrooms, rebuilding libraries, running mentoring and public-speaking programs, even helping to restore deteriorating buildings. Parents are fighting for adequate school budgets, an increasing challenge with barely a third of the nation's families having school-age children, a postwar low.

More importantly, parents are taking a larger role in guiding their children's education.

Most Americans haven't abandoned public schools: 89 to 90 percent of the nation's children attend them. But today's parents want to know what's going on, and they want a voice in their children's education.

We believe this book will help parents help their children. It outlines the legal rights of a public school parent, and tells parents how to use these rights to help their children get the best possible public school education.

We'll look at dozens of practical issues and questions, such as:

- When does your child have to start school?
- Is it legal to educate your child at home?
- Can you choose your child's school? Teacher?
- What are your rights at the school board meeting?
- How do you make sure your child's school bus is safe?
- How can you examine your child's curriculum?
- What do you do if your child has an incompetent teacher?
- What are your rights if your child is gifted and talented? Or learning disabled?
- Can you sue if your child is injured in school?
- What is the school's responsibility for your child's health?
- What if your child's school building doesn't meet building code?
- Can you examine your child's records?
- What if your child is sexually harassed at school?

While we will discuss legal precedents and discuss parents' legal rights, we don't intend the book to be a handbook on how to sue. Lawsuits are expensive and take ungodly amounts of time. And after all that time and money, you can still lose. Actually, you can do worse than lose. In a recent New York case, a woman brought a suit claiming her son was unjustly kept out of the National Honor Society. The judge thought the suit frivolous, and socked the woman with $60,000 in court costs. A Virginia couple brought a legal action against a special education teacher, claiming the teacher was abusive. The teacher came right back and sued the couple for defamation of character.

So while thousands of lawsuits have been filed over education questions, legal action should be a last resort.

In many situations, just knowing your legal rights can prevent lawsuit-sized problems. For example, let's say there's a problem teacher at your child's school. Activist parents would know they had a right to visit the school, and so would likely discover the problem well before the school year started. They could then request their child not be placed in this teacher's class. The principal doesn't have to grant this request, but many do. Most educators want to do the right thing, and most want to avoid legal action. Indeed, good educators are thrilled when parents are interested.

Activist parents know how to effect change at the school board level. In Hamden, Massachusetts, school officials split the town in half and sent the children on one side to morning kindergarten and the other half to afternoon kindergarten. Lynn Champion Schmidt's son was assigned to the afternoon sessions, but he still took an afternoon nap. Lynn Schmidt thought the fairer method would be to switch at the half year. She found some other parents who felt the same way. This is always a helpful first step. There is strength in numbers, and a larger group assuages the fear some parents have that school officials will somehow retaliate against their child if they speak up.

Schmidt and her little band then called the bus company, and learned that changing the morning and afternoon groups would incur no additional expense. They then went to the next meeting of the school committee, as the school board is called in Massachusetts, and asked for the change.

The committee didn't know what to say. They had always done it the old way, but no one could remember why. Because they couldn't come up with a reason not to make the change, and an articulate group of parents wanted it, they voted unanimously to make it. Schmidt won, and people like her win every day.

The key to this small victory was that Schmidt, who also happens to be a teacher, understood that school board meetings are public forums. This is one of the basics for all parents, so let's take a closer look at it.

For years, many school boards were in the habit of sneaking off to quiet locations such as the back rooms of restaurants to make key decisions. They don't do it anymore—or at least they aren't supposed to. Every state now has a "sunshine law," "open meeting law" or "freedom of information act" that requires school boards to hold public meetings. Board members are supposed to make their decisions at these public meetings. In all but a few states, board actions can be nullified if board members don't follow the law.

The sunshine laws differ from state to state, and sometimes local laws are more stringent than the state's law. A few years ago, Nancy Berla and Susan Hall of the National Committee for Citizens in Education wrote *Beyond the Open Door* (NCCE 1989), a book about citizen access to local school boards. They assembled what they consider the best elements of a sunshine law. If your law differs in any substantive way, you or your parents group should contact local and state officials to change it. The ideal law should call for:

- *Meetings open to the public.* These should include meetings of the board and all official committees and subcommittees. Electronic meetings must also be open to public scrutiny. Signing up should be voluntary and no one should have to identify himself or herself as a precondition to attending the meeting.

- *Adequate public notice.* Meeting schedules should be set annually, with the schedule made public. A second notice of each meeting should be published three to seven days before the meeting. Notice of all meetings should include date, time, place and agenda.

- *Convenient meetings.* Meetings must be held at times and places convenient to a majority of the public who might want to attend.

- *Citizen participation.* Subject to reasonable time limits, citizens should be able to participate at the beginning and end of each meeting and ask questions about agenda items.

- *Minutes.* Detailed minutes of each board and committee meeting should be available within 15 days of the meeting. The minutes should include all salient points of the meeting: date, time, place, those present, issues discussed, actions taken. Abbreviated minutes of executive sessions should also be made available.

- *Limited closed or "executive" sessions.* Executive sessions should be called only by formal motion and two-thirds vote of board members, and only for specific and limited reasons. Those reasons should be limited to personnel matters, real estate dealings, pending litigation, and student discipline if requested by the student or his representative. No votes should be taken in executive session.

- *Penalties for violation.* Actions taken in violation of the law should be voidable by the court. Suit should be filed within three months of the action or the discovery that it was illegal. If the suit is upheld, the board should pay court costs and reasonable lawyers' fees. If the suit is found to be frivolous, the plaintiff may be responsible for court costs.

Berla and Hall recommend that parents determine if their state law is being followed, identify the necessary standards and procedures that aren't addressed by state law and local policy, and make recommendations to change them. In other words, if you don't have an ideal law, work for one. Contact your local state legislator or the chairperson of your legislature's education committee. If you make a good case, this isn't a hard sell. Legislators like to take the side of parents. You can also make the same pitch to your city council or county board of governors. Parents who have had to fight a recalcitrant school board can tell you that it is worth the trouble.

As an activist parent you can face and solve many different problems. Parental advocate Jill Bloom suggests a seven-step process for parental advocacy:

- Pick a problem with finite limits.
- Get all the information and gather it carefully.
- Decide on the most appropriate course of action.

- Create a coalition involving the broadest possible base.
- Put everything in writing.
- Develop effective advocacy strategies geared toward desired goals.
- Monitor the results carefully.

Parental activism takes many forms. The majority of problems are solved by a simple phone call to the teacher or principal. When an individual parent can't make a change, a group of parents often can. Sometimes parents organize around a single issue. They call a meeting, give themselves a name, do their homework, and make their case.

In the early 1970s a group of parents in Philadelphia formed the Parents Union to fight a teacher strike. The group stayed together, and now has more than 2,000 members. They are involved in virtually every aspect of local education, from training parents of special education students to negotiating contracts and removing inept school officials.

If your school has no parents group, organize one. Elizabeth Byrnes of the National PTA offers the following tips:

1. Notify all interested parents and teachers and administrators, and put a notice in your local paper. Make personal calls. Form a planning committee with interested parties and hold a planning meeting.

2. Appoint a chairman and secretary, and organize temporary committees for by-laws, nominations, publicity and hospitality.

3. You may contact your state PTA coordinator for assistance. To get the name of your coordinator, call the National PTA in Chicago at 312–670–6782. You may chose not to affiliate with the PTA; that is up to you.

4. Call an organizational meeting. Again, put an ad in the newspaper and make personal phone calls. Find out who is willing to be nominated for office. Prepare a proposed set of by-laws.

5. At the meeting, move to organize the group. Distribute the by-laws. Enroll members. Ask for nominations from the floor for new officers. Install the new officers. The new president then takes the floor, and opens the meeting for new business. You have a parents group.

Whether the group is called the Parents Union, the Parent-Teacher Organization or anything else, it can become a force for positive change. When a group of parents cannot sway the school board, they may do what a group of Jacksonville, Florida, parents did, and run their own candidates for the board. In each of the areas we discuss in the book, we'll suggest means of possible parental action.

This is a tumultuous time in American public education. Widespread dissatisfaction has led to calls for across-the-board reforms, everything from school-based management to private management of public schools. It's vitally important that parents be part of this process. In the "Goals 2000: Educate America Act" signed by President Clinton in March 1994, "parental participation" in "the social, emotional and academic growth of children" became one of the eight National Education Goals for the year 2000.

Parental involvement is now the law. It may not be easy for us parents to walk in that school door and get involved, because that isn't how the game was played when we went to school. But it is now. Parents who don't get involved take a risk that their children won't get the best their school has to offer. Being good school parents is the best way to ensure our children will be good school students.

Tom Condon   Patricia Wolff

STARTING
SCHOOL

◆ INTRODUCTION ◆

Janice looked at Marian, her daughter, as the child did a chalk drawing on the driveway. Marian was bright and outgoing, but often didn't do what she was told. She seemed not to hear whenever Janice wanted her to do something she didn't want to do. Marian was a September baby, and would turn five years old in the fall. Her mother's dilemma was whether the child should start kindergarten.

Was she mature enough? Would she get along with the other children? Would she take direction from the teacher? Would Marian end up having to repeat kindergarten?

Janice wondered if she should hold Marian back for a year. She even wondered if she should try to educate the child herself, at home.

School is no different from most other ventures in life: one of the hardest parts is getting started. Parents face a host of issues and questions when their children are about to start school, including:

- Must the government provide a certain standard of education for my child?
- Do I have to send my child to school? To public school?

- *Can I choose my child's school?*
- *At what age does my child have to start school?*
- *Can I educate my child at home?*

✦ DISCUSSION ✦

To understand the public schools of today, it's helpful to take a brief look at where they came from.

The folks who passed our country's first public education law, in the Massachusetts Colony in 1647, had one goal in mind—to battle the devil. The law was called the "Old Deluder Satan Act." It aimed to educate young people so that Satan couldn't keep them from knowledge of the scriptures and also so that "learning may not be buried in the graves of our forefathers."[1]

The law ordered villages of more than 50 households to hire teachers to teach reading and writing, and towns of more than 100 households to create grammar schools.

Other colonies copied the Satan law. Thomas Jefferson proposed a Virginia law that would have given scholarships to the College of William and Mary to the brightest of poor children who attended a system of public schools he proposed.[2] The idea wasn't adopted; Jefferson was, as usual, ahead of his time.

The public schools created by the Satan law and its progeny were a start, but they weren't a paradigm of excellence. The children of the wealthy often went to private schools, and the public schools struggled by as best they could. Teachers in the early 19th century needed no qualifications except literacy and a letter from a minister attesting to good character. In many communities, children from ages 4 to 16 were in one-room schoolhouses together.

It wasn't until the 1820s and 1830s that reformers such as Horace Mann of Massachusetts created the "common school"—a publicly funded, publicly controlled school for all the children of a community.

Hordes of youngsters didn't immediately flock to these schools; the majority stayed away. Some parents couldn't get over the idea that their children weren't their property, to be sent to the factory or mine at the age of 8 or 9. Others couldn't live with Mann's idea that the common schools should be nonsectarian. Did he think Satan was slacking off?

It took another generation and compulsory education laws to get most of America's children to school. And while it may be tattered and torn, Mann's dream of public schools for rich and poor alike still lives.

Public schools developed state by state. They are still primarily governed by state law, and run by local boards of education. Recent years have brought some new federal laws on education, in areas such as special education and equal funding of female sports programs, but most legal questions involving schools are still resolved in state courts.

By the same token, there is no *right* to an education granted by the U.S. Constitution. The word "education" doesn't appear in the Constitution.

It looked like the court would create a constitutional right to an education in the famous *Brown* v. *Board of Education* case in 1954, which struck down racial segregation of schools. The court said education was "perhaps the most important function of state and local government,"[3] and it said black children had the right to go to school with white children. But the court never said that children, black or white, had the right to go to school at all.

In 1975, in a case involving a Columbus, Ohio, youngster who claimed he'd been wrongfully expelled from school, the court said a child had a "property interest"[4] in his education, meaning the education was a benefit to which citizens are entitled, and one that shouldn't be taken away without due process. (This is why there must be some kind of hearing before a student is suspended or expelled.)

Although it's not in the U.S. Constitution, there is a constitutional right to an education; it's in each state constitution. Each state grants its citizens the right to a public education. But this right is not absolute; serious misconduct can still get you expelled, as many judges have taken pains to point out.[5] There are, as we shall see, other limitations on the right to an education.

Each state also has compulsory education laws. These laws create both a right and a responsibility. They mean your child has the right to go to school, and you have the legal responsibility to send the child to school, from age 6 or 7 to age 14–18, depending on the state.

On the other hand, compulsory education laws do not mean parents must send their child to public schools. This question was litigated in the 1920s, over an Oregon compulsory education law, which in fact required attendance at public schools. An order of nuns and others who ran private schools filed suit. The court agreed that children could be educated at private or parochial schools, saying not to allow such schooling would unduly interfere with parents' rights to guide their children.[6]

As most parents doubtlessly realize, the law makes your first decision for you. You have to send your child to either a public school or an approved private or parochial school, or educate the child at home under a state-approved home school plan. The government's responsibility is to provide the public school. The next step is to decide which is best for your child.

WHICH SCHOOL TO CHOOSE?

A parent can always choose to send a child to a private or parochial school. Choices in public schools are more limited, but are growing.

Most children still have to attend the public school in the district in which they live with their parents. Residence means where the parents are and where they intend to remain. As a rule, parents can't send a child to live with another relative in another school district, just so the child can attend school in that district.

This isn't a problem for families who live in districts with good schools. It unfortunately becomes a problem for youngsters trying to escape districts with weak schools, or sometimes for youngsters who have left their families, for one reason or another.

To take a fairly typical example, a girl named Johnnie Mae Turner moved from her parents' home in Chicago to live with her brother in the town of North Chicago and attend high school there. She wasn't accepted as a tuition-free student on the basis that her real residence was Chicago, and the court upheld the decision.[7] She finished the year as a tuition-paying student—many districts allow out-of-towners to come and pay tuition if space is available—and then moved back with her parents in Chicago.

However, courts have held that if denial of free schooling would mean the youngster wouldn't get any schooling at all, then they may be eligible. This has sometimes come up in cases involving the children of illegal aliens[8] or children no longer living with their parents.

In a recent case, a 15-year-old in Texas who couldn't get along with her mother moved out and moved in with her boyfriend's parents, in the same school district. This was OK with everyone involved, except for one thing. Under school regulations, she couldn't go to school unless she lived with her parents. The court said enforcing such a law would create a class of kids who weren't eligible to go to school. This, the court said, was wrong and against state law.[9] Parents who are divorced but have joint custody of their child can choose which school the child attends by choosing which parent the child lives with.

But while courts usually have not allowed youngsters to leave their neighborhood schools, legislators are showing increased interest in the idea.

"School choice" is all the rage among many politicos and some educators. Presidents Ronald Reagan and George Bush, among others, pushed for a "voucher" program, in which parents would be given vouchers for tuition payments that could be used at any public or private school.

The idea is that vouchers will create competition among schools, forcing them to improve to survive. Opponents say such a plan will drain money away from the public schools and cause their demise. It's still too early to tell who is right.

Despite the support of two Republican presidents, reluctance by Democrats in Congress to use public funds for private schools has thus far doomed federal voucher programs. However, several states have passed school choice plans in recent years. In Minnesota, where the first choice program was passed in 1985, students can attend schools outside their district as long as the receiving school has room and the move doesn't adversely affect racial desegregation. Some states, such as Massachusetts, give communities the option of accepting transfer students from other districts. This hasn't been an overwhelming success, only about a fourth of the Bay State's school districts participate.

For years, 80 Vermont towns that don't have high schools have paid full tuition for their youngsters who want to attend any public high school in the state, and partial tuition for private schools.

One of the most radical new choice programs was started in 1990 in Milwaukee, where youngsters whose families are within 175 percent of the poverty line can get vouchers to attend any nonsectarian private school in the city. The experiment has been upheld by the Wisconsin Supreme Court. The court noted that 80 percent of welfare recipients and 75 percent of the prison population were school dropouts, and said educators should "give choice a chance" to see if it would improve the graduation rate.[10]

By 1995–96 there were about 1,000 youngsters participating in a dozen schools. The Wisconsin legislature voted to expand the program to schools with religious affiliation. This expansion was promptly challenged in court, where it remained in early 1996. Although it's too early to make a definitive assessment of the program, supporters say it has made a couple of resounding points. Parents love it. The level of involvement on the part of the parents of the youngsters in the program has increased significantly. Also, the program isn't "creaming" the best students. Opponents of the choice experiment feared it would attract the best students away from the public schools. Several observers say that hasn't happened. The students doing well in public schools, usually those who had gotten into the best specialty or magnet public schools, stayed. By and large, parents of students who weren't doing well, for whatever reason, took the vouchers and made the change. While there's some dispute over whether the experiment has resulted in higher test scores, proponents say the "choice" children are graduating from high school at a considerably higher rate. In 1995 the Ohio legislature initiated a choice program for Cleveland that is similar to Milwaukee's.

Boston, after years of forced busing to achieve racial integration, now has a "controlled choice" program, in essence a lottery in which parents and students send in a list of their preferred schools and hope to get into them. Neighborhood location, racial quota and available space are all factored into the program, the success of which is still uncertain. But an older Hub City program METCO, in which 3,000 city youngsters are bused to 30 suburban communities, is considered successful.

New York City, which has had pockets of choice for several years, is starting a city-wide choice program. Results thus far are mixed. Some parents say the commitment and resources aren't there; that there are too few seats in too few good schools. But a choice program in an impoverished East Harlem district resulted in such dramatic improvements at some schools that the program has become a national model.

In 1973 School District Four was the worst-performing of all of New York's 32 school districts. The district was attempting to educate 15,000 students, but only 16 percent were reading at grade level. Dropout and truancy rates were among the worst in the country. But by 1987, 63 percent of the district's youngsters were reading at grade level and the district's test scores had risen from 32nd to 15th in the city.

This remarkable turnabout took place because some gifted educators—and parents—built a network of more than two dozen small, alternative schools, either offering new and progressive teaching methods or a specialized curriculum. Parents could choose which to send their children to, and thousands did. For an excellent account of the experiment, see *Miracle in East Harlem—The Fight for Choice in Public Education* by Seymour Fliegel with James Macguire (Times Books, Random House).

One city in which choice appears to work is Omaha, Nebraska, where the city's seven public high schools have to compete for students, and do so vigorously, with new programs and services. Other cities aren't as enthusiastic. Sometimes choice is meaningless because funding inequities make it difficult for urban schools to compete. Often, urban districts don't afford many choices. It's still not clear that private schools will take youngsters with special needs. Sometimes parents don't choose the best academic program, opting instead for a different program, or a school closer to home, or a school they believe is safer.

School choice can also involve different kinds of schools, such as:

- *Magnet schools*, which are said to "draw students like a magnet" from within or even outside the district by offering specialty courses in such fields as the arts, computers, science, or languages.

- *Charter schools*, which are semi-autonomous public schools freed from most rules and regulations in return for a commitment to meet specific performance goals. Such schools, now allowed by law in 20 states, typically involve a contract between a group that manages the school and a group that sponsors or oversees it. Charter schools can be run by teachers, parents, a college, a theater or museum staff, a labor union, or almost anyone else. They can be sponsored by local or state school officials, universities, or a government agency.

    The contract or charter is a legal agreement that sets standards and expectations for the school. In most charter states, the school manages its own budget, is free from local board supervision, and is allowed to hire a certain percentage of noncertified teachers. If the school fails, as has happened a few times, the charter can be revoked. The charter movement has led to some interesting innovations around the country. In Wilmington, Delaware, five corporations and a hospital have joined forces to operate a new high school emphasizing science and mathematics. The U.S. Drug Enforcement Administration is creating a school for 200 at-risk urban youth in Detroit. Boston University runs a school for homeless children.

- *Privately run public schools*, which have become an option in some communities. A private company, The Edison Project, runs schools in four cities, and plans to take over several more in the 1996–97 school year. A private entity called The Public Strategies Group replaced the superintendent of schools in Minneapolis. Little Alternative Public Schools, Inc., runs a school in Wilkinsburg, Pennsylvania. A number of school systems have contracted with Berlitz to handle language instruction. These experiments haven't all been successful. Educational Alternatives, Inc., of Minneapolis, ran public schools in Florida, Maryland, and

Connecticut, but by early 1996 had lost those contracts and faced an uncertain future.

The private companies claim they can run better schools more efficiently than most school boards can, a claim hotly contested by teachers unions and some others. It's too early to tell who is right.

◆ ACTION STEPS ◆

A parent's goal in choosing a school is to find as good a match as possible between the child and the school. "You want a match between your child's temperament, ability and interests, and what is available at the school," said Barbara Bowman of the Erikson Institute of Chicago, a well-respected graduate program in child development.

Parents should first find out what is out there. They should speak with school administrators, teachers and other parents to find out what schools are available in their town or district. Call private schools, if just for information. If there is a school choice experiment going on, parents should monitor it. If it works, as the Omaha program seems to, it may be a good choice. The point is to get as much information as possible.

SchoolMatch, of Westerville, Ohio, is a private company that helps select schools for corporate and private clients. They pick schools for children of executives of 370 of the nation's largest corporations when these families are being transferred.

Steven Sundre, executive vice-president of SchoolMatch, recommends that parents do not take the word of neighbors or fellow workers as gospel about a school. Listen, but remember these are subjective impressions. Try to get as much factual information as you can.

After you have found what schools are available, visit the schools. "Focus on the visibility of the administrator. Do students cheerfully come up and greet the administrator?" If so, that's usually a sign the school is running well, Sundre said.

He also said to get a sense of the level of parental involvement. The more the better. Finally, he said, compare academic performance.

When SchoolMatch analysts compare schools, said Sundre, they look at four main categories:

- *Academic rigor.* They compare tests and other indicators of student performance. They ask what statewide or district-wide achievement tests are given, and then they ask for the results.
- *Size.* They look at the size of the system, the building and the classrooms. This, said Sundry, is particularly helpful when a student is transferring. Moving a child from one school to another is easier if the schools are roughly the same size, he said.
- *Money.* They compare such things as per-pupil expenditure, commitment to library and other facilities, and financial commitment to instructional programs.
- *Demographics.* They look at such factors as value of the tax base, percentage of families with children in schools and other factors that may affect a community's commitment to its schools.

The Parents Union of Philadelphia suggests school visits, particularly for parents of prospective kindergartners. They recommend that parents examine how safe the school is, and look at such things as how dismissal is monitored and whether children walk with buddies. Parents should also check the classrooms and bathrooms to see if they are clean and neat.

Also, parents should talk with a teacher, and ask about school procedures for such things as inclement weather, sending children home and leaving school early. If there are procedures and they make sense, that's another sign the school is well run.

For another approach to selecting a school, the National Association for the Education of Young Children has a brochure titled *Good Teaching Practices for Older Preschoolers and Kindergartners* that offers a comparative checklist of appropriate and inappropriate teaching practices.

The brochure emphasizes open, positive, developmentally appropriate teaching, and can be had by calling 1–800–424–2460.

WHEN TO START SCHOOL

For parents of 4-, 5-, and 6-year-olds, the question is when to start kindergarten. This is an area in which experts disagree vehemently.

The law varies from state to state. Children are eligible to start kindergarten if they turn 5 anywhere between July 1 and December 31, depending on the state (some districts also allow 4-year-olds into kindergarten if they pass the readiness test). However, children don't have to start when they turn 5. Parents have the right to hold them back for a year, a practice parents are beginning to call "red-shirting" from the sports term. Remember that compulsory education laws don't kick in until a child is 6 or 7, so legally, a 5-year-old doesn't have to go to kindergarten at all (although most do).

The trend in the past two decades has been to hold kids out longer, so that parents of autumn babies would hold their children back a year so they would be a little older and more mature when they started kindergarten. Now, in some parts of the country, parents are keeping "summer babies" out for a year. Is this a good idea?

One of the principal advocates of keeping children back is the Gesell Institute of New Haven, Connecticut. Dr. Louise Bates Ames, one of the founders of the institute, says a child should start school when his or her "behavioral age" is 5, not their chronological age.

She said the behavioral age can be determined by a series of tests developed by the institute and offered by some schools both here and abroad. If chronological age is used, girls shouldn't start unless they turn 5 by September, and boys, who she says develop more slowly, shouldn't start unless they turn 5 by June, she said.

This position is hotly disputed by many other experts, including Bowman of the Erikson Institute. "There's no evidence that waiting does any good, and it may do some harm," she said. "There seems to be a correlation between waiting and high dropout rates, at least in some communities." She said testing young children usually isn't productive, and doesn't predict how quickly children will develop.

Bowman said schools should be ready to accommodate the entire range of differences among 5-year-olds. Unless the 5-year-old has an unusual, handicapping condition such as a sudden emotional problem at home, the child should start kindergarten when the child reaches the appropriate legal age.

Sue Bredekamp of the National Association for the Education of Young Children, the country's largest professional association of early child educators with 90,000 members, agrees.

She said continually moving back the age for kindergarten entry keeps creating another "youngest group," which threatens to reach a point of absurdity. "It doesn't make sense to have kindergarten for older kids. There ought to be a standard date for kindergarten," she said.

Bredekamp said because children develop so quickly, readiness tests given in April cannot reliably predict what a child will do in October. She believes schools must accept children who are age appropriate for kindergarten. However, some schools try to counsel parents into sending their children to other programs, such as pre-kindergarten programs, and the quality of these varies dramatically. According to Bredekamp, if a school is trying to disallow many students from entering kindergarten, the problem is most likely with the school. "Err on the side of sending kids to school," says Bredekamp. "School is for kids. If you suspect there's a problem such as a learning disability, that's all the more reason to get into a school system, where the child can be evaluated," she said.

Bredekamp has an ally in family psychologist John Rosemond. Rosemond says the problem is that much of what used to be taught in first grade has been "pushed down" to kindergarten, particularly reading skills. So what used to be a year of socialization and readiness is now a year of academics that some 5-year-olds may not be ready for.

He thinks the answer is to push the curriculum back up to the first grade and let kids enroll in kindergarten when they reach the legal age to do so.

Rosemond also likes the idea of transitional K-1 programs, for youngsters who aren't ready for the academics of first grade. He said much development and growth, including some catching up, go on in the sixth year of life.

On the other side of the coin, Bowman said there's also no evidence that "pushing" a child to enter kindergarten early does any good. Again, the reason is the unpredictable rate of development of young children. "They don't even stay consistent with their own patterns of development. A slow learner or developer can become a fast one and vice versa."

The different age limits for kindergarten in different places sometimes leads to legal problems. One such case occurred in Pennsylvania. Nathan O'Leary was allowed to enter kindergarten at the age of 4, then wanted to transfer to another kindergarten that had a minimum age limit of 5. He was refused and his family sued. They lost. The court held that since there was no statutory right to kindergarten, and because the 5-year-old limit didn't single out Nathan for discrimination—it applied to everyone—Nathan had to wait until he turned 5.[11]

◆ ACTION STEPS ◆

If you are concerned about whether your child is ready to start kindergarten, you can:

- Talk to your child's nursery school teachers. Tell them your concerns, and ask them how your child compares with other youngsters entering kindergarten that fall.

- See if your school district does preschool screening for school readiness. Go to the screening session if you can, and talk with the educators doing the screening. If there's any indication of the presence of a learning disability, you might want to follow up with testing by a learning specialist in your area.

- See if your district offers a pre-first-grade program. This is where teachers evaluate children after kindergarten and may offer them a transitional year of school before putting them in the first grade.

- Check out the kindergarten programs in your district to see if they are full-day or half-day. A half-day program might not be as academic, but may be less stressful for a younger child. Ask about such things as class size, and how the staff can meet any special needs your child may have.

- Finally, go with your instincts. You know your child better than anyone else.

◆ DISCUSSION ◆

THE HOME SCHOOL ALTERNATIVE

Can you just keep your kids home and teach them yourself? If you have the time, talent and inclination, the answer is yes.

The home school movement in this country has been growing in recent years. According to officials of the Home School Legal Defense Association of Paeonian Springs, Virginia, there are as many as 500,000 youngsters being educated at home, and the number is growing at the rate of 20 percent a year.

Most of the parents of these children are educating them at home for religious reasons. According to one survey, the vast majority of home school parents are born-again Christians. But there seems to be a group of parents who have brought their children home because of perceived or real problems with the public schools. Advocates claim home students do much better than average on standardized tests, and manage to learn social skills from the family environment.

The home school advocates have had to fight through literally hundreds of lawsuits and arrests, and do considerable lobbying to get where they are today, and many claim they are still being harassed with over-regulation.

In many early cases, such as the 1937 case of *Stephens* v. *Bongart*,[12] the court held that school went beyond mere instruction, and included such things as interaction with other children and availability of facilities such as libraries and laboratories that weren't found in the home. Thus, home instruction wasn't the equivalent of public education and wasn't to be allowed.

Home school teachers have often tried to convince courts, with mixed results, that they should be viewed as private schools. The danger in losing was that many parents faced prosecution for criminal truancy for pulling their children out of school.

When Texas home school advocates filed suit a few years ago to make home schooling exempt from the state's compulsory education law, 125 parents had been arrested for violating the law, and about 80 had been convicted.

But the home school forces won and got home school put on the same legal plane as private or parochial schools.[13]

The home school movement, as many educators and more than one judge have pointed out, raises interesting questions. Does a school have to be a red brick building? Is a child supposed to go to school to get an education? How is a child best educated? Will the age of home computers boost home schooling?

If you are interested in home schooling, check your state regulations, because they vary dramatically. Some states, such as Massachusetts, heavily regulate home schools. Others, such as California, don't.

States may require, for example, that parents have bachelor's degrees and are certified teachers, that they teach required subjects for a certain number of days and hours each year, that they submit to home visits and curriculum inspections, and that their children take standardized tests.

Home schoolers and state regulators are involved in scores of lawsuits over these regulations. New Mexico officials brought an action against a woman whose oldest daughter was teaching her younger siblings in a building behind their house. It turned out she met the minimum qualifications for a private school, which involved children being taught in a building not their home by someone not their parent.[14]

Although home schoolers are winning more cases now than they used to, parents clearly still are safer by complying with the law before pulling their children from school. In a recent Ohio case, all the court had to know was that parents kept their child out of school without permission, and the parents were found guilty of "contributing to the unruliness and delinquency of a minor."[15]

Failing to follow required procedures, such as filing reports or having your home-schooled children take standardized tests, can also land you in court.[16] What should be clear from this is that, in most states at least, you can't keep your kids home from schools and just claim you are educating them. You really have to do it.

◆ ACTION STEPS ◆

If you are interested in home schooling, check with your school board. Someone there should be able to provide you with a copy of your state's home school regulations or refer you to someone at your state department of education who can provide the regulations. They may also be able to provide you with the name and address of a home school group in your community or your state. You can also contact the National Center for Home Education (see address at end of chapter) for help in starting a home school program. Also, meet with local school officials, either your district principal or a school board official. Your local district may have a program that supports parents who teach their children at home.

◆ SELECTED QUESTIONS ◆

If there is no choice option available in my district, and I can't afford private school, am I stuck with my local school?

Possibly not. Some districts will allow you to send your child away from your district school for particular programs. Let's say there are two middle schools in your town, Washington and Jefferson. You're in the Washington district, but would like to send your child to Jefferson. See if there's a program only offered at Jefferson, a particular language, perhaps. If your child agrees to take the program, and the board allows the transfer, you're in.

Can a child be withdrawn from public schools for religious reasons?

Obviously, parents can place their children in religious schools, providing the school meets the state's requirements for private schools. Parents can also educate their children at home, provided they follow their state's home-school laws. But in most instances they cannot simply pull their children out of school for religious reasons.

However, the Supreme Court did carve a narrow exception to this principle, for members of the Old Order Amish and Amish Mennonite people of Wisconsin.[17]

Wisconsin's compulsory education law required attendance in school until the age of 16. The Amish wanted their children at home after the eighth grade, to prepare them for lives in the Amish community. The court was often called on to balance one interest against another. Here, it was the free exercise of religion versus the benefits of mandatory education.

The court found that since the Amish were a three-century-old religion and that the community would continue an informal, vocational training that was within the intent if not the letter of the compulsory attendance law, they were exempt from the compulsory attendance law. But the court stressed that the Amish were almost unique in their circumstances, and suggested other groups would be very hard pressed to receive the same treatment.

However, most states allow parents to withdraw their children from individual classes that offend their religious principles. This comes up most often in the sex education area.

If I can't pick a school, can I at least pick the teacher I want?

Usually not, but you can influence the school's decision on which teacher your child gets. Most schools make their own classroom assignments. But that is just the official policy. You have a right—it's the law in more than 30 states, most districts and every school that receives federal Title I funding (nearly all urban districts)—to visit the school and watch classes, subject to reasonable guidelines.

Go, see your child's potential teachers, decide, if you can, which would be the best for your child and then arrange an appointment with the principal. Suggest, don't demand, that your child would be happiest with this particular teacher. The principal may have a counter-argument that makes sense, or may just go along with your suggestion. Principals like to make parents happy. Squeaky wheels get oiled. So squeak up.

What happens when parents are divorced and one wants to home school, and the other doesn't?

If the case gets to court, the judge probably will do what judges do in custody cases, and try to determine what is in the best interest of the child. In a recent case from Kinston, Arkansas, a woman wanted to take her daughter out of school and educate her at home, and the divorced father objected. He said the woman worked three days a week, and that the plan would interfere with his visitation rights. This and other evidence convinced the judge that the child's bests interests were served by remaining in school.[18]

What if a child just doesn't want to learn, and won't go to school?

This is a complicated question, and probably calls for individual or family counseling. In the harshest of circumstances, a child can be brought before a juvenile court judge in most states and ordered to attend school. If he doesn't, he can be subject to penalties for contempt of court such as incarceration in a juvenile detention facility.[19]

If my home is a home school, do I have to follow the building codes for a school, with fire doors, etc.?

This question was recently litigated, and the court said no.[20] If your home is predominately a home, you have to follow the building code for homes. But check state regulations for other requirements of a home school.

Does a school have to be a one-story brick building with square classrooms and rows of desks?

No. A school is a constructed thing; there's no law that it look a certain way or operate in a certain manner. Many educators believe the traditional classroom with a teacher in front of rows of desks was modeled after the factory layouts that were being built as the common schools were being developed.

In the past 25 years, many have suggested different arrangements. Albert Shanker, the New York educator and teacher union leader, has recommended a class that was led by a master teacher, who was surrounded by apprentice teachers and students.[21] This isn't a completely new idea; it is much like the schools of Renaissance artists hundreds of years ago.

I'm a single mother of two living in public housing. What help is available for low-income parents?

A fair amount, depending on where you live. For openers, President Clinton has expanded the Head Start preschool program, one of the top government education programs for low-income youngsters. Your local school board can put you in touch with the Head Start agency in your community.

You may also qualify for free or reduced-price lunch programs, tutoring assistance, out of district education programs or local scholarship programs. Call your school board for details.

I've read that it's necessary for me as a parent to have frequent conferences with my child's teacher. Do I have a legal right to teacher conferences?

In about a third of the states, and in many local districts, you do have a legal right to a minimum number of teacher conferences. But teachers say this is rarely a problem. Most teachers are more than happy to talk about your child's progress with you on a regular basis. The more severe problem, they say, is parents who can't find the time to talk about their child's education. You should call your child's teacher and make arrangements. In some schools, teachers leave voice-mail messages that cover the days homework and principle activities; in others, teachers use computers to publish weekly newsletters for parents.

Our son Adam is biologically ready to start kindergarten in the fall, but he is not socially ready. He doesn't share well with

his friends, can't sit still, is teased often and is easily distracted. We had him tested by a specialist. The specialist said his intelligence was fine, but that his social development was slow, and that he could use another year in nursery school. We're thinking of that, but aren't we admitting that he isn't as bright as other kids? Isn't there a stigma here?

Certainly not. As we've said, experts differ radically on whether children such as Adam should start kindergarten. Remember also that children develop at different rates of speed. It's possible that Adam will spurt in the next few months and be ready for kindergarten, and it's possible that he won't. There's certainly no stigma in looking out for your child's best interests. If you feel his self-esteem will suffer because he isn't grasping ideas as quickly as more intellectually developed (not necessarily smarter!) kids are, then keep him out for another year. You know Adam better than anyone.

My husband and I both work full-time, and we're anxious for our daughter Mary to start kindergarten. We know she's ready. Unfortunately the cutoff is December 1, and her birthday is December 5. Can we get her in anyway?

You can ask, but the district is well within its rights to say no. A few districts offer readiness tests for youngsters born after the cutoff date who want to start kindergarten, but most do not. Most likely, your only option will be private school.

FOR FURTHER INFORMATION

National Association for the Education of Young People
1509 16th Street NW
Washington, DC 20036
202–232–8777 or 1–800–424–2460

Association for Childhood Education International
11501 Georgia Avenue
Wheaton, MD 20902
301–942–2443

Erikson Institute
25 W. Chicago Avenue
Chicago, IL 60610
312–755–2250

Gesell Institute for Human Development
310 Prospect Street
New Haven, CT 06511
203–777–3481

Children's Defense Fund
25 E Street NW
Washington, DC 20001
202–628–8787

National Association of Elementary School Principals
1615 Duke Street
Alexandria, VA 22314
703–684–3345

National Center For Home Education
P.O. Box 125
Paeonian Springs, VA 22129
703–338–7600

SchoolMatch
5027 Pine Creek Drive
Westerville, OH 43081
1–800–992–5323

Institute for Responsive Education (information on charter schools)
605 Commonwealth Avenue
Boston, MA 02215
617–353–3309

NOTES

1. Massachusetts Colony Laws and Statutes, Chapter 88.

2. Alf J. Mapp, Jr., *Thomas Jefferson, A Strange Case of Mistaken Identity* (Madison Books, 1987).

3. *Brown* v. *Board of Education*, 347 U.S. 483, 74 S. Ct. 686 (1954).

4. *Goss* v. *Lopez*, 419 U.S. 565, 95 S. Ct. 729 (1975).

5. *C.L.S. by and through S.S.C.* v. *Hoover Bd. of Education,* 594 So. 2d 138 (Ala. Civ. App. 1991).

6. *Pierce* v. *Society of Sisters,* 268 U.S. 510 (1925).

7. *Turner* v. *Board of Education, North Chicago Community High School District 123,* 294 N.E. 2d 264 Sup. Ct. Ill. (1973).

8. *Plyler* v. *Doe,* 475 U.S. 202, 102 S. Ct. 2382 (1982).

9. *Major* v. *Nederland Independent School District,* 772 F. Supp. 944 (ED Tex. 1991).

10. *Davis* v. *Grover,* 480 N.W. 2d (1992).

11. *O'Leary* v. *Wisecup,* 364 A. 2d 770 (Pa. Cmwth. 1976).

12. *Stephens* v. *Bongart,* 15 N.J. Misc. 80, 189 A. 131 (1937).

13. *Texas Education Agency* v. *Leeper,* 843 S.W. 2d 41 (Tex. App. Ft. Worth 1991).

14. *Strosnider* v. *Strosnider,* 686 P. 2d 981 (NM App. 1984).

15. *State* v. *Wood,* 580 N.E. 2d 484, 63 Ohio App. 3d 855 (1989).

16. *State* v. *Skeel,* 486 N.W. 2d 43 (Iowa 1991).

17. *Wisconsin* v. *Yoder,* 406 U.S. 205 (1972).

18. *Clark* v. *Reiss,* 831 S.W. 2d 622 (Ark. App. 1992).

19. In the Interest of J.E.S., 817 P. 2d 508 (Colo. 1991).

20. *Birst* v. *Sanstead,* 493 N.W. 2d 690 (1992).

21. Albert Shanker, interview with Thomas Condon, March 7, 1987.

TAKING THE SCHOOL BUS

◆ INTRODUCTION ◆

Watching as her kindergarten-age son traded insults with his buddies as he disembarked from his yellow bus, a friend lamented, "All the work and discipline they do at school, and it all goes down the drain while they're riding the bus."

Another friend drives her daughter to school every day, because she simply doesn't trust the school bus.

Are they right? Are school buses little more than rolling free-for-alls? Can parents trust their children to school buses?

If your child is one of the 23 million who climb on a school bus every school day, you and your school parents group should be paying attention to school bus issues. With the economic problems facing many school districts, good bus service can no longer be taken for granted. Some districts are extending the minimum distances they'll bus students, changing schedules to get more mileage out of buses, putting more kids on buses and charging for bus service.

Because your child may well spend hundreds of hours on buses, you should explore the following issues:

- *Are school buses safe?*
- *How can parents be sure drivers are properly trained?*
- *Can bus monitors or other measures or devices make school buses safer?*
- *Can parents get bus schedules changed?*

◆ Discussion ◆

Every school day in the United States, 23 million youngsters board school buses, according to estimates of the National Safety Council. Every year, some 400,000 school buses roll up more than 4.4 billion miles while transporting youngsters to and from school.

Considering the number of miles, accident and injury rates are very low. The National Safety Council reports that during the 1993–94 school year, approximately 11,000 pupils were injured in bus accidents; 45 pupils were killed. Of the youngsters who were killed, only 10 died while riding in buses. The rest were either walking to the bus or away from it; about half of them were struck and killed by their own bus. That's why the so-called "danger zone" is around the bus, not in it.

The relatively low injury rate among bus riders is a testament to the tough standards for school bus construction that have been developed over the past 20 years, both by the private sector and the federal government. Many experts today liken school buses to Sherman tanks. Indeed, when school buses are involved in collisions with automobiles, most often students escape with no injuries or minor cuts and bruises, while the car's driver isn't as lucky. This wasn't always the case; some innovations in bus design were the direct results of tragedies that revealed fundamental flaws in the way buses were built. School bus transportation was born in the rural areas of this country as small, local school districts consolidated into county and regional districts, drawing pupils from much larger geographic areas. Today school buses are used in even the most compact cities.

In 1939 a group of people representing state education departments, local school districts, bus operators and other interested professional organizations met for the first time for a national conference on school bus transportation. That first conference was called to put together a recommended set of standards for school buses carrying 20 or more passengers.[1]

Since then, conferences have been called in 1945, 1948, 1951, 1954, 1959, 1964, 1970, 1980 and every five years since to review recommended standards both for bus construction and operation. The report of the last conference in 1995 is titled, "1995 National Standards for School Buses and Operations." (The report is available through the Missouri Safety Center, Missouri State University, Warrensburg, Missouri 64093, 816–543–4830.)

The recommendations of the national conference have covered aspects of bus construction, from color (National School Bus Yellow) to location of mirrors, turning radius, number and location of emergency exits, the fire block test that must be performed on bus seat upholstery—you name it. The recommendations are used by most states as the basis of their own school bus regulations, although some states modify them, most often to make them more stringent.

The federal government got into the act of regulating school bus construction with the enactment in 1966 of the National Traffic and Motor Vehicle Safety Act. The National Highway Traffic Safety Administration, part of the U.S. Department of Transportation, is charged with promulgating standards, called Federal Motor Vehicle Safety Standards, for all sorts of motor vehicles, including school buses.

Between 1967 and 1973, the federal agency issued 19 safety standards for school buses. In 1977 the agency got tougher and required bus manufacturers to make a number of new changes, including:

- installing stronger, higher-backed and better padded seats
- improving the body strength of buses
- adding mirrors to improve drivers' ability to see dangerous areas around the buses
- establishing the structural strength of buses to withstand rollover-type accidents

- improving the hydraulic brake systems
- providing crash protection to the fuel tank and tank system

The importance of the last change came into focus 11 years later. A pick-up truck plowed into a school bus being used by a church group on an interstate highway in Carrollton, Kentucky, in 1988. The gas tank on the bus exploded. Twenty-seven people in the bus died, 24 children and three adults. The bus was built two weeks before the 1977 requirements went into effect.

The accident and publicity surrounding it accelerated the replacement of pre-1977 school buses. Most of them that are still on the road have been converted from school buses and are being used by church groups and the like, says Paula Hanna, executive director of the National Association for Pupil Transportation, an organization of school officials who oversee school bus transportation. She estimates that only about 5 to 6 percent of the buses used for school transportation around the country were built before the 1977 standards went into effect.

With each passing year, that number continues to decline. Nevertheless, federal authorities have recommended strongly since the Kentucky crash that school districts replace *any* buses built before 1977.

The Kentucky crash pointed up another deficiency in bus construction, one that has only recently been addressed by federal officials. That's the small number of emergency exits required on school buses. A 1989 accident in Alton, Texas, that cost 21 lives underscored the problem, and eventually prompted the federal government to act. A bus, struck by a truck, fell into a water-filled gravel pit. The bus had only one emergency exit, at the rear. The front door was jammed.

Three years later, in 1992, the National Highway Traffic Safety Administration issued a new standard, requiring an additional emergency door on the left side of a typical, 65-passenger school bus. The standard took effect on May 2, 1994, and affects only buses manufactured after that date. As a result, it will be some years before all buses have the extra emergency exit.

Some people think the federal government hasn't gone far enough with the new rule. The standards now call for emergency exits on both sides of the bus and two roof hatches in buses that carry 23 to

65 passengers, and two emergency exits per side and two roof hatches in buses with passenger capacity of 66 or more. In any case, parents should be aware of the recommended standards, and urge school officials to improve their bus fleets if they aren't well equipped for emergency evacuation.

◆ ACTION STEPS ◆

Your parents group should have a transportation committee that works with school officials on busing issues. Also, your school should be represented on a district-wide parents transportation committee that monitors broader bus issues.

As a first step, the committee should find which state agency regulates school bus transportation. Usually, it's the department of education or the department of transportation. The agency should be able to provide you with a copy of the school bus transportation regulations your local district is supposed to adhere to. See if they are being followed.

The committee should immediately find out if the district has any pre-1977 buses in use. If so, the parents should press school and government officials to send these dangerous dinosaurs to the bone yard and replace them.

The committee can also work with school officials to create a school-based bus safety education program. This should include an orientation program each fall, perhaps during National School Bus Safety Week, for young bus riders. The safety program should also include evacuation drills a couple of times a year.

The committee should also encourage parents to "cover" their bus stops, that is, either be there when their children are dropped off or make sure that another adult is there.

THREE CHEERS FOR THE BUS DRIVER

Driving a school bus is a job loaded with liabilities and short on rewards. Any parent who has driven even one unruly child any distance can appreciate the problems inherent in trying to safely deliver eight, or 15, or 60 children to and from school. Driving a school bus

Safety experts suggest parents teach their children these rules and follow this advice in and around buses:

- Arrive at your bus stop early to avoid getting hurt while running to catch the bus. While waiting, don't horse around with other youngsters and stay away from the road.

- As the bus approaches, line up away from the street. Wait until the bus has stopped completely and the door is open before walking toward the bus.

- If you have to cross the street to catch a waiting bus, do so only after the bus has stopped completely and its red lights are flashing and stop arm is extended. Make sure all traffic has stopped, too, before crossing.

- While on the bus, sit in your seat quietly. Loud noise can distract the bus driver. Don't put bookbags or backpacks on the floor where someone might trip on them. Never put arms, hands or head out the bus window.

- Wait until the bus comes to a complete stop before getting up from your seat to get off.

- If you have to cross the street after getting off the bus, take three giant steps away from the bus, then 10 giant steps along the side of the road until you can see the bus driver's face. Cross the street only after the driver has signaled you to walk.

- Before leaving school, store all papers, pencils and other belongings in a backpack. Never stop to retrieve something you've dropped under or near the bus. If you do drop something, tell the bus driver about it. (Parents should assure youngsters that they won't get angry about lost papers or other items misplaced around the bus.)

- Stay away from the rear wheels of the bus at all times.

isn't a job that attracts many enthusiastic candidates, except from the ranks of people with an exceptional love for children, or the desire for a part-time job that can be easily wrapped around another job or homemaking. In short, that's why there is so much turnover in the ranks of bus drivers, and why maintaining a generally high level of driver proficiency is a tough task for school districts.

Nevertheless, probably no factor is as important to school bus safety as the driver's skill. Mechanical problems cause only a fraction of bus accidents; driver error is responsible for the majority of school bus accidents. Consequently, improvements in driver training pays off: The number of accidents in New Jersey fell from 675 to 562 in just three years (1977–80) after the state used federal funds to expand driver training programs.

Screening of applicants for drivers' jobs is critical, too. No parent wants to find out the hard way that the school district hired a driver with a history of substance abuse. The 1990 National Standards for School Buses and Operations recommend that procedures for selecting drivers include:

1. An application form that covers personal and occupational history
2. A check of the applicant's driving record, with criteria established in advance of what is an acceptable driving record and what is unacceptable
3. A criminal background check
4. At least one personal interview
5. A physical examination that includes tests for drug and/or alcohol use and communicable diseases, such as tuberculosis

Many school districts, or the bus companies they hire to transport their students, go even further, with provisions in their employment policies for random, at-will and post-accident checks of drivers for substance abuse.

Drawing up—and enforcing—the requirements for bus driver training is left to state governments, and experts say the extent of training programs varies widely. The only requirement imposed by the federal government is that a driver of a school bus carrying 16 or more people have a commercial driver's license in addition to a state driver's license.

Bill Loshbough, a school transportation consultant based in Austin, Texas, says that 40 hours of pre-employment training for new bus drivers is approximately the industry standard. Recently, the National School Transportation Association (NSTA), based in Springfield, Virginia, whose members are school bus companies, prepared a sample training curriculum for bus drivers. Karen Finkel, the NSTA's executive director, says the sample curriculum was created after the group's safety committee reviewed training programs across the country. It covers the following areas:

- Company (or industry) orientation
- Pre- and post-trip inspections
- Defensive driving techniques
- Passenger loading and unloading procedures
- Special defensive driving techniques, including how to handle loss of traction, skidding, driving at night or in adverse conditions, and tire or vehicle failure
- Emergency procedures
- Passenger management, including how to handle unruly passengers and communicate with students, their parents and the public
- Behind-the-wheel training
- Transporting special-needs children

Also, courts tend to hold school bus drivers to a high standard. In a 1992 Tennessee case, bus drivers could choose where to stop at an intersection. In this case, a first-grader got off the bus, was hit by a car and injured. The court held that the driver must know the direction children are headed when they get off the bus, in order to assure their safety. The driver doesn't have to memorize their addresses, but must know the general direction they normally take when leaving the bus, and then choose the stop area appropriately.[2]

In another remarkable case, a very rowdy teenage boy got off a bus, crossed in front of it, and from the left side of the road dropped his pants and "mooned" the bus driver.

In response to this extreme provocation, the driver pulled the bus out into traffic, initially in the direction of the boy. The driver didn't intend to hit the boy, just get close enough to shout something out the window. But the driver was disciplined for momentarily heading the bus toward the student, and it held up in court.[3]

◆ ACTION STEPS ◆

Your transportation committee should review the hiring and training practices used in your bus operation and see if they meet national and industry standards. These standards should absolutely include pre-employment drug testing and random drug testing during employment. If your district doesn't measure up, the parents organization must begin working with the school board and local legislators, if necessary, to bring the district up to snuff. Some states restrict workplace drug testing, but most make exceptions for jobs such as airline pilots, railroad engineers, bus drivers and other jobs where dereliction could cost lives.

SAFETY MEASURES

THE RHODE ISLAND EXPERIMENT

As the Tennessee case indicates, the most dangerous part of a bus driver's job isn't when the bus is moving in traffic. It's when the bus is starting and stopping. The most dangerous part of any child's bus trip comes as he or she disembarks and heads away from the bus toward home, either by crossing in front of the parked bus or by walking toward the rear wheels of the bus. Getting on can be almost as dangerous, especially if the children are horsing around and not waiting a safe distance from the vehicle.

Indeed, the area around the bus is known to everyone in the school transportation field as the "danger zone." It is where the majority of accidents that cause injury and death to youngsters occurs. Is there a way to cut down on those accidents? Probably. The question, as in every area of transportation, is: How much safety are we willing to pay for?

One state has decided to pay for what has thus far been total safety. Within nine months in 1985, three children were struck and killed by their school buses in Rhode Island. In 1986 the Rhode Island General Assembly voted to require monitors on school buses transporting children in kindergarten through fifth grade. Since monitors began riding buses in the 1986–87 school year and as of this writing, Rhode Island has not had a single child killed or seriously injured outside a school bus.

It was the grief and tenacity of parents who had lost a child and neighbor to a danger-zone accident that led to the passage of the Rhode Island law. Vanessa Pendergast was 6 years old and in the first grade on a rainy day in May 1985 when she was run over and killed by the school bus that had just left her at her stop in Middletown, Rhode Island. The driver had turned around to quiet children who were still on the bus. When he turned back around, he couldn't see that Vanessa was in front of the bus because the hood blocked his view.

The child's mother, Sophia Pendergast, and another concerned parent, Winifred Brady, rallied parents and founded an organization called Families Insisting on Safe Student Transportation (FISST). They galvanized more than 2,000 people across the state to lobby for a set of bus safety bills that included the one mandating monitors. They haven't stopped working, either; they answer requests for advice from parents around the country who are trying to persuade local school boards or state legislators to require bus monitors. (To reach FISST, send a self-addressed, stamped envelope with your letter to: FISST, 2 Maidford River Road, Middletown, Rhode Island 02840.)

Rhode Island's monitor program faces continuous administrative problems, and it costs already strapped school boards a good deal of money—probably between $3 million and $5 million per year, according to Steven Nardelli, who oversees the bus monitor program for the Rhode Island Department of Elementary and Secondary Education. In fact, it is the cost more than any other factor that has deterred many school boards and states from enacting regulations or laws similar to Rhode Island's. A few years ago, the Transportation Research Board of the National Research Council, an independent advisor to the federal government on scientific and technical questions, evaluated the cost effectiveness of various measures to improve school bus safety. The board concluded that "adult monitors on buses offer the smallest safety improvement per dollar invested; for each $1 million spent annually, this measure would save one life, on average, every 50 to 143 years." Money is better spent, the board said, on higher seat backs in buses and programs to teach children bus safety. Of course, such a cost-benefit analysis is usually not persuasive when a child is killed or injured by a bus in your town or city.

Hiring and retaining monitors, who are paid around the minimum wage for only a few hours of work every week, presents many headaches for school districts. Nardelli says many Rhode Island districts employ high school students (the law says monitors must be at least 16 years old), because many districts stagger school hours so that buses can do double duty and transport high school students before doing their elementary-school runs.

Rhode Island has allowed a few districts to use "zone monitors." These are adults at each bus stop who help the driver get the kids on and off the bus safely. They help children cross the street, and they check around the bus when the driver announces over the public address system that the bus is about to leave. The state also allows variances for a few other alternatives, but the vast majority of bus runs in Rhode Island are covered by paid monitors.

Elsewhere across the country, some communities seek out volunteers to work as monitors, either riding buses or overseeing the boarding and unloading of buses at stops. Such an approach, while commendable, isn't foolproof. The number of bus runs and stops in even a small town can mean that hundreds of volunteers are needed. In many places, it is impossible to find enough parents who are able and willing to do such duty. And volunteers usually aren't as reliable as paid monitors.

Despite the cost and administrative headaches, there are compelling arguments for school districts to set up some kind of monitoring program for school buses. In debates over bus monitor legislation in Connecticut, pediatricians laid out for legislators the reasons why even the best bus safety education program won't work on young children. Christine L. Hart, M.D., a member of the American Academy of Pediatrics Section of School Health, wrote to Connecticut legislators in 1993:

"Children under the age of 8 years old are impulsive and easily distractible. Developmentally, they are often incapable of concentrating and judging speed and distance; therefore, educating the children about safety is not enough. They need an adult guide to safely navigate disembarking from the bus and crossing the street."

What's more, said Paul Dworkin, M.D., co-chairman of the government liaison committee of the Connecticut chapter of the American Academy of Pediatrics, "adults consistently overestimate children's street-crossing skills." He referred to the findings of research done by the Harbor View Injury Prevention Center in Seattle. "For example," Dworkin told lawmakers, "parents thought their children would cross at a safe, regulated intersection, rather than an unregulated intersection, much more often than they actually did."

Connecticut has lost, on average, one young child per year to a danger-zone accident for the past 20 years. Nevertheless, legislators have been loathe to lay a requirement for bus monitors on local school districts already crying for relief from state mandates that run up their budgets and residents' taxes, and they failed to pass a monitor law in 1992 and again in 1993.

Advocates of monitor programs point out that children are closely supervised when they're at home and when they're in the classroom, but they take a bus with only one person, the driver, trying to control as many as 65 youngsters at once while he or she operates a heavy vehicle in traffic and in bad weather. Adults monitors do more than reduce injuries and deaths. They can, just by their presence, reduce the amount of horseplay and teasing that occurs on almost every school bus every day. They're also there to help the driver handle emergencies, such as a sick child, a fight between passengers, an accident, or a mechanical breakdown.

THE BLACK BOX AND OTHER GADGETRY

In the absence of bus monitors, many school systems have relied on technology and other gadgetry to make their buses safer and their bus riders better disciplined. Companies that manufacture school buses are always working on design innovations to make buses safer. The costs of such features vary, but you should be aware of what's available in the event your school district is talking about new equipment for buses or new vehicles to add to its fleet. Among the options now available:

Two-way radios or cellular telephones: These allow drivers to stay in touch with their central office and report any problems or emergencies. Such options may have particular appeal in urban and heavily populated areas where there is concern about youngsters carrying concealed handguns or the potential for hold-ups and other crimes at bus stops.

Crossing gates: These are mechanical arms mounted on the front bumpers that swing out when buses are stopped to unload children. The arms, which usually extend automatically when drivers operate doors, stop arms, or warning lights, force children to cross far enough in front of the bus so they remain in the driver's view. A few states mandate that school buses be equipped with arms; more than half allow them as optional equipment.

Video cameras (or The Black Box): Many youngsters now find black boxes mounted in the front of their school buses. Those boxes, with mirrored fronts, are designed to hold video cameras to record the actions of student passengers. The videotape provides evidence administrators need to discipline students who are disruptive—and to have on hand when disbelieving parents argue that their child has been wrongly accused.

The price of video cameras makes it impossible for some districts to install them in every bus. Instead, many districts put the black boxes on every bus, then rotate cameras. Students, unsure whether or not they are being videotaped, are more likely to remain on good behavior. The Bastrop Integrated School District in Texas reported a 65 to 70 percent drop in bus discipline incidents following the installation of video cameras.

Public address systems: Drivers use public address systems to direct students who are outside the bus as the vehicle approaches a stop or gets ready to leave.

Electronic and mechanical sensors: These devices are supposed to detect motion—such as a moving child—in the danger zone and alert drivers with audible or visual signals or both. Many of these are in the developmental stage.

THE SEAT BELT QUESTION

Probably no public awareness campaign has been as successful as the push to make it everyone's habit to buckle up his or her seat belt when getting into a car. And yet seat belts are the exception rather than the rule in school bus transportation.

To advocates of bus seat belts, that makes little sense. Seat belts, they say, would reduce injuries and deaths in the event of accidents, improve discipline on buses (because children would be anchored to their seats), and send a consistent safety message to children, who are accustomed to buckling up when riding in cars. Indeed, a federally commissioned study of nine districts using seat belts found that there was a "carryover effect": Students who rode belt-equipped buses said they used their seat belts more after the bus belts program began. Administrators in the nine school districts that were included in the study also said student behavior improved after buses were equipped with belts. On the other hand, students said their parents, other car companions and mandatory seat belt laws had more of an effect on their use of seat belts in automobiles than school bus belts.

Cost-benefit analyses of seat belt use conclude that the potential benefit of making the belts standard equipment on school buses is not sufficient to justify the considerable investment that would be required. The Transportation Research Board found that if all large buses operated in the United States (those with a gross motor vehicle weight of more than 10,000 pounds, accounting for about 80 percent of the school buses in this country) were equipped with seat belts, one life might be saved and several dozen serious injuries averted each year. But the cost to equip buses with the belts would be more than $40 million per year. The research board noted, however, that some of its members felt that a uniform occupant restraint policy for all motor vehicles was important enough to justify seat belts on buses.

Federal law says that small school buses, such as minivans used for transporting small groups or special needs students, must be equipped with seat belts. But federal regulators have decided that, based on cost-benefit analyses, it's best to leave the seat-belt issue up to states and local districts. They believe that the compartmentalization provided by high seat backs has proven to be sufficient protection in the event of a collision.

Nevertheless, the seat belt issue remains lively in some parts of the country. New York state requires that new buses be equipped with seat belts, although the law leaves it up to school districts to decide if they want to require students to use them. Studies suggest that seat belt use is low, even in the districts that elected to require students to use them. What's more, school districts report that vandalism of the belts is high, making the costs of keeping them in repair a problem.[4]

In 1992 New Jersey became the first state both to require belts as standard equipment on new buses and to make use mandatory. The law's passage culminated a 20-year crusade on the part of one state senator. A few other states have—or are—experimenting with seat belts. Some school districts have bought buses with belts and demanded that students use them. In any case, the seat belt debate appears to have been muted in the past few years because of the other financial pressures facing school districts.

SCHEDULING

Although we have emphasized safety, the most common problem parents have with school transportation is scheduling—when and where their child is picked up or dropped off. When it comes to scheduling, parents have rights. But before marching off to court, parents should be aware that arranging a bus schedule isn't the easiest job in the world.

School bus companies and school transportation officials are involved in a delicate balancing act between safety and economy. If the school bus stopped in front of the home of every child, it would take hours to deliver a full busload of children. It would also add so many miles and manhours to the trip that the cost would be exorbitant.

Officials also have to work within rules and guidelines. Many of these are in the school district's written transportation policy. Others are generally accepted safety guidelines that say, for example, that it's best to discharge students after the bus has made a right-hand turn, rather than before the turn; that there shouldn't be more than 10 students per stop; that buses shouldn't make stops in cul-de-sacs, and that youngsters should not be assigned to bus stops that require them to cross a divided highway.

◆ Action Steps ◆

As we suggested earlier, your parents group should review your district's transportation program. If you determine that safety equipment is needed, the next step is getting the school board to pay for it. Consider a letter writing campaign; it's a way to get a lot of people involved, with reasonable efficiency. Follow these steps:

- Determine who your allies are. These would include parents of children who ride the buses, teachers, and administrators, and possibly community groups that work with youngsters.

- Schedule two meetings, at different times. This allows more people to get there.

- Explain why new equipment is needed, and back it up with research you have done.

- Encourage people to write a personal letter, which generally are more effective than a form letter. However, you may draft a form letter to give them something to work with. In a pinch, make copies of a form letter and ask people to sign them and send them in.

If you have a problem with a bus stop, bring it up either with the head of transportation for the local school district or with the bus company under contract to provide bus service to the district. Most often, they will work with you to find a safe solution.

If you can't reach agreement with transportation officials, you have, in most states, another set of options. You can take the complaint to your local school board. Failing that, you can appeal for a hearing before your state department of education. You may then take a court appeal, if you choose.

Your best chance is at the local level. That's where you present the facts. Should you appeal to a higher authority, they will make judgments based on the facts you presented to the local board. Also, state boards and courts give great deference to local administrators in transportation decisions. To win beyond the local level, you must show that local officials acted in an arbitrary, capricious or unreasonable manner and that you have been aggrieved—you suffered some loss or injury—by their decision. It isn't easy.

For example, a kindergarten boy named Eric Blau of East Hampton, Connecticut, lived on a winding, hilly road with no sidewalk. He was the only school bus passenger on the street. But the school bus wouldn't come up the street. Officials said the bus had nowhere to turn around.

That meant a 6-year-old boy would have to walk down a narrow road with a poor line-of-sight for traffic. Eric's mother, Linda Blau, wouldn't hear of it. She tried to change the ruling. She went to her local board, then the state board, then to Superior Court, then to the Appellate Court, then back to Superior Court again. She had a neighbor sign a statement saying the bus could turn around on his property. She still lost. The courts gave deference to the local board's decision, saying it "wasn't unreasonable."[5]

Linda Blau now drives her children to the bus stop. But the case got her interested in the entire process. She ran for a seat on the board of education, won, and is now in her second term.

◆ SELECTED QUESTIONS ◆

My district is thinking of charging for school bus service. Can they do that? I thought bus service was supposed to be free.

For years, school bus transportation was, in most places, provided free to public school students (and even, in many cities and towns, to private school students) whose homes were far enough from their schools to make the trip on foot onerous. Some districts even bus every child, no matter how short their walk to school, on the thinking that youngsters are safer in a bus than walking along roadsides. The cost of busing was picked up by the local district or even by the state government. Today, however, financial pressures facing most districts have forced many to curb riding privileges for youngsters who could walk, and even to charge parents for the cost, whole or in part, for bus transportation.

The California education code, for example, has long had a provision permitting school districts to charge for home-to-school transportation, although disabled and indigent students must not be assessed. The law was upheld in court despite a challenge from those who said it violated the state constitution, which guarantees free public education. The court said bus transportation is an ancillary benefit and not an integral part of education.[6]

A U.S. Supreme Court decision in a North Dakota case also upheld the right of school districts to charge for bus transportation. A Dickinson, North Dakota, student, Sarita Kadrmas, and her mother challenged a state statute authorizing some school districts to charge a fee for providing bus service.

Kadrmas contended that the state law discriminates on the basis of wealth and violates the Equal Protection Clause of the U.S. Constitution. Their arguments were rejected. The court said, "The Constitution does not require that such service be provided at all, and choosing to offer the service does not entail a constitutional obligation to offer it for free."[7]

Karen Finkel of the National School Transportation Association, whose members are companies that provide bus service to school districts, says some hard-pressed districts are even eliminating bus transportation altogether, or eliminating it for older students.

My son's principal called me today to say that the bus driver said he got into a fist fight on the school bus and that he cannot ride the bus again until I come in for a conference. Can they do this?

You bet they can. Bus transportation is a privilege, not a right, and it can be revoked. The overarching importance of the safety of all youngsters riding the bus outweighs any individual rights. School districts should have policies in writing that spell out what kind of behavior could result in suspension of bus privileges, and what has to be done for those privileges to be restored. Many districts publish booklets outlining safety and behavior guidelines for bus riders and use them in their orientation programs so students understand that breaking the rules could cost them their bus passes.

My daughter attends a special education program in another town. As a result, she spends about two hours a day on a small school bus. Is there anything I can do to see that this time isn't just "dead time" for her?

If your daughter is a special education student, then you are, by law, entitled to be part of a team that develops her Individualized Education Plan, or IEP. This process is discussed at length in Chapter Seven. Be aware that you should make transportation part of the planning process. George Korn is director of special education in a New Hampshire school district and vice president of Safeway Training and Transportation Services, Inc., in Kingston. He recommends that parents of special education youngsters work to get a bus driver who has experience transporting such children and/or a demonstrated sensitivity to their needs. The driver should also have some special training to support students with disabilities, according to Korn. For example, drivers should be able to engage their passengers in games, such as identifying license plates, that can make a long ride less dreary and support some of the youngsters' educational goals. Drivers should also be trained to handle the particular needs and potential emergencies that go along with the physical, mental, or emotional disabilities of their passengers, Korn says.

Secondly, Korn says, parents should see to it that the IEP includes provisions for regular communication among the bus driver, parents and other educators on how the bus ride is going. It may be a separate report, or integrated into the reporting process that is outlined in the IEP. In any case, Korn says, there should be some accountability. Finally, Korn recommends that if a child is going to have a long ride to and from school each day, that there be some goals for the ride included on the IEP that can be reported on as part of the IEP process. Korn also recommends that a special education driver make a visit to the home of every new student to learn from parents about any specific needs or problems.

Our daughter is starting kindergarten this fall, and we're a little nervous about her taking the bus. We're worried she'll be disoriented. Is there anything we can do to get her used to taking the bus?

Yes. Many districts have a "practice ride day" for children such as your daughter. On the designated day, usually a couple of weeks before school starts, you go to your bus stop with your child and ride with your child to the school. You get off, are greeted by a school official, then get back on again and ride back to the stop. If your district doesn't have a practice day, it should. Have your parents group president call the principal in the spring. If the principal cannot arrange the exercise, write to the school board and to the district superintendent.

We just moved to a new house in a cul-de-sac. At our old house, the bus used to stop right outside our door to pick up our daughter. Now they say she has to walk to the end of the cul-de-sac and wait there. Can they do that?

Yes. As we have said, bus schedulers have to balance convenience with expedience and safety. In many areas, school buses aren't even allowed to enter cul-de-sacs.

FOR FURTHER INFORMATION

Families Insisting on Safe Student Transportation
2 Maidford River Road
Middletown, RI 92840

National School Transportation Association
6213 Old Keene Mill Court
Springfield, VA 22152
703–644–0700

U.S. Department of Transportation
National Highway Safety Administration
400 7th Street SW
Washington, DC 20590
292–576–6585

National Safety Council
444 N. Michigan Avenue
Chicago, IL 60611
708–285–1121

National Transportation Safety Board
800 Independence Avenue SW
Washington, DC 20594
202–382–6600

School Bus Manufacturers Institute
7508 Ben Avon Road
Bethesda, MD 20817
301–229–8841

NOTES

1. The Eleventh National Conference on School Transportation, "National Standards for School Buses and National Standards for School Bus Operations" (1991).

2. *Bowers* v. *City of Chattanooga,* 826 SW 2d 427 (1992).

3. *Goss* v. *District School Board of St. John's County,* 601 So. 2d 1232 (1992).

4. Westport (Conn.) School Bus Safety Committee, "Final Report," 1992.

5. *Blau* v. *State Board of Education,* 562 A. 2d 586 (Conn. App. Ct. 1989).

6. *Arcadia Unified School District* v. *State of California,* 2 Cal. 4th 251 (1992).

7. *Kadrmas et. al.* v. *Dickinson Public Schools* et.al., 487 U.S. 450 (1988).

chapter 3

WHAT THEY TEACH

◆ INTRODUCTION ◆

Hundreds of years ago, in the schools of the middle ages, young scholars studied the seven liberal arts. These were divided into the "trivium," the three lower division subjects of grammar, logic and rhetoric, and the "quadrivium," the four upper-division courses of arithmetic, geometry, astronomy, and music.

Fast-forward across many centuries of progress, and we find parents, politicians, and educators battling in the early 1990s on the streets of New York over a curriculum that would teach first graders to respect the gay and lesbian lifestyle.

The debate over New York's "Children of the Rainbow" curriculum—so heated and bitter that it helped bring down the city's school chancellor—proves yet again that Americans have great interest in the educational agenda as a transmitter of learning and values. Power lies in the ability to set that agenda, and we believe parents should share in that power. Curriculum issues parents may face include:

- *Are American children getting enough of the basics?*
- *Can parents force removal of books or classes that offend religious principles?*

- *What can parents do about weak textbooks?*
- *Do bilingual education programs work?*
- *What is the fate of arts and music programs?*

◆ DISCUSSION ◆

In the early 1960s some educational reformers declared that the nation's school curricula hadn't changed enough since the days of the trivium and quadrivium and pushed for new and innovative course offerings.

Many schools did change, offering scores of new courses and alternative modes of teaching. There were alternative schools, schools without classroom walls, schools that let students pick their own books and subjects. Some educators began to argue that schools should teach "self-esteem," as if self-esteem were an academic subject.

After a decade or two of this, many parents and educators felt these reforms had gone too far, that schools had become too permissive and were failing to teach basic subjects.

Indeed, some fairly creative electives had been created around the country, including: The Accomplishments of Leif Eriksson (Illinois), the Political and Economic Contributions of Women (California), Bicycle Safety (Florida), the Worth of Kindness to All Living Creatures (Washington), International Cooking (Maryland) and Consumerism (Wisconsin).

In addition to courses such as these, schools have responded to societal problems with classes on such things as AIDS, sex education and peer mediation/nonviolent dispute resolution. While these classes are admirable and perhaps necessary, critics say they get in the way of a school's main goal of teaching core academic subjects.

In 1982, a year before the landmark study "Nation at Risk" was released, the Educational Testing Service of Princeton, New Jersey, did a survey and found only 2 percent of American high school students completed the "core curriculum" recommended by the National Commission on Excellence in Education, which consists of four years of English, three years each in social studies, science, and math, two years of a foreign language, and one-half year of computer science. Only 13 percent completed a "minimum academic program," the same as the core minus the language and computer courses.

But there's good news. ETS released a study, titled "What Americans Study: Revisited," on June 7, 1994, saying those numbers were up. Analyzing 1990 data, they found that 17 percent of high school students completed the core curriculum and 40 percent finished the minimum academic program.

"We're improving, but we're not doing enough. We're still not nearly where we need to be," said Patte Barth of the Council on Basic Education, a Washington-based public interest group that promotes the teaching of core academic subjects.

"Our elementary schools aren't too bad, although they still don't spend as much time as they should on science and history. But our high schools still have too much other stuff that takes away from time on core subjects."

The curriculum has traditionally been set via broad mandates from the legislature to school districts, who then decide how many hours per day or week should be devoted to what subjects. Your parents group should work with your school on curriculum issues. To see how your school compares to national curriculum standards, you should examine "A Standards Primer," a chart produced by the Council for Basic Education (CBE), at 1319 F Street NW, Suite 900, Washington D.C. 20004–1152. Using a compilation of the best available curriculum materials, CBE created a guide to what children in the 4th, 8th, and 12th grades should know.

Another resource is the "core knowledge curriculum" devised by Prof. E. D. Hirsch of the University of Virginia. Hirsch, author of the best-selling book, *Cultural Literacy*, feels too much time is spent in schools on such things as problem solving, at the expense of factual knowledge. Hirsch isn't against problem solving, but he thinks students need a body of information, the shared knowledge of our culture, to work from. He has created a curriculum that lays out the factual information each child should learn in each subject, for grades K through six.

For example, instead of merely teaching first graders "map skills," Hirsch would insist they know the names of the continents and oceans. Instead of teaching youngsters "about plants," he'd make sure they knew the difference between evergreen and deciduous trees. Hirsch's core knowledge curriculum is being used at about 100 schools around the country, and he says reading scores at most of these schools have improved markedly. Hirsch's curriculum is called "Core Knowledge Scope and Sequence," and can be had by sending $12.50 to the Core Knowledge Foundation, 2012-B Morton Drive, Charlottesville, Virginia 22903, or calling 804–977–7550. If your school doesn't adopt the Hirsch curriculum, it can at least be a resource to help develop teaching goals for each grade.

Also, the National Education Goals Panel is developing a voluntary set of national standards—proponents say they'll be "world class" standards—of what elementary and secondary school children should be taught in 11 disciplines, including English, history, geography, mathematics, science, foreign languages and the arts. By early 1996, all but two of these voluntary standards were completed and submitted to the U.S. Secretary of Education.

By way of background, President Bush convened the nation's governors in Charlottesville, Virginia, in 1989 to address what many believed was a crisis in public education. This "education summit" agreed to set national education goals for the year 2000.

In 1990 six goals were announced. In the next three years, the goals panel was created, the number of goals was raised to eight (see box on page 50) and officials began work on the national education standards, and a means to assess their attainment.

In March of 1994, President Clinton signed the Goals 2000: Educate America Act, which makes the goals a part of federal law, and creates the National Education Standards and Improvement Council to review and certify voluntary state and national education standards.

Some states have already written their own standards, and others are in the process. The "standards movement" is controversial; the standards produced in a few states have been criticized as too mushy and "feel-good," and not academically rigorous enough. The history standards have come under blistering criticism for being too diffuse and emphasizing the important moments in Western Civilization.

Nonetheless, the standards are another resource for parents who are examining their school's curriculum.

◆ ACTION STEPS ◆

Your parents' curriculum committee should compare the CBE, Hirsch, and Goals 2000 standards with what is being taught at your school. Hopefully, this will open a dialogue on the school's curriculum. If the core courses are missing, if for example there is no computer class, the discussion should center on how to start one.

The nature of parental activism will be different depending on the school and the state. In schools using site-based management with parent councils, parents can vote to change the curriculum. In at least two states, Massachusetts and Rhode Island, parents can petition for courses to be taught. If they get enough students to sign up, the school has to offer the course. If nothing else, parent groups can simply ask for new courses. If the request is well researched and has strong backing, it will succeed more often than not.

TIME

How can we teach more core subjects? Barth and many other educators think the answer lies in how schools use time. They feel the country needs a school day that is both longer and differently arranged.

The case for a longer school day was made convincingly in a 1994 report by the National Education Commission on Time and Learning titled, "Prisoners of Time."

The report, which is remarkably readable for a government document, says the "uniform 6-hour day and 180-day school year is the unacknowledged design flaw in American education." Japanese, German, and French youngsters not only spend more days in school than their American counterparts, but they also spend more of each day on core academic subjects. High school students in the U.S. spend an estimated 1,460 hours on core subjects. In Germany, France, and Japan, those hours spent are 3,528, 3,260, and 3,170, respectively.

The authors of "Prisoners" surveyed 42 states and found that U.S. high school students spent an average of 41 percent of their time on core subjects, which include English, math, history, science, civics, foreign languages, arts, and geography. They spend slightly less than three hours a day on these core subjects. For American kids to be competitive, the commission feels the number should be somewhere around 5.5 hours a day.

Julia Anderson, deputy director of the commission on time and learning, says there are a number of experiments being tried around the country to get more time for academic subjects. One obvious method is to clear all the nonacademic classes out of the current six-hour school day and offer them afterward. Thus there would be an academic day, offering only core subjects, followed by another part of the day for driver education, family life, pep rallies, assemblies, tutoring, peer counseling, AIDS education, and other activities.

"There are several models, and each community should look for one that meets its needs," Anderson said. For example, a high school in Alexandria, Virginia, simply added an extra class period, known as "eighth period." Schools in Murfreesboro, Tennessee, are open from 6 A.M. to 7 P.M., in response to a problem with too many "latchkey" children with no place else to go. An elementary school in Albuquerque, New Mexico, operates on a 12-week-on, 15-day-off schedule all year, with enrichment and remedial programs offered during the 15-day break. All are doing quite well, said Anderson.

The lesson is that there is no magic in the rigid schedule of 180 six-hour days. This hide-bound arrangement often leaves slow learners behind and inhibits kids who learn quickly. It often encourages teachers to cover material at an unrealistic pace, to "finish the book" by June. A longer day, and a longer school year, offer the chance for more innovative scheduling, and for new programs and teaching techniques. It would give teachers more preparation and professional time. And for many youngsters, it would give some structure to their after-school time.

Education consultant Connie Muther said the present arrangement in most schools of a new teacher taking over every fall following a 10-week layoff creates considerable downtime. "September through

December is review and makeup. May is a wash. So the only new instruction happens from January through April. More continuity of time and teacher would greatly improve the learning curve."

As a parent, one of the best things you can do to help your child is to simply ask your child's teacher what your child is supposed to learn this year. What is it your child should know at the end of the year, in all subjects, that he or she does not know now? What are the performance goals for the year?

Get a list of them, subject by subject. Then you can tailor your home support to these goals. If your child is learning multiplication, you can practice. If your child is studying penguins, you can plan a trip to an aquarium. In other words, if you know what your child is supposed to be learning, you have a clear idea of what help to offer.

◆ ACTION STEPS ◆

Your parents curriculum group should examine the school's schedule. If you feel that too much of the school day is devoted to nonacademic subjects, you should consider adding a class period to the day and moving nonacademic classes to that period. This usually requires a series of presentations to the school board and negotiations with the teachers union. But that's okay; every parents group in the country should help their administrators look for ways to find more core subject instructional time.

NONSTANDARD CURRICULUM

MONKEY BUSINESS

Perhaps the most heavily publicized curriculum issues in this century have involved efforts by parents and others to make schools lessons conform to religious beliefs. Many of these cases have gone to court. Can religion limit school curriculum?

One of the most notable areas of conflict is the clash between evolution, widely considered the unifying principle of modern biology, and the literally interpreted biblical story of creation. History buffs will recall the famous "Monkey Trial" of the 1920s, when a young teacher named John Scopes was arrested in Dayton, Tennessee, for the crime of teaching Darwin's theory of evolution. Fundamentalists had gotten Tennessee and two other states to pass laws against the teaching of evolution.

The trial—some called it the trial of the century—pitted legendary orator and former presidential candidate William Jennings Bryan against renowned trial lawyer Clarence Darrow, and drew the greatest journalists of the time, such as H. L. Mencken.

Most of us may think the Scopes trial is a historical curio, but it isn't. The issue refuses to go away. In the late 1960s a young Little Rock, Arkansas, biology teacher named Susan Epperson demanded in court that the state's anti-evolution law be held void so she wouldn't be fired or jailed for teaching Darwin's theory that man evolved from a lower order of animals. The case made it to the U.S. Supreme Court in 1969. Justice Abe Fortas noted that the only reason the anti-evolution law was on the books was that it conflicted with the Book of Genesis account of the origin of man, as interpreted by certain fundamentalists.

This was, in effect, a law establishing religion, which is contrary to the First Amendment. Government, he said, must be neutral in matters of religion. It may not be hostile to any religion, but also cannot "aid, foster or promote."[1] any religion, either. Because the Monkey Law promoted a religious theory, it couldn't stand.

That was by no means the end of it. Many Christians began to think the teaching of evolution was a big reason why the country was going to hell in a handbasket. In 1981 Arkansas passed another law ordering the schools to give equal time to evolution and to "creation science," a fancy name for the literal Book of Genesis view of creation.

The court tossed this one out as well. Even though proponents called what they believed "science," the court held that the idea of the universe being suddenly created from nothing was an inherently religious concept, and that "creation science" was another effort to impose a certain religious theory on the youth of the state.[2]

But the issue lives on. In 1992 a California court upheld a school board's right to order a teacher to teach the evolution lessons that were in the curriculum, and not to offer his own creationist views. Students, the court said again, have a right to be free of religious influence or indoctrination in the classroom.[3]

Don't think the fundamentalists have lost. Because of their influence, the coverage of evolution in elementary and high school science texts has been reduced considerably in the past two decades, according to Dr. Gerald Skoog of Texas Tech University and other experts. They've also managed to keep detailed discussions of sex out of many biology books.

BOOK BANNING

Religious fervor has been behind many, if not most, of the efforts to ban textbooks and school library books.

In 1983, in Hawkins County in eastern Tennessee, the school board adopted the Holt, Rinehart & Winston basic reading series as the first- to eighth-grade reading textbooks.

Vicki Frost, a parent from Church Hill and a born-again Christian, read the books and was appalled. The books contained ideas and concepts such as feminism, mental telepathy, evolution and pacifism that offended her religious beliefs.

After some give-and-take with school officials, she and a half-dozen other parents ended up in court. They claimed the offensive materials burdened their right to free exercise of their religion. Frost objected to the students being exposed to the offensive materials. She said certain political themes or issues have theological roots, and that there was "no way" certain themes such as evolution or feminism could be presented without violating her religious beliefs.[4] The case garnered much national publicity; some called it "Scopes II."

A federal judge agreed with Vicki Frost and her fellow plaintiffs, but his decision was reversed on appeal. To accede to her demands would again promote one religious view, the court said, which schools must not do. Also, schools should teach tolerance of divergent religious and political views, something that cannot be done if these views are stricken from the curriculum.

Every year, hundreds of parents around the country challenge the presence of certain books in school libraries.

Sometimes these cases end up in court. A New York school board removed nine books from the school library, including *Slaughterhouse Five* by Kurt Vonnegut and *Soul On Ice* by Eldridge Cleaver. The board said these books were vulgar, immoral, irrelevant, and in bad taste: Hence, inappropriate for high school students.

The case got to the U.S. Supreme Court. The court said the board could use the curriculum to transmit community values, which includes promoting respect for social, moral and political values.

Therefore, if board members really removed the books because they were pervasively vulgar, then they were on solid ground. But if they removed the books to suppress certain ideas they disagreed with, then they went too far, and their actions were unconstitutional.

Did the board conduct a systematic review of all books under objective standards of educational suitability, or of vulgarity? It didn't appear so. They were, in fact, removed because they were put on a hit list developed by a group of conservative parents. The court frowned on such selective censorship, and the parents group lost.[5]

Every year, the American Library Association and other groups put out lists of books being challenged. These often include classics such as Mark Twain's *Huckleberry Finn,* Ken Kesey's *One Flew Over the Cuckoo's Nest,* or even Shakespeare's *The Merchant of Venice.*

Sometimes books are found to be obscene, which means they offend community standards by appealing to the prurient interests of minors, describing sexual conduct in an offensive way and *having no serious literary, artistic, or intellectual value.*

But most of these challenges fail. Happily, most of the books that are challenged remain available in school libraries. Sometimes they are pushed to an upper-grade reading list, or are ordered to be read with parental permission. But it is still a struggle.

◆ ACTION STEPS ◆

If you object to the content of a book, or the material being taught in a class on religious grounds, most states and school districts give you an option. You can usually withdraw your child from the class, or from the portion of the class you find offensive. In the case of offensive books, most schools now offer an alternate reading list, from which you can choose another book. If you are faced with this situation, your school principal should be able to tell you the rules for your district.

Also, at many schools around the country, parents serve on school library acquisition and book evaluation committees. To serve on such a committee, call the head of your parents organization, and ask to be considered. But in determining whether or not to remove a book from the library or reading list, remember the message in the cases we examined. It is that courts view the classroom, like our democratic society as a whole, as a marketplace of ideas, in which all ideas should be considered so the best can be chosen.

If a book, film, or tape is pure gutter trash, the decisions support removal. But if it has some intellectual value, and removing it will constrict or limit the body of knowledge available to students or will promote personal religious views, most courts won't allow it.

GAY AND LESBIAN ISSUES

Along with religion, no subject touches off controversy like the very mention of homosexuality in schools. New York's battle over the Rainbow Curriculum came about after the school chancellor formed an advisory committee on multiculturalism in the late 1980s. It had no representative from the gay and lesbian community, so members of that community protested. They eventually gained representation on the committee, and were able to include a small section on acceptance and respect for their lifestyle in the 443-page curriculum.

Those passages met with substantial protest, notably recommendations that teachers bring the subject up, and that the lessons be offered to first-graders. The chancellor, William Fernandez, revised the curriculum, but didn't still the criticism. One tough, conservative school board in the borough of Queens has adamantly refused to teach anything about the gay and lesbian lifestyle. *The New York Times* calls the whole dispute an "explosive mix of educational philosophy, political calculation, religious principles, clashing moral values, and bureaucratic inattention."

Perhaps more typical has been the controversy in Fairfax County, Virginia. The county has a state-mandated "family life education" program, which teaches youngsters about sexuality and related health matters. The lessons are integrated into other courses, such as biology and physical education. Parents are given the chance to "opt-out," or remove their child from any family life lesson. It is a conservative program that spends only a couple of hours throughout four years of high school discussing homosexuality. Teachers explain that their are people who are homosexual, that they, like heterosexuals, have a risk of sexually transmitted diseases such as AIDS, and that they shouldn't be subjected to bias and stereotyping.

Despite this minimal effort, a small group of conservative Christians has attacked the program at every turn. They hounded a school librarian out of office whose only crime was keeping a gay publication in the library on First Amendment grounds. They went after an administrator who helped develop a national lesson plan on tolerance toward gays and lesbians. The group "has kept our lives miserable for years," said school board spokeswoman Dolores Bohen.

The victims of this kind of intolerance are young people who are gay, or who are conflicted about their sexuality. Advocates say gay and lesbian youth have for years suffered from isolation, ridicule, harassment, family difficulties, and physical assault. They are two to three times more likely to attempt suicide than heterosexual youths.

However, the movement for gay and lesbian civil rights has begun to include children. Massachusetts is probably the leader in this area. The Bay State passed a Gay and Lesbian Civil Rights Bill in 1993, which prohibits any form of discrimination based on sexual orientation. Teachers in Massachusetts must also undergo sensitivity training in dealing with gay and lesbian youth before being certified. In other parts of the country:

- New York has an alternative public high school, The Harvey Milk School, for gay, lesbian, and bisexual youths. It is run by the city and the Hetrick-Martin Institute, an advocacy group for gay and lesbian youth and their families.
- In San Francisco, the school health department has appointed a director of support services for gay and lesbian youth, plus a staff person at each middle school and high school, to work with gay and lesbian young people.

- Minnesota also bans school discrimination based on sexual orientation, and has a governor's task force working to create a safe school environment for gay and lesbian children.

These and a few similar efforts aside, much of the country has done nothing to stop the stereotyping and harassment of gay and lesbian youngsters. "Coaches still use terms like 'pansies and sissies.' It's the one last bit of persecution that goes relatively unchallenged," said Harvard professor Arthur Lipkin, who has developed several curricula dealing with gay and lesbian issues in schools. (For issues surrounding gay and lesbian teachers, see Chapter Four.)

◆ ACTION STEPS ◆

Because an estimated 10 percent of the population is gay, the chances are there are at least a couple of gay children in your child's class in school. You certainly want them treated with tolerance and respect. Your parents group should review your school's family life program to see that it offers an adequate, age-appropriate introduction to gay and lesbian people. If it doesn't, you can get curriculum materials to improve the program by contacting the Harvard Gay and Lesbian School Issues Project, 210 Longfellow Hall, Harvard Graduate School of Education, Cambridge, Massachusetts 02138, 617–491–5301.

Parents of gay and lesbian children can get helpful material from the Hetrick-Martin Institute, 2 Astor Place, New York, New York 10003–6998, 212–674–2400; or Parents, Families and Friends of Lesbians and Gays, 1101 14th Street NW, Suite 1030, Washington, D.C. 20005, 202–638–4200.

Teachers, both gay and straight, who want to help end homophobia in schools can contact the Gay, Lesbian and Straight Teachers Network, 122 West 26th Street, Suite 1100, New York, New York 10001, 212–727–0135.

TEXTBOOKS

It is sadly ironic that most of the controversy over schoolbooks has to do with evolution, sex, or dirty words. These draw attention away from the real problem. That problem is textbooks. According to several experts, the majority of elementary- and secondary-school textbooks used in this country are poorly written, superficial and often laced with errors and oversimplifications. Experts such as former U.S. Education Secretary Terrel Bell say that many of today's texts have been "dumbed down," and aren't as challenging as books used by earlier generations.

"It's a disaster," said Harriet Tyson, author of *A Conspiracy of Good Intentions: America's Textbook Fiasco* (Council on Basic Education). Tyson, an author and consultant who has studied textbooks for more than two decades, said the fault does not always lie with book publishers.

She said school systems force publishers to cover so many curriculum guidelines and standardized test questions that the result is often an incoherent mishmash.

"There's a book out with two sentences on the Nixon Administration. One of the sentences is: 'Nixon got in trouble for helping his friends.' Kids read that and ask, 'What's wrong with helping your friends?' It's ridiculous," she said.

Read your children's textbooks. You'll find more bad writing, more dull, lifeless prose than good writing. Why is this?

Journalist Bruce DeSilva examined scores of textbooks and found:

- Many publishers prepare their books according to "readability formulas," which are mathematical balances of age-appropriate vocabulary and sentence length that are supposed to make books easier to read. However, experts say relying on these formulas makes books both artless and more difficult to read.

- Schoolbooks are often hastily written or rewritten to get new copyright dates that school officials demand. Many schools won't consider a book that is more than two years old. Some publishers change books for the sake of changing books, which often leads to sloppy writing and to factual errors.

- Many texts aren't written by authors, but rather are assembled by editors from bits and pieces of writing from teams of contributors. Thus, the book lacks the "voice" of a single author.

- In the same vein, most texts aren't written by professional writers, but rather by ex-teachers, moonlighting teachers or publishing house employees, few of whom are accomplished writers.[6]

The result is a disservice to the kids. Research by Professor Michael Graves of the University of Minnesota shows that children will remember considerably more information from a well-written text than from a poorly written one. Also, a poorly written text won't encourage kids to read another book.

In addition to being dull, many texts are hopelessly superficial. Because publishers are pressured to cover hundreds of curriculum guidelines and standardized test areas, many texts end up as virtual laundry lists of facts, often unrelated, and don't delve into important points. Tyson said different states have literally hundreds of curriculum guidelines to cover, and some states have hundreds of other guidelines, and publishers have to cover them or risk not selling the book. Every textbook publisher has a horror story of a good, well-written textbook that didn't sell.

In addition, there's the power of the "adoption states." At present, 22 states have laws that require them to adopt textbooks on a statewide basis. These are mostly Southern and Western states, and include Texas and California. Because those are huge markets, officials there have a great deal of say in what goes into textbooks. In other words, if a subject is controversial in Texas, such as sex education or evolution, it isn't likely to be covered in detail.

There is a host of other reasons why mediocre textbooks get into schools. Sometimes teachers on school selection committees pick books because of the accompanying materials—the audio-visual aids or the workbooks—rather than the books themselves. Sometimes books are selected on the basis of their illustrations. Sometimes principals want books that are "teacher-proof," that is, they have so many aids and materials that even a weak teacher can keep a class going with them. Sometimes price is a deciding factor. Sometimes schools get free English books if they buy a certain set of science books. "It is exceedingly complex and not very promising," said Tyson.

There is a little hope on the horizon. Thanks to critics such as Tyson, some schoolbooks are better written today. Also, for the past decade, California officials have tried to force publishers to produce better textbooks, with some success. William Honig, the state's superintendent of schools, believes textbooks can be well written, make key points, and provide depth where appropriate. He and other officials made headlines in 1985 when they refused to adopt science books that had no mention of evolution. In 1986 the California Board of Education gave textbook publishers one year to improve the elementary school math books being used in the state, because they didn't meet the state's new standards.

Tyson praised the efforts of Honig and other California officials, but said it's too early to tell if this "top-down" method of textbook reform will improve learning.

◆ ACTION STEPS ◆

This is a tricky area, because some of what seems like it will work simply doesn't. Faced with weak textbooks, some well-educated parents have gone to PTA meetings and suggested teachers use more original materials, and not rely on texts. This suggestion is almost always hooted down. Many parents, said Tyson and Muther, want their kids to have a big, thick textbook just as they did, and feel cheated if their child doesn't have one.

Another option, done at many schools around the country, is to place parents on the textbook selection committee. The problem here is that the school often plays to special interests, and puts someone from every special interest group on the committee. This is sometimes called "political insurance." But the result is more points to cover, more sensibilities to genuflect before, and more mishmash.

Tyson said the best parents book group she found was one in Ohio, where the school located experts in each subject area from among parents and community leaders, and had them review prospective textbooks.

To organize such a group at your school, arrange a meeting with your parents group, your principal and your curriculum director.

Explain the idea. Bring a textbook you find inadequate. If you can't form a panel of experts, perhaps you can at least have parent representation on the school's textbook selection committee.

If you can get on your school's textbook selection committee, here is how to approach the job. First, establish what it is the book is supposed to teach. Make a list of the main ideas and concepts the children are supposed to get from a textbook in that subject and that grade. Then, copy sections covering the same subject from each book and put them next to one another. For example, if you're reviewing biology books, take the part on sex education. If you're considering history, take the Civil War. Refer to the list of what information the kids are supposed to get from the book. Read each section. Which does the best job of getting that information across?

Narrow the books down to three finalists, then let a group of students make the final choice, using the same criteria. Kids said kids will almost invariably pick the book that is the best written and most informative.

Another option is to turn to experts in some fields who review textbooks. The National Center for Science Education puts out a newsletter called "Bookwatch Reviews, Candid Appraisals of Science Textbooks," in which scientists review science texts. Gilbert Sewell of the Social Studies Review (475 Riverside Drive, #518, New York, New York 10115) reviews social studies and history books. William Bonetta of the California Textbook League (P.O. Box 51, Sausalito, California 94966) puts out a newsletter, the California Textbook Letter, in which scientists and historians review texts.

If nothing else works, and you are stuck with a weak textbook, the only option is to overcome it. Meet with the teacher. Again, get a list of main facts and concepts that your child should know by the end of the year (this is something you should do anyway). Then ask for other books, background materials, computer files, films, anything that will help get these ideas across to your child.

THE BILINGUAL EXPERIENCE

What about children who don't speak English? Officials estimate that by the year 2000, at least 10 percent of the nation's public school students will be language-minority children. Most educators and parents agree that these children must be taught standard English if they are to have a chance for the American dream. But how to teach them English, how fast to teach them, and how much of their native language to use in the process have been controversial issues in many parts of the country.

In the early 1970s some non-English-speaking Chinese-American students in San Francisco went to court to ask for instruction in the language they understood.

The case got to the U.S. Supreme Court, and the court agreed that failure to provide meaningful public education was violative of the 1964 Civil Rights Act. "Those who do not understand English are certain to find their classroom experiences wholly incomprehensible and in no way meaningful," the court said.[7]

At about the same time, the federal government passed the Bilingual Education Act, which was supposed to solve the language assimilation problems by providing three years of simultaneous English instruction and course instruction in the native language. Several states followed with more expansive bilingual (or bilingual-bicultural) mandates.

There are a number of different bilingual programs around the country, and some are quite promising. Authorities such as James Crawford, author of *Bilingual Education; History, Politics, Theory and Practice* (Crane, 1989) feel that bilingual programs have overcome numerous challenges and are generally doing the job. But other experts say parents of minority-language children who need to learn English should be extremely careful before putting their child in a bilingual program.

Why? Because a lot of the time, they say, these programs simply don't work.

The standard program in many states is called transitional bilingual education, or TBE. The plan is for a youngster to start with one English class a day while getting the rest of his or her instruction in the native language, let's say Spanish (although there are more than 150 languages being taught in bilingual programs across the country).

As the child progresses, the bilingual teachers are supposed to use more and more English, until the child is "mainstreamed" into regular English classes. That's the theory.

In practice, the kids often stay in the bilingual classes for years and years, never learning English very well, and they aren't able to get decent jobs after they graduate, says Rosalie Pedalino Porter, a teacher in Springfield, Massachusetts, and author of a courageous book titled *Forked Tongue: The Politics of Bilingual Education* (Basic Books).

Porter, who taught fifth- and sixth-grade Hispanic students, said that most bilingual programs offer two basic premises: they will make students literate in two languages and they will preserve their cultural identity. They do neither, she says.

The reason is a matter of common sense. If youngsters spend most of the day speaking Spanish, that's the language they'll be good at, not English. Often, the bilingual teachers who are supposed to phrase in English don't, because they themselves aren't fluent in English.

Porter cites studies by the U.S. Department of Education that show the TBE approach doesn't work as well as other methods, yet she says the department continues to fund TBE programs, apparently because they have become a Hispanic political sacred cow.

As for improved models, she cites early childhood "immersion" programs being used in several cities and the Canadian Province of Quebec, and says each city should have a choice of language education models. In Quebec, the "dual immersion" system of placing English and French speakers together, and teaching half the day in each language, has had remarkable results. Many school systems opt for the "English-as-a second-language" model, in which students are taken out of their regular class for part of the day to study English. ESL, as it is known, has its advocates as well. Communities with large bilingual programs make a sacrifice. The programs require new teachers, both in regular and special education classes, as well as counselors and other professionals. The cost is partly defrayed by federal and state grants, but the programs are still expensive.

◆ Action Steps ◆

It's a great gift to have mastery of two or more languages, one parents should want for their children. The first thing parents should know is that federal law requires schools systems take "appropriate action" to help their children overcome problems they may have with the English language. The federal law no longer specifies what this action should be, it can be TBE or ESL or any other sound, successful system. Sometimes, state law dictates that a particular method be used.

Second, parents have a choice, under federal law, whether or not to put a child into bilingual classes. It's up to you. Most systems will test a child for English proficiency. If your child is a borderline English reader, you should check the programs available in your community. Ask to look at numbers, specifically the average length of time children spend in bilingual classes. Children who start kindergarten in a bilingual program should be mainstreamed by at least the end of the third grade. Also, visit classes and talk to teachers. Ask at what point bilingual students begin taking standardized tests, and see if the school has a record of results. See if your child's prospective teacher is truly bilingual. Clearly, bilingual programs have helped countless children. But they've also held some back. Make a careful decision.

HAS THE MUSIC STOPPED?

One of greatest tragedies befalling public school curriculums in this country is the limiting or elimination of art and music classes.

In New York City, a mecca of the performing and visual arts, two-thirds of the public schools no longer have any arts or music teachers. Arts and music education always seems to take the first hit when budgets get tight, especially in major cities. Some states have maintained strong commitments to arts and music, but others are letting them slide into oblivion.

According to Cathy Welling of the Music Educators National Conference, the percentage of junior and senior high school students taking music has declined by a third since 1950. Only 29 states have graduation requirements that involve the arts, and because most colleges don't require arts courses for admission, college-bound students have little interest in taking them. Fifty-five percent of the nation's school districts are either unserved or served part-time by a music specialist. And the federal government spends 29 times more on science education than it spends on the arts.

Some school officials might not see a problem with this. They view the arts as curriculum icing, as a frill. We emphatically disagree. The arts are forms of beauty, ways of connecting the imagination to the core of the human spirit. Studying the arts allows students to find and develop their powers of creativity and self expression. This leads to a more well-rounded education.

History bears this out. Music was part of the quadrivium, and was part of the curriculum when Horace Mann started the "common schools." Educators have sensed the importance of music for hundreds of years, and modern research proves them right. Studies by Howard Gardner of Harvard University and others indicate music may be a form of intelligence, rather than just a manifestation of it.

Along with being a form of intelligence, music seems also to enhance overall intelligence. According to several years records abstracted from the College Entrance Examination Board results, students who have taken four or more years of music instruction score an average of 34 points higher than their peers on the verbal portion of the Scholastic Aptitude Test (SAT) and an average of 18 points higher on the math portion of the SAT.

Those results may have to do with what goes on when a child studies music. He or she learns to interpret symbols and develop problem-solving skills. Just as important, students develop self-discipline. Homework never went out of style with music lessons; students must practice to achieve. When they master a piece, bravo! Their self esteem takes a well-deserved jump. Children who study dance, theater, and the visual arts garner most of the same benefits. Conversely, youngsters who don't get the chance to study the arts miss a great deal. What can parents do to see that this doesn't happen?

◆ ACTION STEPS ◆

The fight to restore and strengthen arts education has been led in large measure by music educators and the music industry. In the late 1980s the National Conference of Music Educators, the National Academy of Recording Arts and Sciences, Inc., and the National Association of Music Merchants formed the National Coalition for Music

Education to teach the public about the value of music education. The coalition was instrumental in getting arts education included in the Goals 2000: Educate America Act, meaning that arts education for all children is now a national educational goal.

This was a major victory, but the coalition and other arts educators are still trying to win victories on the local level.

Parents who want to fight to retain or expand arts classes should write to the Coalition at 1806 Robert Fulton Drive, Reston, Virginia 22091–4348, for the Coalition's Action Kit, that includes videos (one features the late Henry Mancini), brochures, books, and other information to heighten awareness of the need for music education. For materials supporting arts, contact the American Association of Arts Educators, 1916 Association Drive, Reston, Virginia 22091 (703–860–8000).

The music coalition's tips for effective lobbying of the school board and school administration, in part developed by JoAnna Newhouse of the Los Angeles City Elementary School Music Association, are particularly helpful for any parental advocacy movement. They are summarized here:

- Be positive. Look at the issue you face as a chance to educate the board or administration on the value of the arts.
- Be adamant that the arts are not frills, but are essential components of the core curriculum.
- Do NOT suggest cuts in other school programs. It doesn't work and polarizes your community. Show that you are willing to work for the good of all students. Keep the issues students-centered, not teacher-centered.
- Find a standard-bearer. If you're fighting for music instruction, find a board member or other civic leader whose child is taking piano lessons. Human nature suggests that board members probably will be more attentive to a peer than they would be to someone they don't know.
- Be current on board issues, attend meetings and keep your group up to speed.
- Get to know your board members personally. Be involved in their campaigns. Have a small group visit board members at

home. Invite board members to concerts and arts shows. Let them experience what the children are doing.

- Have a "telephone tree" of phone numbers to be ready for a crisis. Make sure you can network hundreds of phone calls in a day.

- Have a speakers list ready to address the school board, and have four times as many speakers as you'll need for any given meeting. Meetings will be postponed or rescheduled, and you don't want to be caught short.

- Know board rules on such subjects as how far in advance speakers must sign up, and how long they can speak for.

- In fighting for a music program at a board meeting, use a "trilogy" or three-step approach. Have a parent talk about the value of music education in school. Then follow with a student who talks, without prompting, about the value of music in his or her life. Then wrap it up with a teacher or professor who talks about the value of music in the curriculum. When you have a list of speakers, make sure they don't repeat themselves, but instead approach the subject from different angles.

- Have community leaders write the board. Petitions are okay, but phone calls and letters do the job.

    Don't use form letters in writing to administrators or board members. Write individual letters. Always use proper titles, such as "Madame Chair" or "Mr. Superintendent." Write and thank board members when they offer positive comments or otherwise send a positive message about the arts.

In addition to these suggestions, you might also:

- Ally with arts institutions and corporations in your community. Museums, theaters and galleries don't want to see arts programs shut down, for both esthetic and self-interest purposes. No arts education means no audience a generation hence. Virtually all the major New York arts groups are involved in trying to save arts programs in the schools.

- Become a cost center. Make money. One New York high school is paying for its arts supplies by selling drawings, paintings, ceramic works, hand-painted t-shirts, calendars, buttons and other objects of art at fairs and fence shows around the city. This not only provides income for the kids and the program, but teaches kids that in the real world, art is a business.

- Consider a legal challenge. Although the idea is in its infancy, there's some law on the side of those who want arts education. At least 42 states require arts education, and 30 states specifically requires arts courses for graduation. So a state that has mandated arts education but refuses to fund it is at least vulnerable to a legal action.

Some schools have attempted to sidestep this requirement by having teachers not certified in the arts stumble through the courses. In many states, this practice is against regulations. Often, a parent can file an administrative appeal to the state education department and force the local board to hire a real arts teacher.

◆ SELECTED QUESTIONS ◆

Can teachers use dirty words in class?

It depends. If the word is used in a serious educational context, it's probably okay, as courts have held. If the word is used gratuitously, the teacher may get into trouble. If your child tells you this happens in class, call the teacher immediately and explain your concerns. If the problem continues, write a letter to the principal.

———————

Can parents inspect curriculum materials?

Generally, yes. A federal law allows parents to inspect certain curriculum materials used in experimentation or research. Many if not most school districts allow parents to review all curriculum materials.

———————

Will there be more use of television in classrooms?

It's hard to say. In 1992 a New Jersey judge issued an advisory opinion on Channel One, a classroom television news service that includes commercials, that said using the service in public schools violated the state's compulsory attendance law and the state constitution's guarantee of a thorough and efficient education. However, Channel One claims to be in 12,000 schools in 47 states, and a 1994 Michigan study found that two-thirds of teachers using the show strongly recommended it.

Also, several schools are experimenting with sharing classes by television or video. This has proved troublesome in many places, because it's been hard to keep two schools on exactly the same schedule every day.

Whether by television or not, there is without question an effort by scores of companies to get their names in front of the nation's school children, often by providing posters, maps and teaching aids with the company's logo on them. There are nutrition programs from food companies, photo programs from camera companies, you name it. School officials must review these materials carefully and use them judiciously, if at all.

_____

We're appalled. Our son's fourth grade teacher recently showed a film about abortion, with extremely graphic representations of aborted fetuses. Shouldn't he be fired for this?

In a similar situation in New York, parents complained to the school board and demanded the teacher be fired. The board investigated. They reprimanded the teacher and demanded a formal apology, which the teacher gave. But the teacher, who was tenured, was allowed to go on teaching. You should by all means complain. But in most instances, administrators won't try to fire a tenured teacher without an extremely strong and well documented case, and one instance of bad judgment may not be enough.

_____

Will more schools be changing to an all-year schedule?

At present, 1,500 to 2,000 schools, mostly in California, use some form of all-year schedule. Most of these schools were motivated by the desire to save money. Nonetheless, it shows that all-year scheduling is possible. Whether the all-year schedule will be used to increase the length of the school year remains to be seen.

FOR FURTHER INFORMATION

California Textbook League
P.O. Box 51
Sausalito, CA 94966

Connie Muther & Associates
257 E. Center Street
Manchester, CT 06040
203–649–9517

Gilbert Sewell
Social Studies Review
475 Riverside Drive #518
New York, NY 10115
212–870–2760

Association of American Publishers/School Division
220 E. 23rd Street
New York, NY 10010
212–689–8920

Harriet Tyson
3702 Ingomar Street NW
Washington, DC 20008
202–966–0906

National Education Goals Panel
1850 M Street NW Suite 270
Washington, DC 20036
202–632–0952

National Education Commission on Time and Learning
1255 22nd Street NW
Washington, DC 20202-7591
202–653–5019

Educational Testing Service
Princeton, NJ 08541
609–734–1615

National Coalition for Music Education
1806 Robert Fulton Drive
Reston, VA 22091
703–860–4000

American Association of Arts Educators
1916 Association Drive
Reston, VA 22091
703–860–8000

NOTES

1. *Epperson* v. *Arkansas,* 393 U.S. 97 (1969).

2. *McLean* v. *Arkansas Board of Education,* 529 F. Supp. 1255 (ED Ark.1982).

3. *Peloza* v. *Capistrano Unified School District,* 782 F. Supp. 1412 (1992).

4. *Mozert* v. *Hawkins County Board of Education,* 827 F. 2d 1058 (1987).

5. *Board of Education, Island Trees Union Free School District No. 26* v. *Pico,* 457 U.S. 853, 102 S. Ct. 2799 (1982).

6. Bruce DeSilva, "Schoolbooks—A Question of Quality," *Hartford Courant,* June 15–18, 1986.

7. *Lau* v. *Nichols,* 94 S.Ct 786 (1974).

TEACHER COMPETENCE

◆ INTRODUCTION ◆

In the first two grades, Janie was a bright and aggressive student, eager to go to school. But after only six weeks in the third grade, she had changed.

She moped in her room in the morning, and no longer looked forward to getting on the bus.

"What's wrong?" her mother finally asked.

"Everything," she said. "All our teacher does is yell at us and make us do punishment stuff. She's a monster!"

Answers such as this, or nonverbal behavior such as pretending to be sick or fighting with siblings or friends, often mean there's a problem with your child's teacher. The parental antennae have to go up immediately.

We are not suggesting that you go to the next school board meeting and demand the teacher's resignation. You don't as yet know what the problem is, and it may not be the teacher's fault. Most teachers are bright and dedicated people who do a good job. Nonetheless, it is possible to get a weak teacher. It's also possible to get a once-competent teacher who's burned out or suffering the effects of illness, substance abuse or personal tragedy. It's also possible to get a decent teacher who happens to be a bad personality match with your child.

71

Parents want the best possible teacher for their child, and so should be aware of major issues involving teachers. These issues include:

- *How does someone become a teacher?*
- *What is tenure?*
- *What rights does a teacher have?*
- *Can an incompetent teacher be fired?*

◆ DISCUSSION ◆

BECOMING A TEACHER

Men and women who become teachers must meet the license or certification requirements of their state and school district. This means they must: attain a certain education level, usually a bachelor's degree, with a minimum number of courses in the subject they are to teach; be of good moral character; and be a U.S. citizen. Prospective teachers often must agree to continuing education requirements. Sometimes they must agree to live in the school district. Increasingly, they are asked to undergo a criminal background check. Also, almost half the states have set up an alternate certification process, in which nonteachers qualified in certain subject areas can be brought into the system without meeting the normal requirements for education courses.

In an effort to weed out incompetents and attract talented teachers, all states now also use competency tests for beginning teachers, and a handful of states use them for the recertification of experienced teachers. Courts have upheld the use of such tests, as long as they are valid tests and aren't used to discriminate.

Most states have a two- or three-tiered certification process. In the first two, three or five years, a teacher is on probation. If the teacher meets the requirements for tenure, it is granted after that period. Tenure in essence offers a teacher continual employment unless the teacher is removed for just cause, such as immorality or incompetence. That removal can only come after what is called procedural due process—meaning the teacher has a right to a hearing on the charges, along with the right to present evidence, be represented by counsel, cross examine witnesses and review the evidence. The teacher can then appeal the decision in court. Because this is expensive and time-consuming, it translates into substantial job protection. Tenure was created in the early 20th century as a good government measure, to keep political bosses from using teaching jobs for political patronage. Many think it now offers too much protection to the wrong people.

TEACHERS' RIGHTS

As role models for young people, teachers in the past were prohibited from such public activities as drinking, smoking, or, in the case of female teachers, being seen with any male other than a father or brother. Teachers who got married or got pregnant had to resign. And teachers weren't supposed to speak out in public.

The courts have now decided that teachers, as citizens, do have constitutional rights. In 1968 a high school teacher named Marvin Pickering in Will County, Illinois, wrote a letter to the editor of the local paper attacking the school board's handling of fund-raising issues. The board responded by making Pickering a former teacher. He sued.

In this landmark case, the court said there is a balance between the interests of a teacher as a citizen and the teacher as an employee. In other words, while there might be times when a teacher would be best advised to keep a low profile, there are also times when he can speak out, as long as he's not interfering with his classroom teaching or the operation of the school. Pickering was ordered rehired.[1]

TEACHER COMPETENCE

When a teacher is dismissed, it is usually for incompetence, or for some criminal or immoral act or conduct. Incompetence manifests itself in several ways, including:

- *Lack of teaching ability.* Teachers have been dismissed because of their own poor spelling, grammar, or basic math skills. A Minnesota math teacher who gave a lot of low grades tried to claim his dismissal was an infringement on his First Amendment rights to give low grades. The court disagreed. The grades were accurate, because the teacher hadn't imparted the curriculum knowledge. In other words, the kids had low grades because he hadn't taught them anything.[2] His dismissal was upheld.

- *Lack of discipline.* This was the holding when a teacher's students were found daydreaming, walking about the classroom and leaving the room at will, without permission.[3]

- *Excessive discipline.* A few teachers have also been fired for too much discipline, usually for employing excessive corporal punishment or allowing injuries through such activities as "hazing." (See Chapter Nine.)

- *Insubordination.* In a 1991 New York case, a teacher was fired because she "entered the principal's office without permission and altered warnings in her personnel file without authorization; ignored established procedures for disciplining students despite prior warnings; refused to meet with troubled students' parents; refused to send progress reports to parents; did not have her lesson plan book available as required by district policy on at least three occasions; and graded students improperly.[4] It is, perhaps, a commentary on the system that this case even got to court.

- *Immorality.* Many districts allow dismissal for behavior defined as immoral. This can mean sexual behavior, or other behavior, such as lying or cheating. Since teachers are supposed to set standards for youth, courts are generally tough with teachers who have any kind of sexual contact with students. As for sexual behavior with nonstudents, the court will try to determine how the conduct affects a teacher's fitness to teach. In something of a classic case, a California teacher was dismissed after she was seen and arrested for performing oral sex three times at a "swinger's club." She appealed.

  The court upheld the dismissal, saying teachers were exemplars for children, and that this wasn't the kind of example society wanted to set.[5]

  With homosexual behavior, courts in the past 25 years have tended to uphold dismissals or decertifications for open and flagrant homosexual behavior or student contact, as they would for flagrant heterosexual behavior or student contact. Whether teachers can be removed simply for being homosexual isn't clear. In some jurisdictions, courts have upheld the removal of gay or lesbian teachers from the classroom. A few states still have criminal anti-sodomy laws on the books, which, as recently as the 1980s, have resulted in the firing of gay teachers as criminals.

The trend, however, is otherwise. Sexual orientation is increasingly being protected by state antidiscrimination statutes, so dismissal for the mere status of homosexuality is less likely but still possible, particularly in more conservative districts. There are gay teachers; most are good, conscientious professionals, just as most heterosexual teachers are. If your child has a gay teacher and this is an issue, discuss it with your principal.

- *Criminal behavior.* Courts are likely to find criminal behavior unduly affects the ability to teach, especially if the crime is a felony.

  In an Ohio case, a teacher who managed a second income by applying for welfare with a false application—and got away with it for five years—was fired. She appealed. The court said her conviction supported the board's finding of conduct unbecoming a teacher.[6]

  In a similar case, a Kansas teacher named Hainline was suspended after he was caught burglarizing a furniture store. He appealed. The court upheld the suspension, saying: "One of the goals of education is to instill respect for the law. Teachers are role models for their students. Hainline's burglary offense was publicized . . . There is at least the presumption that the felonious conduct has sufficient relationship or nexus to Hainline's fitness to teach to warrant action by the board."[7]

TEACHER DISMISSAL

It is much easier not to renew a probationary or nontenured teacher's contract than it is to dismiss a tenured teacher. The unsung heroes of education are administrators who spot inept teachers while they are on probation, and either improve them or remove them. Because once a teacher is tenured, it is a different story. As we mentioned above, tenured teachers typically have the right to notice, a hearing and a court appeal before being removed. This process can take years (often while the teacher is still getting paid) and can sometimes cost hundreds of thousands of dollars in legal fees.

Horror stories abound. Officials of the National PTA in Chicago told of a situation in their state in which it took more than two years to remove a teacher who had suffered a nervous breakdown and was unable to teach. In New York, according to *The New York Times,* a teacher was convicted of selling drugs, and was fired. But he appealed his dismissal to the education commissioner and to court. The process took years; the man received his salary while in prison, and was reinstated to his job after a two-year suspension. In the small town of Ridgefield, Connecticut, a teacher fired in 1992 was still in court three years later, and still being paid as she appealed. The panel hearing the case held 29 days of hearings, which produced more than 5,000 pages of transcript and more than 400 exhibits. The town's legal costs? So far about $250,000.

Cases such as these are the reason New York and several other states, including Michigan, Texas and New Jersey, are attempting to streamline the teacher dismissal process.

But the present system is so onerous in many places that some administrators will put up with almost anything rather than face the dismissal process. The easiest solution, and often the worst, is to keep transferring bad teachers from one school to another, or to encourage them to move to another district.

For a variety of reasons, the odds are your child's teacher won't be fired. Remember that the vast majority of teachers do a good job, and the majority of student-teacher problems aren't serious enough to warrant such action.

Also, many districts are implementing remedial strategies to help teachers who are struggling for one reason or another. These include remedial training programs and mentoring programs, where an experienced teacher is paired with a newer teacher to act as a professional counselor and confidant. This common-sense step, used in private industry, is long overdue and rapidly gaining popularity.

◆ ACTION STEPS ◆

AVOID THE PROBLEM

What do you do if you have a problem with a teacher? First, do everything you can to avoid it. We can't emphasize enough the importance of visiting a school before your child attends it. In almost every district in the country, you have a legal right to visit a classroom while it is in session.

Robert Pressman of Harvard University's Center of Law and Education says more than 30 states explicitly recognize the right of a parent to visit the school at any time with notice to the school. A few other states have different versions of this right; one limits it to resident parents. Beyond these state laws, many communities have established the right of parents to visit the school, either by local ordinance or in their teachers' contract.

Also, schools using funds from certain federal programs, such as Title I of the Federal Compensatory Education Program, are required by federal law to allow parents to observe in the classroom. So if you look hard enough, the law is on your side. That's as it should be. It's a public school. You are the public. A school visit can take you a long way toward avoiding the problem of having your child taught by an inappropriate teacher.

Each fall your child enters a new grade. Rosemary Baggish, director of education at The Institute of Living, a nationally known psychiatric hospital in Hartford, Connecticut, tells parents to visit the school in the preceding spring and see all the child's prospective teachers in action. "Parents know their children better than anyone else does. They should be part of the placement process, especially in the younger grades, where personality plays more of a role," Baggish says.

It doesn't have to be a long visit; stay for 15 to 20 minutes to get a feel for the teacher's style and relationship with the students. Set up your visit ahead of time with the school principal. This usually involves calling the school's office and explaining that you want to observe, say, each of the first grade teachers teach a class. Many schools set aside a day to do this, but you can ask to go on your own as well.

Many parents are hesitant to do this, but shouldn't be. We have done it, and found most schools welcome visitors.

Next, use your school network. Your network is made up of other parents in your car pool, those in the parent-teacher organization and those you meet through sports, religious, community and other activities. Talk to parents whose children have had the teachers your child may get.

For help with a variety of school problems, find out who your "super-parents" are. Virtually every school in the country has at least one, and sometimes several, parents who are at the school almost every day, volunteering in the classroom or working on committees, and have gained a thorough knowledge of the school. Sometimes these parents wield remarkable power. Get to know them, and they can give you the lay of the land.

The information you get won't be infallible. You may hear something about a teacher that simply isn't true. Beware of gossip and rumors. Sometimes a parent just didn't hit it off with an otherwise good teacher. Also, each child responds differently to adults. Even so, this will help you get a general idea of what the teachers are like.

Comparative scores on achievement tests or state mastery tests usually aren't available until the second, third or fourth grade. Nonetheless, ask school officials how they keep test scores. You'll want to know how each teacher's students do on these tests. At some point, the information will be useful.

By this point you'll know something about the teachers. Take a few minutes to write down what you know about your child. What type of child is he? Does he need structure or will he function better in an open environment? Is there a child she should not be with? What are her academic strengths and weaknesses?

When you have finished the list, make a copy. One will be for the principal, the other for you.

Now it's time to visit the principal. A good principal will welcome your sense of involvement, and want to work with you. But don't just walk in and demand a particular teacher, no matter how tempting that may be. Most of the time, that isn't a good idea. The principal is trying to fit hundreds of kids with a handful of teachers, and doesn't want to be backed into a corner. "Tell me *what* you need, not *who* you need," one principal told us. In other words, tell the principal what kind of learning environment your child succeeds in. Give the principal your written description of your child.

At the end of the discussion, tell the principal the teacher or teachers you would be comfortable with, and why. Why is that important? If you don't get one of those teachers, and a problem ensues, you've got an argument. You can return and say, "As I suspected . . ."

When your child does get a teacher assignment, make arrangements to talk with the teacher as soon as possible. The teacher should be made aware of any special information. For example, if your child is extremely sensitive and will cry easily, the teacher should know that. Emphasize your willingness to work with the teacher. To a good teacher, you're a partner. To a bad one, you're a squeaky wheel. In either case, the teacher will know your child is there. As one principal tells us, "It's a given that we flag kids whose parents have visited us. We have to keep reminding ourselves that we owe the same duty to the children of silent parents."

IF THERE IS A PROBLEM

The spring visit to the school can avoid many problems, but unfortunately not all of them. Let's say your child has come home with a complaint about the teacher.

If the complaint is of an urgent or criminal nature—"The teacher touched me in a no-touch place," or "The teacher punched Peter," or "The teacher made fun of me because I have an accent"—then you have to go right to the principal.

Such complaints aren't unheard of, but fortunately they are rare. More common complaints have to do with a teacher's style, mannerisms, method of teaching, personality or—kids will always pick this up—lack of knowledge of the subject he or she is teaching.

When you hear complaints such as these, the first thing you have to do is assure your child you are there to listen and help. And, do listen. Investigate a bit. Your child may be complaining about school to mask another problem. She may have had a fight with her best friend, and be mad at the world.

But if it appears there really is a problem at school, call the teacher immediately. The majority of such problems are misunderstandings, or problems the teacher doesn't know about. For example, the teacher may not realize she is using too many big words. A teacher may be having a personal problem and not be aware it's affecting classroom performance. A student in the back of the class who can't hear can be moved, if the teacher learns about the problem. In one New York school, a teacher wasn't aware that parents wanted to know what was going on in the class. When a group of parents told her they were, she started a weekly newsletter.

You should also call the teacher—usually by leaving a message at the school office—if you begin to see problematic behavior. If, for example, you begin to see poor grades while your child doesn't seem to be doing much at home, find out if things are going smoothly in the classroom. If your child doesn't want to talk about school, call the teacher and talk about it. He or she may know of something that happened—a fight on the playground or an accident in the cafeteria—that can help you work with your child.

How do you talk to a teacher? As you would to a friend. Don't talk down to the teacher. No one likes to be treated like a dumbbell, or be put on the defensive, or be accused of doing something wrong. Begin the conversation by saying something like, "I'm having a problem with Claire, and I wonder if you can suggest something I (or we) can do to solve it." Then outline the problem.

Rosemary Baggish suggests telling the teacher not what the problem is, but what your perception of the problem is. This way you set a nonaccusatory tone, and you'll be able to carry on a rational conversation. If you are angry, cool off first. This is the person who has your child all day, so there's no point in being more aggressive than necessary, or setting the stage for a bad relationship.

Sometimes, unfortunately, teachers will make excuses rather than solve problems. If the teacher complains about how hard she has to work, or how hard it is to teach today's kids, that teacher should be doing something else.

But some excuses may be valid. The class may be too crowded. The school may not have enough resources. It's hard to believe that school districts with multimillion-dollar budgets don't have enough money for textbooks, writing paper or even toilet paper, but it happens more often than we would like to believe. And sometimes parents groups can help solve these problems.

End your meeting with the understanding that you'll talk again in a few days, to see if the problem is getting better. This meeting with the teacher will solve a majority of problems. Even teachers who offer a litany of excuses will try to make things better after personal contact with a parent.

But if the problem persists, you have to monitor it. Talk with your child regularly, over the next several days or weeks. Ask if it's happening to other kids, and if so, talk with their parents.

Go to the classroom and observe, if you can. Everyone will be on their best behavior, more than likely, but as journalists say, there's nothing like being there to get the story. You may spot subtle clues. You can also offer to help with reading or math groups, or help chaperone a class trip. The more contact you have with your child's class and teacher, the better the chances are of resolving any problems.

While you are monitoring and investigating, it's important that you continue to support the teacher, says Dr. Kenneth S. Robson, a child psychiatrist who specializes in family issues. Here's why. In trying to be a pal, many parents forget how much influence they have over their children. Children do what their parents do, think what their parents think, and pick up the same prejudices and ideas their parents espouse. This often leads to the following scenario:

A child comes home from school and says, "I don't like my teacher, she's a grouch." The parent, trying to be supportive, chimes in with, "Yeah, you're right. I know her from tennis and she's not one of my favorites, either."

This parent has inadvertently created a learning dysfunction in her own child. "Once a parent announces he or she doesn't like a teacher, the child won't listen to that teacher again," Robson says. If children are around, parents even have to be careful how they discuss teachers on the phone with other parents.

This is the same kind of dysfunction that sometimes happens with certain subjects. For example, a child comes home and says she's having a hard time with arithmetic. The good-guy parent says, "What the heck, I was never any good at it, either." If the parent dismisses mathematics, so will the child.

By this point you have listened to your child, spoken with the teacher, visited the class and perhaps spoken to other parents. What do you do if the problem persists?

THE PRINCIPAL CAN HELP

If your child's problem hasn't been corrected in a reasonable amount of time, usually a couple of weeks, go to the principal. Tell your child's teacher, but do so in a diplomatic way. Say something like, "I think we're at an impasse. I know you're trying to find a solution, but I'd like to get the principal involved, to see if she has any ideas."

This is wise. The principal often does have an idea, and it's usually something only the principal can implement.

When going to see the principal, remember a couple of things. Most principals have heard it all. Yours may have just gotten off the phone with a parent complaining the school gives too much homework, and that call may have followed one complaining the school gave too little homework.

Anger won't get you anywhere. If you're angry and can't cool down, bring someone with you. You want to make a cogent, rational argument. You want the discussion to be as positive as possible. You want ideas that will help your child learn, and you've come to a professional for help.

One parent of a third-grader was concerned when her son, a whiz in math, was bored stiff by what was being taught. His mother feared he would lose interest and ultimately fall behind. She went to the teacher.

"I've got 23 kids and I can't individualize," the teacher said. The teacher suggested home tutoring. The parent didn't bite. "I've got 23 kids," is an excuse. Home tutoring, while it might help, doesn't address the problem of being bored in school. The mother went to the principal.

The principal had two ideas. One was an advanced placement, in-school tutoring program, using sixth graders. The other was a math league, for youngsters such as this one who wanted the challenge. It worked.

If several parents have the same complaint, there's always strength in numbers. In one case, several second-grade parents went to the principal with the complaint that their children's teacher was weak, had no personality, and was poorly prepared, and consequently their children weren't learning anything. They all wanted their children transferred to the other second-grade teacher in the school, who had a much better reputation.

The principal knew the first teacher was weak, but, as is often the case, there was nothing she could do immediately. And principals can't put all the kids in one class. But this principal found a middle-ground solution. She created a team-teaching situation, in which all the kids got some benefit from the good teacher.

If the problem has to do with inexperience, the principal may be able to provide your child's teacher with additional training or an experienced teacher as a mentor. The school psychologist may be able to provide counseling.

THE HARD PART

Of course, there is that small percentage of incompetent teachers who aren't going to be helped by a conference with you or the principal.

If you have tried everything else and are still convinced you have a teacher who isn't teaching, abuses children, fails to maintain discipline, or doesn't follow major policies, you should go to the principal with a clear, well-documented case and file a complaint. Stick to the facts, don't engage in characterizations or name-calling (the teacher could turn around and sue you for defamation of character). You should have a written chronological account of your experience with the teacher. Have anyone else familiar with the situation write in support of your position, particularly other parents.

It is possible that other complaints are pending against the teacher, and yours is the one that will cause the teacher to resign or retire.

The initiation of disciplinary proceedings causes a good number of resignations. Also, some principals are good at encouraging incompetent teachers to resign or retire.

But if the teacher is inclined to fight it, and the teacher is tenured, it is going to take time.

In many districts, the board and teachers union have worked out a process for handling complaints. Typically, a teacher will go from "continuous" evaluation to "intensive" evaluation. There will be a conference, and the teacher will do a self-evaluation. Then evaluators—administrators, or, in progressive districts, fellow teachers—will spend up to 50 hours evaluating the teacher.

The teacher gets a chance to improve. Then comes another evaluation process. Only then do formal disciplinary proceedings start. That involves a hearing before a state board or commission. The district presents its evidence and the teacher and his lawyer have a chance to rebut. If the teacher is dismissed, and appeals in court, the process can take years.

This is an unwieldy system. If filing a complaint does nothing else, it may lead to a change in the evaluation process in your district. With educational budget cuts in many states, evaluation of teachers has suffered. Complaints may be the best way the administration has of finding out who isn't doing the job. Filing a complaint may also be a way to get parents involved in the teacher selection process, if your school has enough autonomy to select its own teachers.

It should. As business people know, hiring is the critical step in assembling a competent workforce. It's the same in education. The best schools are those with the best teachers in the classrooms. Parents can be helpful in finding those teachers, and preventing the school from hiring weak teachers.

Ideally, your district has a system in which complaints are handled swiftly, teachers are removed from teaching, if appropriate, during the process, and a just resolution is quickly reached.

But what if that doesn't happen? What if the principal backs the teacher and dismisses your complaint? Then you have to make another decision.

TO TRANSFER OR NOT TO TRANSFER?

The decision you have to make is whether or not to get your child out of the class. Some experts are very reluctant to suggest moving a child from a class during a school year. They say:

- It could cause the child to think the teacher doesn't like him.
- It could damage the child's self-esteem, because the child sees the transfer as her fault.
- The child could miss his friends.
- A transfer could interrupt the learning process.

Those are considerations, to be sure. But remember that your child is in school to learn. We think a parent has to ask two basic questions:

- Is learning going on?
- Is my child suffering?

Think it through. What if you transfer and your child is still unhappy? Talk it over with your child. "Kids have amazing good sense. Ask your child if he or she wants to stay. And if they say they want to stay with their friends, that's not necessarily bad, because a lot of kids learn from their friends," says Chrissie Bamber, an expert on problem teachers.

One parent thought about moving her child because the child felt the teacher was "boring." Still, as she found out, the child did her homework, did well on tests, and didn't find school oppressive. Every teacher can't be electrifying. Boring isn't the worst thing in the world, as long as the kids are learning and working. The parent ended up keeping her daughter in the class, and didn't regret it.

But if your child is suffering, or if there's no learning going on in the class, go to the principal and get a transfer. Some principals are reluctant to transfer students. They may not want to do the paper-work, or may fear a grievance from the teachers union if a lot of parents go in looking for transfers. Most principals will make trans-fers if pushed hard enough. Tell the principal, if you must, that the teacher and your child are a bad personality mix. The important thing is to stay with it, and do it as quickly as possible so your child will adjust to the new environment as soon as possible.

◆ Selected Questions ◆

We thought our daughter's fourth grade teacher was terrific. We thought she fostered a love of learning and a sense of independence in the kids. But some parents felt she wasn't structured enough. The long and short of it is that she isn't being recommended for tenure, but will come back as a probationary teacher. What can we do?

Get as many parents as you can and mount a letter-writing campaign to the superintendent and each member of the school board. Outline in detail why you think the teacher was exceptional. Then follow up with a meeting with the school principal. Let them know that a sizable number of parents support the teacher, and watch what happens when the tenure question comes up again.

In our school there are three second-grade teachers. Everybody knows Ms. Roberts is the best. All the children of the teachers and administrators end up in her class. It is clear to us that this is fixed, and that they are just taking care of one another. What can we do?

Confront the principal and ask who is in charge of placement. Explain the problem as you see it. Fight for your own child, while you're at it; that's why you're there. Talk about whether your child's needs are being met. If the other teachers are inadequate, tell the teacher why. This is a classic example of why parents ought to be involved in placement. We think the principal will want to meet you halfway on this one. If not, you've got options. It's not the kind of case that lends itself to a lawsuit. But there's always the threat of taking the complaint to the school board, in front of the media. Most school administrators loathe bad publicity.

I saw a fellow parent in the store the other day and she said, "I understand Ms. Albert is having a very difficult time with your son John paying attention in class." I was stunned. I asked where she heard this, and she said Ms. Albert told her at the last parent-teacher conference. I'm so upset I don't know what to do.

Go right to the teacher. If it happens again, go to the principal. This is called "labeling," and it is completely unprofessional and unacceptable. It is also illegal in most cases to reveal such confidential information; it violates the Buckley Amendment (see Chapter Five). Some teachers, after spending all day with youngsters, need to talk to adults. So they talk about their students, and do so rather indiscriminately. Sometimes they don't even realize they're doing it. You've got to tell them. And if a teacher is labeling another child in your presence, you've got to make it clear you don't approve.

I've read that teacher performance can be enhanced by using a merit pay plan in which the good teachers get extra money. Do these plans work?

The concept is a good one, but making it work has been difficult. Merit pay plans were in vogue in the mid-1980s, but have since fallen slowly by the wayside. Florida, for example, started a master teacher program, then dropped it a few years later. Critics, who often include teachers unions, say the plans are divisive, that it is difficult to fairly determine who should get the extra money and who shouldn't. Also, merit plans are sometimes eliminated by budget cuts.

Is there such a thing as educational malpractice?

It has been talked about, but it has not achieved the same legal standing as medical or legal malpractice. Parents have tried to sue when they've felt their children have gone through school and not gotten an adequate education, but courts haven't looked with favor on these suits. In a California case, a young man who graduated from high school reading at the fifth-grade level sued, claiming the school failed to provide him with adequate instruction.

The court couldn't find standards to measure adequate instruction. There are hundreds of educational theories, and countless reasons why young people don't learn, and not all of them have to do with the school. Therefore, the court reasoned, there was no definitive way to show the school's negligence was the cause of the youngster's failure to learn. He lost the case.[8]

But in a different kind of malpractice, where a girl was improperly placed in a special education class, a Montana court held the state was not immune from a lawsuit.[9] More recent decisions is cases such as this, where grossly negligent testing, evaluation or classification has held a youngster back, seem to be favoring the students.

FOR FURTHER INFORMATION

National Education Association
1201 16th Street NW
Washington, DC 20036
202–833–4000

American Federation of Teachers
555 New Jersey Avenue NW
Washington, DC 20001
202–879–4400

National Center for Research on Teacher Learning
Michigan State University
East Lansing, MI 48824-1034
517–353–9337

National Coalition of Education Activists
P.O. Box 405
Rosedale, NY 12472
914–658–8115

Center for Context of Teaching
CERAS Building
Stanford University
Stanford, CA 94305-3984
415–723–9613

NOTES

1. *Pickering* v. *Board of Education,* 391 U.S. 563 (1968).

2. In Re Johnson, 451 N.W. 2d 343 (1990).

3. *Board of Director of Sioux City* v. *Mroz,* 295 N.W. 2d 447 (Iowa 1980)

4. *Jackson* v. *Sobol,* 565 N.Y.S. 2d 612 (1991).

5. *Pettit* v. *State Board of Education,* 10 Cal. 3d 29, 513 P. 2d 889 (1973).

6. *Stelzer* v. *State Board of Education,* 595 N.E. 2d 489 (1991).

7. *Hainline* v. *Bond,* 824 P. 2d 959 (1992).

8. *Peter W.* v. *San Francisco School District,* 131 Cal. Rptr. 854 (1976).

9. *B.M. by Burger* v. *State of Montana,* 649 P. 2d 425 (1982).

chapter 5

TESTS AND RECORDS

We all remember the nervousness, the anticipation of taking tests in school. Have two sharpened pencils. Clear everything else from your desk. Don't look at your neighbor's paper. Ready—go!

It seemed simple enough, and hopefully it was, if you studied and were a good test-taker. But did it do much good? Tests, particularly standardized, multiple-choice tests, have come in for increasing criticism from parents and some educators who say they are biased against females, minorities and non-native English speakers, emphasize rote memory skills rather than analytical ability, and even take control of the curriculum. This chapter takes a look at issues surrounding testing and the role parents can play to make tests more meaningful. We also look at how parents can gain access to student records.

◆ DISCUSSION ◆

Standardized testing began, some educators believe, in Boston in the mid-19th century, as a supplement to oral exams. Others claim a renowned French educator, Alfred Binet, first used standardized tests to measure the achievements of mentally retarded children in 1904.

The real explosion in standardized testing began about 1960, as politicians and school administrators sought evidence that our expensive public education system was working. Now standardized testing pervades public education.

The two most common kinds of tests in grades K–12 are called "norm-referenced" and "criterion-referenced tests." In "norm-referenced tests," students are compared to others who took the test in the past, and are deemed to represent the national norm. A student scoring in the 60th percentile is said to have done better than 60 percent of the students who have taken the test in the past, and worse than 40 percent.

But sometimes these tests are "normed" years before the test is given, which gives teachers the chance to align their lessons to the test, or even teach to the test. This sometimes creates a false reading of the test's effectiveness, because all the children score above average. Norm-referenced tests are created by private, for-profit testing companies such as CTB-McGraw-Hill or Riverside.

"Criterion-referenced" is a fancy name for a test given by teachers to see if children have learned what they have just been taught in class. If children were taught spelling words on Monday through Thursday, then given a quiz on those words on Friday, the quiz is a "criterion-referenced" test. Students who score a 90 on a criterion-referenced test are deemed to have mastered 90 percent of the material. Also, many state competency tests are considered criterion referenced, because they attempt to assess knowledge of basic skills all students are supposed to be taught, such as multiplying three-digit numbers or gleaning the main point from a paragraph. If criterion-based tests are multiple-choice, they can fall into the same traps as norm-referenced tests. Of course, criterion-referenced tests can offer essay questions, or open-ended problems that require analytical thinking to solve.

Another well-known form of test is the aptitude test, which is used to predict a student's future performance. The best known of these are the Scholastic Aptitude Test and the American College Test, which are designed to predict how a high school student will perform in college. While these tests also come in for criticism, they are beyond the scope of this book.

Courts have consistently held that schools can and should develop tools to gauge the effectiveness of their programs, and that tests are such a tool. But as in every other area of education, tests, although they are legal, have caused lawsuits.

Traditionally, courts have steered clear of intervening in school testing. However, the increase in competency testing for high school diplomas has increased judicial interest in the testing process. Courts are now more likely to examine tests to see if they do in fact test what students are supposed to learn (not always easy with the variety of curriculums out there) and to determine if the tests are discriminatory.

Tests can discriminate in subtle ways, said Pamela Zappardino, executive director of FairTest, Inc., a Cambridge, Massachusetts, watchdog group that works for more accuracy and less bias in testing. Tests often ignore the subtle differences in language found in poor and upper-middle class neighborhoods. For example, a question on one test asks what children should do if they get a cut on their finger. The answer is to put a Band-Aid on it. But many urban youngsters answer: "Go to the hospital," because they think it means a serious cut. When told it doesn't, they get the right answer.

Cultural background plays a role in test results. "If you get a math question on stocks and bonds, and you don't know what they are, it will take you a little longer to answer the question. Get just four or five questions such as this in a timed test and you're behind," she said. "If reading passages deal with your cultural background, it's easier to answer the questions. Most test numbers simply tell you how well a student can take the test. Test results correspond to family income; the higher the income, the higher the test scores. The way tests are constructed institutionalizes the status quo."

The effect of discrimination against poor, minority or female students is often to relegate them to lower "tracks" or curriculum paths than their real abilities demand. We'll look more closely at "tracking" in Chapter Six. Also, research by Stanford professor Claude Steele has identified "stereotype vulnerability," which means if a certain group knows they are expected to do poorly, they will. Steele's research was done with white males as well as minorities and females.

Indeed, one-time, norm-referenced multiple choice testing can hold back middle-class white males, who might be sick on the day of the test, or just not good test takers. Of course the fact that such tests are coachable usually favors students from affluent school who have more coaching resources.

Many schools now find themselves "teaching to the test," as, for example, they prepare students for their state's mastery tests. This isn't necessarily bad; some mastery tests are well constructed and have the effect of raising standards in some schools. But it still takes away some of a teacher's options and control of the class. That isn't necessarily good.

Educators such as Gary Marx of the American Association of School Administrators say we put too much emphasis on the numbers. "We have a scoreboard mentality, we treat testing like we treat football games," he said. "We have communities with disadvantaged children. At the schools, teachers are working to make up for the social and economic problems the kids bring to school with them. And those teachers are making progress. But the test results might say they're failing. Is that fair? Standardized tests might be helpful as a benchmark, but we should never stop there. We need to know if students have mastered certain skills, to know where each child is, and standardized tests don't always tell us."

◆ ACTION STEPS ◆

Parents should learn all they can about the tests their children will have to take. Most experts allow that there's a place for some multiple choice testing, but say it should be part of a broader testing program that includes a strong and continual emphasis on thinking, and that children should be asked to write essays and solve problems.

So get a file folder. Place copies of the tests your child brings home in the folder. After you've accumulated some tests, look them over. If they are all multiple choice, take up the matter with the teacher and with your parent group's curriculum committee. There should be a balance of multiple choice questions with essay questions and problem solving questions.

In the elementary grades, tests should also emphasize two subject areas, says Professor John Wick of Northwestern University in Evanston, Illinois, a leading expert in testing. Those areas are reading comprehension and math concepts, such as changing fractions to decimals and using letters for variables. These are the building blocks for the child's educational future and must be solid. Check your file to see if your child's tests are emphasizing reading comprehension and math concepts. If not, you need to ask, "Why not?"

Wick also recommends parents ask what teachers do with test results. The results can be a helpful diagnostic tool, if they are used as such. For example, if a test shows a child is behind in, say, vocabulary, is the there a plan to improve vocabulary?

Many schools have tried to move away from strict multiple choice testing to alternative assessment tools that measure learning and progress over a longer period of time, and measure a child's ability to apply what he or she has learned. Instead of doing a fill-in-the-blank math test, it could mean applying a formula and developing a geometric diagram. In science it could mean designing an experiment. Advocates say a group project teachers such skills as teamwork, use of references and consensus building—skills highly valued but almost never emphasized or tested in school. Another method of assessment growing in popularity is the individual portfolio, a file of a student's essays, tests and other materials that stays with the student over a period of years and can provide a longitudinal look at a child's development.

South Brunswick, New Jersey, has an early childhood literary portfolio for youngsters in kindergarten through second grade. The portfolio travels with the child and is continually upgraded. It includes a number of instruments, such as a word awareness test, an interview and a word and sentence identification test, that measure a child's literary development. Each year the child takes the test and receives a score from one to six, based on a scale developed by the district and the Educational Testing Service. When a child reaches a score of six, he or she is ready for the third grade.

In the third grade, the students start a "best works" literary portfolio, that will stay with them through the eight grade and into high school. Twice a year, the students select what they feel are their two best written works, and the student and teacher select a third work, for the portfolio. Part of the student's grade is based on the literary work in the portfolio. The school also gives standardized tests. Dr. John Haymond, director of testing, said his districts like the results they've gotten with the portfolios, and said a similar portfolio program is being developed in math.

He said the developing portfolio allows a teacher to observe the development of the child and to identify strengths as well as areas that need more work.

Not everyone agrees that portfolios, or other such projects, should be a part of testing. Wick, for example, thinks a teacher judging a portfolio is too subjective to provide any meaningful comparison among students. But he enthusiastically agrees that portfolios are excellent teaching tools.

Your curriculum committee, working with your school administration, should examine a portfolio program, if you don't have one, and also push for a greater percentage of performance assessments, in which children do something or produce something, rather than fill in blanks.

Because one-time, multiple choice tests are often unreliable, parents should always raise a red flag when any decision about their child is made based on such a test, or any time a decision is based on one indicator, period.

Finally, there are going to be tests of one kind or another, and parents shouldn't forget the basics of helping their children prepare. Sometimes it helps children to see real life examples of what they are studying. For example, if your child is studying for a math test, pull out the gas bill or the water bill and explain the importance of family math. Also, make sure your child has a quiet place to study, has left enough time to study, gets plenty of rest the night before the test, and has a good breakfast.

STUDENT RECORDS

Test results become part of a student's record. Before 1974, student records were not always available to parents. For example:

- A parent was told she had no right to see the records that were used in the decision to put her child in a special education class for students with mental retardation.

- Another parent who was told his child needed psychological counseling had to get a court order to see his son's records.

- A father went to a parents meeting and learned his son's records said he was inordinately interested in girls and had strange political ideas—in the fifth and sixth grades. Did they confuse his son's records with those of Hugh Hefner?

- A father who was told his son needed psychological counseling had to get a court order to see his child's school records.[1]

In these and countless other cases, the parents were shocked. Often, schools would make records available to law enforcement agencies or other government agencies, but not to parents. Most parents had no idea what was in school records, what the records were used for, and what damage an incorrect or poorly kept record could cause. Parents continued having these problems even though several major court cases said parents should have access to their children's records.

Something had to be done, and something was. U.S. Senator James Buckley, a New York Conservative, proposed the Family Educational Rights and Privacy Act, known as FERPA or the Buckley Amendment. It's one of the most important legal tools for parents, one every parent should be familiar with.

The FERPA law is essentially this: The U.S. Department of Education requires that schools receiving federal funds:

- Grant to the parents of present or former students the right to inspect and review the educational records of their children.

- Do not release educational records or other personally identifiable information about the student, with some basic exceptions, without written permission of the parent (or the student, if he or she is over the age of 18).

If a school violates either of these basic precepts, the ultimate penalty is the cutoff of federal funds.

The act begins by requiring that every school or institution that receives federal funds (public schools and colleges and most private colleges and universities) must establish procedures that give parents access to student records within a period of 45 days. Some parents think they have a right to view records immediately. They don't, under FERPA. The school has 45 days to provide the records.

Under the act, a school can still release some information about students without parental permission. Mostly, this is what is called "directory information," and it is the kind of stuff that might be found in a school yearbook. It includes: Name, address, telephone listing, date and place of birth, major field of study, participation in official activities and sports, dates of attendance, weight and height of members of athletic teams, degrees and awards received, and most recent educational institution attended by the student.

Also, parental permission isn't required to release students' records:

- To other school officials or teachers who have a legitimate educational interest in the student

- To other schools where the students seeks or intends to enroll, as long as the student's parents receive notice of the transfer and receive a copy of the records if desired, and have a chance to challenge the content of the records if they so desire

- In connection with a student's application for, or receipt of, financial aid

- To authorized representatives of certain government agencies including the state education department

- To accrediting organizations in order to carry out their accrediting function

- To state and local officials pursuant to laws passed before November 19, 1974

- To parents of a dependent student as defined by law

- To appropriate persons in case of emergency, if the knowledge is necessary to protect the health and safety of the student or others

Beyond these exceptions, schools cannot release personally identifiable information without the written consent of parents, specifying what records are being released. Schools must also keep a record of what information from a student's records has been released and to whom. Parents have access to this document.

In addition, schools have to tell parents what information is in their child's file, and explain it to the parents if need be.

VIOLATIONS

Parents who feel their child's school is violating the act have a right to demand a hearing. Parents may wish to challenge the records because they are inaccurate or misleading, or to challenge the school's policy of releasing information. The hearing would provide the opportunity to correct or delete any information found to be incorrect or inappropriate. The parents do not have to hire a lawyer, but may if they choose, at their own expense.

The law isn't specific on who should conduct the hearing; it can be any school official who isn't involved in the matter at hand. The hearing officer must provide the parents with a full opportunity to present their evidence. The school has to reach a written decision based solely on the evidence. If the school decides it is correct, it must offer the parents the chance to put a letter in the file stating their objections to the record in question.

If the parents still are not satisfied, they can file a complaint with the U.S. Department of Education's Family Policy Compliance Office (4000 Maryland Avenue SW, Washington, D.C. 20202–4605), charging the school isn't complying with the act. Under regulations adopted in 1993, the individual filing the complaint has 180 days from the time he knew or should have known of the problem to file the complaint.

According to LeRoy Rooker, the office's director, the office receives hundreds of complaints a year, but many are without merit. He said many parents demand records immediately, not realizing the school has 45 days to provide them. He said some parents also demand copies, not knowing they're only eligible for copies if they can't come to the school and read the records.

The office ends up investigating about 100 cases a year. In a recent case, a small Midwestern district had a special education student they were sending to a special school out of state. They discussed the particulars of his case at a public meeting. Rooker's office investigated, and found the board had violated the student's privacy and the Buckley Amendment. The school was given a warning and ordered not to discuss the case in public in the future.

When a school is in violation, Rooker's people tell the school what it has to do to comply. If the school doesn't comply, it faces loss of federal funds. That is a big stick. In 20 years, no school has bucked the compliance office and had its funds cut off.

The Buckley Amendment is generally quite a successful reform measure. It has put a different spin on many school situations:

- At one time, for example, it was common for schools to post grades after examinations. The grades were usually posted next to the names of students. Now, under the act, that might be viewed as a violation of the student's right to privacy. A New York court resolved this by ordering the grades scrambled and the names removed before they were posted.[2] The case allowed parents to compare grades and find out how the class was doing overall, without knowing names. The decision suggests that it's okay to post grades, as long as a code is used so the students aren't readily identifiable.

- Then there's the matter of law enforcement investigations. Before the act, the FBI and other agencies had pretty much free access to student records. That has now changed. If the FBI, the Drug Enforcement Administration, or another agency presents the school with a subpoena for records, the school has to honor it. The one big difference is that the student or parent must be notified.

This makes it hard for investigators who are trying to do undercover probes, who are trying to find out what a student's grades are or who his classmates are. But the law is the law, and the school has to report requests for student records.

◆ ACTION STEPS ◆

FERPA is an excellent law, so use it. The Parents Union for Public Schools of Philadelphia offers the following tips on inspecting your child's records.

First, remember that in addition to having the right to examine your child's records, you can also bring a parent advocate with you, get copies of records, and challenge false or misleading information. To examine the records:

- At least once a year, call your child's counselor or the principal's office and set up an appointment. Plan to spend from 30 minutes to two hours. Someone will probably explain the various forms to you. Then go through them yourself, looking at both the front and back.

- You can take notes about the materials or get copies, so that you can write directly on them. You may have to pay for the copies, but the school must provide copies if you need them and cannot pay.

Most, if not all, student records will be in the pupil packet, known in some states as the "cume" or cumulative record. You have access to all records kept in this file and elsewhere in the school. These records should consist of:

- Test results
- Medical records, which are usually in the nurses office
- Attendance records
- Grades, from the current year and former years, along with teacher's comments

The records may also include:

- Counseling record, which in all likelihood is in the counselor's office
- Psychological record, which may be in the pocket or elsewhere
- Discipline record. If acquired at another school, it will most likely be in the packet. If acquired at the present school, it may

be in the principal's office. Ask to see any other forms or records pertaining to discipline

Remember that if you find any false or misleading information, you have the right to demand that it be removed. If school officials refuse to remove it, you can insert your own written statement into the file, and can pursue a hearing. One note of caution: a teacher's personal notes that aren't part of any other permanent record aren't subject to FERPA. In other words, a teacher's notes to herself or himself, that aren't part of grades or other formal records, don't have to be released (although most teachers are happy to share them with parents).

◆ SELECTED QUESTIONS ◆

What happens if parents are divorced? Who gets to see the records?

The law says information in the records must be released to both parents, custodial and noncustodial, unless there is a court order to the contrary.

This sometimes causes difficulties when one parent is trying to get the address and phone number of the other, and that information is in the student's file. Barring a court order or other legal document to the contrary, the information is available to the other parent.

What if a school withholds grades as a punitive measure? Does that mean parents can't see them?

Some schools do withhold grades as a disciplinary measure, for not paying fees, returning library books or somesuch. The act does say that parents must be able to see their child's records. But it also allows the school to claim a "legitimate cause" to deny copies of records. The withholding policy would be such a cause. So a parent would be able to see the grades, but might have to bring pen and paper to the school to copy them down.

Our state university is interested in our daughter as a soccer player. What records are they entitled to see?

Parents of high schoolers being recruited as college athletes should remember that if their child is a minor, the college needs their written permission to get your child's records. Obviously, colleges need such information as grade point averages and SAT scores. But you can monitor what information is released to the colleges and challenge anything you believe is incorrect.

Will there ever be national student testing?

Possibly, at least on a voluntary basis. At present we have the National Assessment of Educational Progress, also known as The Nation's Report Card. This test was created by Congress in 1969 to measure student achievement in the fourth, eighth, and twelfth grades. It is given periodically in most states in reading, writing, math, science, and history/geography.

With the test showing students making little progress in 20 years, the movement for national standards and national testing has gained momentum. In 1992 a Congressional panel called for national standards and a national system of tests. The Goals 2000 legislation in 1994 established a voluntary set of standards, but the question of national testing is still being debated.

What about report cards? Should we make a big deal out of them, as our parents used to?

Many parents make too much of report cards, in the wrong way. John Wherry of the Parent Institute in Fairfax Station, Virginia, a company that helps schools develop ways to work with parents, said incidents of child abuse rise on the day report cards come home from school. Hitting a child for a bad report card isn't very helpful. First of all, if you are in touch with your child's teacher, the report card shouldn't be a surprise. Use it as a diagnostic tool. If there are weaknesses, ask the teacher what is being done about them, and what you can do at home to help.

FOR FURTHER INFORMATION

FairTest
342 Broadway
Cambridge, MA 02139
617–864–4810

Educational Testing Service
Center for Assessment of Educational Progress
Rosedale Road
Princeton, NJ 08541–0001
609–921–9000

Ruth Mitchell (testing consultant)
725 15th Street NW
Washington, DC 20005
202–547–4393

National Assessment of Educational Progress
PO Box 6710
Princeton, NJ 08541–8710
1–800–223–0267

State Education Assessment Center
Council of Chief State School Officers
1 Massachusetts Avenue NW Suite 700
Washington, DC 20001–1431

John Wick (testing expert)
Professor of Education
Northwestern University
Evanston, IL 60201
708–835–2065

The Parent Institute (provides schools with materials on parental involvement, but deals *only* with schools)
P.O. Box 7474
Fairfax Station, VA 22039–7474
1–800–756–5525

NOTES

1. David Schimmel and Louis Fischer, "Parents, Schools and the Law" (National Committee for Citizens in Education, Washington, D.C.)

2. *Kryston* v. *Board of Education,* 77 A.D. 2d 896, 430 N.Y.S. 2d 688 (1980).

WHO IS ON TRACK?

◆ INTRODUCTION ◆

Elaine's daughter Jeanne came home from the fourth grade with news. The teacher was going to split the class into three reading groups. Elaine started thinking. She'd read to Jeanne since the child was eight months old. She wanted Jeanne to be in the top reading group. Should she call the teacher? Or would it make any difference, because it's only the fourth grade?

Yes, it does. Many experts we spoke with had two pieces of advice for parents such as Elaine. The first is to do everything she can to get her daughter into the highest group she can handle, in reading and in any subject where the kids are divided into groups.

The second step is to get your parents group to work to do away with grouping by ability. These two ideas may seem contradictory, but they aren't.

◆ DISCUSSION ◆

The idea of grouping students by ability has been around for most of the 20th century. In the 1920s some high schools had as many as eight tracks, everything from classical to general secretarial. Today, an estimated 80 percent of schools use some kind of tracking or ability grouping. Some students are tracked as early as kindergarten, by being placed into high, medium, or low reading groups. This may continue right through high school, with "academic" versus "general" diplomas.

But in recent years, tracking and ability grouping have come increasingly under fire. Hundreds of studies have been done, and studies have been done of the studies, and they still don't agree. Nonetheless, an increasing number of experts say tracking doesn't work and lessens educational opportunities for many children.

The terms "ability grouping" and "tracking" are sometimes used interchangeably, but there is a distinction.[1]

Ability grouping, also called homogenous grouping, usually refers to the separating of same-grade children, usually by test scores and records, into different aptitude or ability groups. These groups may be separate classes for children of high, medium and low aptitude, single-subject grouping, cross-grade grouping for reading and math, special classes for gifted and talented students, or in-class groupings.

The term "tracking," which once was used to describe categories of elementary school groupings, is now mostly used for junior high school and high school programs in which a student chooses college preparatory, general or vocational programs, based on their own objectives.

Chapter Seven will discuss issues surrounding education of children with disabilities, and whether they should be grouped together in special education classes, or with so-called mainstream children. This chapter focuses on the mainstream children, whether they should be grouped by aptitude, and whether their parents can influence the process.

So what's wrong with tracking and ability grouping? The first problem recognized by the courts, as we said in Chapter Five, is that grouping can discriminate against poor, minority or immigrant children. This has been a problem for years.

If you walk around Washington, D.C., you can still find some blocks with two old school buildings on them. This is because until 1954 our nation's capital had racially segregated schools. After the Supreme

Court outlawed segregation, the District of Columbia school system began a track system, with four tracks, beginning in elementary school. The tracks were: Honors, for the gifted and talented; Regular, a college prep track in the high schools; General, the college prep track in the elementary and junior high schools; and Special Academic or Basic, for the slow learners.

A group of black parents brought suit, saying a disproportionate number of black students were ending up in the Basic classes, in effect resegregating the schools. The court found the situation outrageous. Indeed, there were a disproportionate number of blacks in the lowest track, and most couldn't get out. The kids in the Basic track were supposed to get remedial help, but most weren't. In some schools, the kids had no chance of moving up to a higher track. In many predominantly black schools, there was no Honors track. Also, many black youngsters couldn't start kindergarten because of overcrowding, a lesser problem at predominantly white schools.

The court also found that the testing used to place children in the various tracks was flawed. The court held the track system was a violation of the plaintiffs' constitutional rights and "simply must be abolished."[2]

The issue was raised again in the 1970s in California. The parents of a group of black elementary school students in San Francisco sued because their children were placed in classes for the Educable Mentally Retarded. The parents said their children weren't retarded, they were placed in the EMR classes on the basis of biased tests, particularly the school's system's IQ test.

The school system couldn't provide a "compelling justification" for the placement system. Also, psychologists testified that when they worked with the youngsters to make the test more consistent with their cultural backgrounds, they scored much higher on it. So the court ordered the school system to stop what it was doing.[3]

These kinds of problems have continued into the 1990s. Advocates broke up a segregated tracking system in San Jose, California, that had many minority youngsters in the lower tracks. According to the consent decree, the school district must eliminate ability grouping in grades K–9 and have open enrollment for all types of classes.

The district will also recruit minority students for all advanced programs.[4]

These resegregation cases may be extreme, but they reflect trends that exist in many districts around the country. While at one time it was believed that tracking worked and was democratic, that it provided students with the education that best suited their abilities and provided the nation with the workers it needed, it's now becoming clear it does neither of these very well.

New evidence strongly suggests that almost every child can reach every worthwhile educational goal. Tracking is thus only a "social structure," based on an outmoded and inaccurate view of children's abilities.

UNTRACKING

Is tracking or ability grouping doing more harm than good? Yes, says Anne Wheelock of Northeastern University in Boston, in a persuasive book titled *Crossing the Tracks* (The New Press, 1992). She urges schools to get about the business of "untracking," and many schools around the country are doing just that.

Wheelock says tracking creates an unequal distribution of effective schooling, giving the most meaningful and challenging curricula, top instruction and highest expectations to the students who already have the greatest advantages. Meanwhile, students who face more of life's struggles are given the short end of the stick, and over years lose ground to the top-track children, creating a school society of haves and have-nots.

We can do better, says Wheelock. We can create a system of mixed ability classes in which not only do the former low-track students rise to the level of instruction and expectation, but also the former top-track children do better still. It requires a substantial shift in the way we think of school. It calls for shifts in curricula, and particularly new teaching methods. But to do it is to release intelligence rather than quantify it, nurture effort rather than define ability, and build strengths rather than sort according to weakness.

"If you combine heterogeneous grouping with a high content curriculum, it will stretch the minds of all children," Wheelock said in an interview.

Most of the time, the hardest sell for "untracking" is to parents of children in the honors or gifted and talented classes. They worry that being in classes with a mixed groups of students will hold their children back. If untracking is done incorrectly, that could be right. If, for instance, a teacher hands the slower developing kids three pages to copy and the kids who are further along six pages to copy, and those children are bored, then obviously the thing isn't working.

But if teaching methods change with untracking, then there are numerous advantages. Teachers will use methods in which the students challenge themselves instead of competing with one another. They'll work in teams to solve problems. They'll work on projects and papers, and get extra work if appropriate. In these circumstances, the so-called brighter kids can cull several advantages:

- They'll learn more problem-solving skills.
- What they learn will stay with them, because they have to explain their answers and point of view to others.
- Students will be encouraged to take more risks. One of the social pitfalls of current "high" tracks is that many students are afraid to ask questions for fear of appearing stupid.
- Students will learn greater acceptance and appreciation of others.
- Students can unlearn some self-limiting notions, such as, "If I can't learn it quickly, I'm not smart."

The conclusion, says Wheelock, is: "You can create a situation that challenges everyone. You can give extra time and attention to the slower children, so you don't have to water down the curriculum."

One of the bedrock ideas behind the untracking movement is that all children can be successfully taught. Researchers such as Ronald Edmonds have said since the 1970s that the knowledge is available to create schools that will effectively educate all students, from the urban poor to the wealthier suburban youngsters. This has been the touchstone for the "effective schools" movement of the 1980s. This movement has produced programs such as the Accelerated Schools Project developed by Henry Levin at Stanford University, the Coalition for

Essential Schools developed by Theodore Sizer at Brown University and Success for All created by Robert Slavin and others at Johns Hopkins University.

All these programs are compatible with untracking. Success for All, for example, is a school-wide pre-K to 5 program that ensures virtually every student reaches the third grade with adequate reading skills. It employs tutors, cooperative learning, frequent assessments and family support teams to see that no student falls through the cracks. The program began in Baltimore in 1986. Extensive evaluation indicates children in the program are doing significantly better than students in a control group in all grade levels from first to third. The program has shown similar good results in several other cities around the country.

Does the success of such programs mean that all grouping of any kind should be done away with? Not necessarily. Robert Slavin of the Center for Effective Schooling for Disadvantaged Students at Johns Hopkins says that while there's no evidence that the traditional forms of ability grouping, such as dividing a reading class into high, medium and low groups, works, some temporary grouping in math may be beneficial, because young children learn the concepts—that numbers stand for things and can be added, subtracted, multiplied and divided—at different developmental speeds. Also, the so-called Joplin Plan, which groups students across grade lines for reading, has its defenders as well. The keys to a successful group are flexibility, frequent reevaluation and mobility between groups. Groups that tend not to work are those that are inflexible and allow for little adaptation. Simply putting kids together is not beneficial. It's what's being taught with what degree of skill that is the big question.

Massachusetts has come as close as any state to banning ability grouping. The state board of education told local officials in 1990 it would no longer offer certain categories of grants for ability grouping programs.

The board sent an advisory to the districts, which reviewed the materials on grouping and reached the following conclusions:

- There is little evidence that ability grouping or tracking improves academic achievement, while overwhelming evidence exists that ability grouping retards the academic progress of low- and middle-ability groups.

- Ability grouping can lead to lower expectations, fewer demands and a lesser education for the low ability group.

- Ability grouping can lead to lower self-esteem, predetermined failure and developmental problems for those placed in the low-ability groups. The groups can also serve as a form of racial, economic, gender or language segregation.

- Ability grouping is an ineffective means of addressing individual differences. Also, it's unclear if grouping makes teaching easier.[5]

◆ Action Steps ◆

The first thing parents must realize are the implications of the placement process. Parents usually understand that having their children placed in "high" groups can have long-term benefits. Most of these parents don't have to be told to fight for a better placement for their children. The first step is to get the facts about the tracking policy in your school. Call your principal, the head of the parent organization and your child's teacher, and ask:

- What is the scope of the school's tracking policy? Is that policy set within the school or by the district?

- How many subjects and grades are tracked, and how many tracks there are in each?

- How are teachers assigned to classes?

- How are decisions made about track placement?

- What materials are used in each curriculum?

- How many children move from low tracks into higher tracks each year?

- How many students are enrolled in each track, by race and by grade?

- Where are the expectations for students in each track?

Having done this, you will have the kind of information that can provide the basis for discussion. Discussion is merited if the system isn't serving all the students equally.

At this stage your parents organization can take the initiative, and, working with the administration, can sponsor a forum or a series of discussions on tracking versus untracking. Bring in experts. Discuss the pros and cons. Talk to officials from schools who have untracked (*Crossing the Tracks* has a list of such schools).

Barbara Oates, principal of the Ray A. Kroc Middle School in San Diego, says you will have to sell the idea to the parents of gifted and talented children, but says many can be won over. One tactic is to show these parents how difficult, and sometimes arbitrary, the selection process is for gifted and talented programs. Many will come away thinking there need to be such programs for all students.

Oates said the untracking of her school has been "very successful." The key, she said, "is that we never lowered our standards."

When a school uses tracking, fight to get your children into the highest groups and classes the children can *reasonably be expected* to master. If the placement decision has already been made, don't be shy about asking for a teacher conference to override the decision. Until we reach the point where we're doing our best with all of our children, this is the game parents have to play.

GIFTED AND TALENTED

For many parents, the way to get some individual programming for their children is to get them into a gifted and talented program, if their school has one. "GATE" programs, as they are sometimes known, are often the target of budget cutters.

Gifted and talented programs have been around in some states for decades. Proponents say they are a way to challenge the best and brightest; critics have charged the programs are elitist. In the 1970s a federal grant provided seed money for experimental programs and teacher training. The federal government has continued to provide this level of support; the most recent federal law on the subject, the Jacob K. Javits Gifted and Talented Students Act of 1988, funds training, research and demonstration projects regarding gifted children.

However, there's never been a federal mandate to identify and serve gifted and talented students. As a result, the availability of gifted and talented programs depends on where you live. More than half the states have laws, backed by some level of funding, that require school districts to identify gifted youngsters and create appropriate programs for them. Also, some school districts have started gifted programs even though their state doesn't require them.

What is a gifted and talented child? Definitions vary from state to state, say Frances Karnes and Ronald Marquardt of the University of Southern Mississippi in their fine book, *Gifted Children and the Law* (Ohio Psychology Press, 1991). Most definitions include references to high general intellectual ability and aptitude for outstanding performance in one or more subject areas. Some states still use the IQ test, but newer definitions of gifted children also make reference to creative and problem solving ability, leadership ability, and outstanding ability in the performing arts. However the definition is worded, it is usually set to include anywhere from 2 to 12 percent of the school's population in the gifted program.

As we'll see in Chapter Seven, youngsters with learning disabilities, or handicaps that affect learning, must have individual education programs developed for them. Ten states require the same thing for gifted and talented students. Also, several states have policies under which exceptional students can be accelerated, either by whole grade or by individual subject.

The special programs for gifted and talented children vary from school to school, but may involve separate tracks, or pull-out enrichment classes, or individual projects with specially trained teachers.

If you want to get your child into a gifted and talented resource program, and you're pretty sure your child can handle it, call the gifted and talented teacher yourself. Often these programs have room for more children, and the teacher can expedite your child's admission.

COURT CHALLENGES

The courts have not been particularly sympathetic to parents with complaints about gifted and talented programs. For example, let's look at a Pennsylvania case that gifted and talented advocates consider a big victory.

A boy named Terry Auspitz had been identified as gifted and talented in reading and math. His school program included two and a half hours a week in an enrichment class with other gifted children.

His parents felt he should have an individualized program in math and reading. They went through various levels of administrative appeals, and then sued. The case got to the state Supreme Court. Pennsylvania mandates gifted and talented education, and state law requires an individualized program for gifted and talented children. The court held that an enrichment program wasn't enough, and that the school had to design an individual program for Terry.

This was a victory, but with a Pyrrhic quality. It took six years to work its way through the courts. And while the court did say Terry needed an individual program, the justices said the school only had to create this program within its current capabilities. If, for example, the school didn't have specialized tutoring or off-campus programs, they didn't have to create one for Terry. "The school district is not required to become a Harvard or a Princeton for every student with an IQ over 130," the court said.[6]

Still, the court did require an individual program for gifted children. Courts do seem reluctant, however, to make schools create programs they don't already have. In another Pennsylvania case, a gifted 14-year-old had taken all of his school's math courses by the end of his sophomore year. The school had nothing else for him.

His parents enrolled him in a college program, and at the same time went after the school to either create a program for him, or reimburse them for the university program. The case got to court, and the judge in effect turned them down, saying the school could have an off-campus college program, but had done all it was legally required to do for the boy.[7]

Parents whose children weren't selected for gifted and talented programs have also brought lawsuits. One Pennsylvania family brought several cases involving their children not being selected for gifted and advanced programs and courses.

They challenged the standardized tests that were used to pick the students for an advanced communications course. They lost. The court said the test just had to be "rationally related" to the educational purpose of the program, and it was.[8]

The family said it wasn't getting an equal share of taxpayers' money by not being in the gifted program. The court said sorry, you have a right to have access to the educational system, but not to a particular level of instruction. The court said the state did its job by creating the school system. They could leave questions about how money was allocated for education to the educators.

The argument made by the parents in this case is still heard in many quarters. If precious resources are lavished on a small percentage of youngsters at the top, and on youngsters with disabilities, some parents ask, don't the kids in the middle have a right to ask for something as well?

Another problem that irks parents of gifted children is the qualifications of the men and women who teach in gifted programs. Some states require certification of gifted teachers, and some do not. Where there is no separate certification, gifted teachers are sometimes the first to go in a budget crunch. In fact, gifted and talented programs are being challenged all over the country, and are often being cut out of school budgets. What is the long-term answer?

Many experts, such as those who advocate untracking, think it's time to do away with the term "gifted and talented," and provide programs that challenge the ability and potential of every child. "Somewhere in the rhetoric about improving schools, we seem to have lost sight of an ideal upon which our education system . . . is based. This ideal asserts that the uniqueness and individuality of every individual should be honored and respected," writes Joseph S. Renzulli, director of the National Research Center on the Gifted and Talented at the University of Connecticut.[9]

Renzulli agrees with critics who say criteria for gifted and talented programs have been drawn too narrowly, and have relied too much on tests such as the IQ test. Research by scholars such as Howard Gardner of Harvard University suggests there are more kinds of intelligences that could respond to different kinds of programs.

Renzulli recommends taking the techniques developed in gifted and talented programs and using them to help all students develop "higher-order thinking skills and pursue more rigorous content than is typically found in today's 'dumbed down' textbooks." It's a great challenge for teachers, but we think schools must develop programs that will challenge every student.

GRADE SKIPPING

With gifted and talented programs falling to budget cuts around the country, many educators have rediscovered an old and not as expensive alternative: acceleration. There are several forms of acceleration, including starting school early, skipping entire grades, acceleration in certain subjects and advanced placement courses.

Grade skipping was popular in this country until the 1920s, when concern over developmental problems and the Great Depression's shrinking job market made early graduation less attractive. Now, new research on acceleration is making believers of educators who work with gifted children.

It makes sense that if a youngster in the third grade can do sixth grade math, the youngster ought to be challenged in his or her ability range, say experts such as Robert Slavin. But some educators worry that advancing younger children may leave them socially isolated, with fewer opportunities for extracurriculars or student leadership posts.

That could all happen. Advocates of acceleration say it isn't for everyone, and that a thorough psychological assessment is essential to determine if a child is ready for acceleration.

Precocious youngsters who are ready to be moved along will have a period of adjustment, but ultimately will benefit, experts say. Lots of acceleration programs have become well established, such as New York City's Special Progress program, which allows students to complete grades seven, eight and nine in two years. Many educators expect to see more acceleration, as gifted programs are cut and parents demand more challenges for their children.

◆ ACTION STEPS ◆

If your child is not being challenged in school and is bored, then you have got to do something. "Do what you'd do for any child with any problem. First, get into the school and find out what is going on," advises Peter Rosenstein, director of the National Association for Gifted Children in Washington, D.C.

First, talk to the teacher. Find out why your child is bored. If the teacher can't help, move up the ladder. Talk to the principal, the superintendent, then members of the school board.

If your child is gifted in music, and there's no music program, then advocate for one. Talk to other parents and educators and see what programs are out there. Join groups. See what programs exist in other school districts in your area. You may be able to switch into another program.

Work with your child at home, to be involved in homework as well as what's going on in school.

The existence of gifted and talented programs and the rules that govern them vary from state to state, and often from district to district. Find out what you've got in your district. If you feel your child has been improperly tested or improperly excluded from a program, there most likely is a set of nonjudicial procedures to resolve disputes between parents and the school over the program.

This typically starts with a parent-teacher-principal conference. If that doesn't resolve the problem, the next step might be mediation. If that fails, there may be a formal hearing. Should the case not be resolved, it could then go to a state department of education review. Only if all this fails should you even consider a court action.

◆ SELECTED QUESTIONS ◆

In my state, schools are required only to identify gifted and talented students. They don't have to provide any programs. A lot of schools don't even bother identifying gifted children. Is it worth it for me to push my school to identify gifted children?

It can be. Here's a hypothetical situation. Suppose your child is very bright, but is shy, or has a behavioral problem. Then let's say you have to change schools, or get a new teacher who doesn't understand what the problem is. The "gifted and talented" designation would be a message to the new teacher that another teacher thought highly of your child. That message likely would encourage the new teacher to look more closely at your child, and could keep your child from being misclassified.

In my daughter's school there is only one teacher available to teach gifted and talented children. As a result, even though there are six kids in my daughter's class who qualify, only three are chosen to receive the special teaching. How can I make certain that my daughter, who qualifies, isn't left behind?

Your child's intelligence doesn't guarantee a placement in gifted and talented programs. If there are only so many slots in the program, by all means do your homework and make an immediate appointment with the teacher who handles gifted and talented children. Get to know the teacher. Make the best pitch you can for your child.

What can I do for my child at home?

Plenty. Don't wait for the school to fill the void in gifted and talented teaching. Speak with your child's teacher and the gifted and talented teacher. Get suggestions for extra reading and math assignments, or work in the area in which your child is gifted or advanced. Then, if your child can handle it, become your child's teacher away from school. Do a project with your child that involves reading a book, solving some problems, writing a story or learning a piece of music. Use a half hour a day, or a couple of hours a week. Look for concerts, films, museum exhibits, or plays that will fit in with your home teaching project. Some experts such as Howard Gardner believe children learn best while doing projects. Mom and dad may learn something as well.

What about grade retention? Are children still kept back?

Sue Bredekamp of the National Association for the Education of Young Children, among other experts, says grade retention is an increasingly discredited way of dealing with a child's problems. She said considerable research—almost unanimous research—shows grade retention doesn't help improve academic success, but does harm a child's self-image and his or her attitude toward school. She said retention in many cases has long-term negative effects. One such effect is that kids who become over age for their class are likely to drop out.

Also, if a child had a difficult year, there's usually not much point in doing the same thing over. The result will likely be the same. The better intervention, Bradycamp said, is to work on the youngster's particular problem. For example, if a teacher is thinking of keeping a youngster back because of a reading problem, the better solution is to develop an after school and summer reading program that will help the child get up to speed.

"Retention is a lazy way to deal with a problem; it's almost giving up on the child, almost blaming the child. It should be a real last resort strategy," she said.

FOR FURTHER INFORMATION

Anne Wheelock
23 Lake Hall
Northeastern University
360 Huntington Avenue
Boston, MA 02115
617–373–5666

Success for All/Center for Effective School for Disadvantaged Students
3505 N. Charles Street
Baltimore, MD 21218
410–516–0370

National Association for Gifted Children
1155 15th Street NW Suite 1002
Washington, DC 20005
202–785–4268

Center on the Gifted and Talented
University of Connecticut
Department of Educational Psychology
Storrs, CT 06269–2007
203–486–5279

Graham Child Development Center
105 Smith Level Road
Campus Box 8180
University of North Carolina
Chapel Hill, NC 27599
919–962–7374

NOTES

1. James A. Kulik, "An Analysis on the Research on Ability Grouping; Historical and Contemporary Perspectives" (National Research Center on the Gifted and Talented, Storrs, CT, 1990).

2. *Hobson* v. *Hansen,* U.S. Court of Appeals, 269 F. Supp. 401 (D.D.C.), 1967.

3. *P.* v. *Riles,* 343 F. Supp. 1306 (N.D. Cal. 1972) aff'd per curiam 502 F. 2d 963 (9th Cir. 1974).

4. *Vasquez; et. al.* v. *San Jose Unified School District,* Case no. C71-2130 RMW (SJ) Order February 18,1994.

5. Dan French and Sheldon Rothman, "Structuring Schools for Student Success: A Focus on Ability Grouping" (Massachusetts Board of Education, 1990).

6. *Centennial School District* v. *Department of Education,* 517 Penn. 540, 539 A. 2s 785 (1988).

7. *Scott S.* v. *Department of Education,* 512 A 2d 790 (Penna. Cmwth. Ct. 1986).

8. See *Doe* v. *Commonwealth Board of Education,* 593 F. Supp. 548 (1984); *Lisa H.* v. *State Board of Education,* 447 A. 2d 669 (1983); and *Roe* v. *Commonwealth Department of Education,* 638 F. Supp. 929 (1987).

9. Joseph S. Renzulli, "Schools are Places for Talent Development: Applying 'Gifted Education' Know-how to Total School Improvement" (essay sponsored by Javits Act Program, administered by U.S. Department of Education's Office of Educational Research and Improvement).

SPECIAL CHILDREN, SPECIAL NEEDS

◆ INTRODUCTION ◆

The Smiths have a daughter, Ellen, who is in the third grade. She was getting by in school, but not doing particularly well and not enjoying it very much. The Smiths were at their wit's end. They knew something was wrong, but they didn't know what. They asked the teacher for help, and then went to the principal. Both said they thought Ellen was doing fine, and would grow out of the little doldrum she happened to be in.

But Ellen's parents knew her and knew something was wrong. They had her tested at a private diagnostic facility, where their suspicions were confirmed. Ellen had a learning disability. With the facts in hand, not only did they get the school to design an individual education plan just for Ellen, but they also got the school to pay for the testing. This is because of a remarkable law known as IDEA, which has made a huge difference to countless thousands of children with disabilities and their parents.

◆ DISCUSSION ◆

Until the 1960s and even the 1970s, persons with mental or physical disabilities were often segregated in dank "training schools" that were little more than human warehouses. Hundreds of thousands of handicapped children weren't even allowed in public schools. Many who were in public schools didn't have trained teachers or support services. Parents often had to send children with disabilities to expensive private schools. This began to change in the early 1970s, with a case well known to most mental retardation workers.

The Pennsylvania Association for Retarded Children (PARC) and the parents of 17 children with mental retardation brought an action against the state, challenging a law that allowed students with disabilities to be kept out of school if they were deemed "uneducable and untrainable" by school psychologists.[1]

The plaintiffs presented considerable expert testimony that most persons with mental retardation were in fact so educable and trainable that they could reach a level of self-sufficiency, and that those who couldn't could still reach some level of self-care.

The parents also argued that the law violated due process and equal protection, and that since the state constitution guaranteed a free public education to all children, they couldn't exclude children who happened to have a disability.

The court agreed, saying the state had to provide a "free public program of education and training appropriate to the child's capacity."[2]

The PARC case opened the door, and other cases soon followed. In 1972 some Washington, D.C. parents challenged a similar situation that was keeping thousands of youngsters out of school. The district school board said it didn't have the money to educate these children.

The court said those youngsters had a right to attend school, and that if the district couldn't raise more money, it had better use what it had to get some kind of education for all the children.[3]

Congress figured out which way the wind was blowing, and passed a major piece of legislation, the Education for All Handicapped Children Act, in 1975.

This law, renamed the Individuals with Disabilities Education Act (IDEA) in 1990, provides that all children in the country who have a disability and require special services be provided with a free appropriate public education, with necessary support services, in the least restrictive environment. In other words, it requires special education for the youngsters who need it. In addition to the federal law, each state has also passed its own version of IDEA, so that procedures sometimes differ from state to state, but the basic rights remain. Thanks to IDEA and its state counterparts, parents of children requiring special education have the greatest array of legal rights in any area of education.

In the 1993–94 school year, the last for which U.S. Department of Education figures are available, 5.4 million youngsters received services under federal education programs for the handicapped. The largest group, 51.1 percent of these youngsters, was classified as learning disabled, meaning they had a particular learning disability. Another 21.1 percent were speech or language impaired, while 11.6 percent were described as mentally retarded and 8.7 percent as seriously emotionally disturbed.

About 40 percent of disabled children receive services in regular classrooms, while 31 percent are served in "resource rooms" for part of the day and 23.5 percent are in self-contained "special ed" classes. The others are in separate schools or residential facilities. Almost 85 percent of youngsters receiving services are between the ages of 6 and 17.

Teachers specialize in one or more disabling conditions, which range from hearing, speech or visual impairment to mental retardation or emotional problems. There remains a shortage of special education teachers in the country.

Children eligible for special education services include those with the following categories of disabilities: speech or language impairment, visual disability, hearing impairment, learning disabilities, serious emotional disorder, orthopedic or other medical impairment, mental retardation, physical disability, multiple handicaps, neurological impairment, autism, and traumatic brain injury. The most common forms of learning disabilities are dyslexia, which is a broad term encompassing any difficulty with reading; dysgraphia, difficulty with handwriting; and dyscalculia, difficulty with mathematics.

Some states now include students who need special education services because of social or emotional maladjustment, pediatric AIDS, attention deficit disorder, drugs in utero, and even disorders that arise from reactions to vaccines.[4] In many states, pregnancy makes a female student eligible for special education services.

◆ Action Steps ◆

IDEA is of paramount interest to parents whose children have one or more of the conditions that inhibits learning and requires special education. It's important to remember that not all disabilities inhibit learning. Slightly more than one in ten children receive special education services, so the first step is to determine if your child requires special education. Some conditions are apparent at birth or in infancy. Others won't reveal themselves until a child has started school. If a child is unhappy, or receiving unusually poor grades, or isn't getting along with other students or teachers, it may be a sign of a hidden disorder. The Council for Exceptional Children of Reston, Virginia, the nation's largest advocacy group for disabled children, lists five behaviors that may signal the need for special education:

- The child does not seem to learn, lags well behind others in basic skills and is not helped by the usual learning experience.
- The child does not seem to make friends, and both avoids others and does things to keep others away.
- The child talks or behaves like a much younger child.
- The child seems unhappy or tired most of the time.
- The child gets sick because of school or personal problems.

Other behaviors that may indicate a need for evaluation include:

- *A short attention span:* The child is not able to concentrate long enough to finish a task.
- *Listening difficulties:* The child turns away while others are talking and doesn't seem to be interested.

- *Repetitive or ritualistic behavior:* The child repeats the same action or word over and over, and doesn't seem to be able to stop.
- *Avoiding adults:* The child won't go to adults for attention.
- *Excessive resistance to discipline or direction:* The child destroys things or hurts other children deliberately.
- *Speech problems:* The child's rate of speech is unusually fast or slow, he or she has trouble making clear sounds, or doesn't talk at all.

These conditions don't necessarily mean the child needs special education, but they are indicators that further examination may be warranted. If you suspect your child needs special education, you should immediately contact your local school district's director of special education. If your child hasn't yet started school, call anyway. The federal law requires services to begin at age 3, and you can get an evaluation before your child reaches 3. Some states now provide special education services for infants and toddlers from birth to 3.

Before your child is referred for an evaluation, school officials may want to try "pre-referral" strategies. That is, they may intervene in the youngster's regular class with a plan, perhaps involving tutoring or counseling, to solve the problem then and there. They may suggest an informal "strategy session" with the teacher and perhaps the school psychologist, another teacher familiar with your child, a special education teacher familiar with your child's symptoms, and an administrator. These strategy sessions can be very helpful.

If the difficulty persists, the next step will be to refer the child to a planning and placement team—it may be called a screening committee or evaluation committee—for a special education evaluation. Before this takes place, parents must be notified and give their written approval.

THE TEAM

The team must have an administrator and a teacher and perhaps a staff member. It may also have the student's classroom teacher, an appropriate professional such as a psychologist or a speech and hearing specialist, or the school nurse or anyone else who knows the student and can be helpful.

The team's job is to refer the student for evaluation and determine if special education is necessary. After an initial meeting, the team may ask that certain tests, such as a speech and hearing test, or a physical examination, be performed. These must be explained to the parents, and parental consent must be granted. When the tests and evaluations are completed, they will be reviewed with the parents and, if appropriate, the student.

Parents who disagree with the evaluation can ask for an independent evaluation, by a professional not employed by the school district, at public expense. The district can ask for a hearing to defend its evaluation. If the hearing officer finds in favor of the district, the parents can still get an independent evaluation, and it must become part of the file, but they have to pay for it.

INDIVIDUALIZED EDUCATIONAL PROGRAM (IEP)

If it is determined that the child needs special education, then the team will schedule a meeting at which an Individualized Educational Program (we're trying to keep the alphabet soup to a minimum, but this is called an IEP) will be developed.

The IEP is a written plan that outlines and describes the special education program for the student who needs it. The plan will include such things as the student's current education level, special needs, types of classes and instructions to meet these needs, annual instructional goals, short-term instructional objectives, modifications of the program that may be necessary, and nonacademic and extra-curricular activities. Parents must be notified of IEP meetings, can invite any advisor they want, can tape them, and are encouraged to take part in the preparation of the plan. Parents must give their approval for the initial placement in special education.

Special education services can be delivered in a variety of ways. If there's no appropriate special education program available in a child's neighborhood school, the child may be referred to a regional or central planning team for placement in the nearest appropriate program. If the team places the child in a private school, the district has to pay for it, and the parent has to approve.

Problems

Some parents feel it necessary to be confrontational with school officials over questions of special education. This is partly explained by the difficult and emotional experience of giving a child with special needs over for schooling. Also, in the early days of special education there weren't as many trained professionals as there are today, and parents had to be more alert.

But today, in most school districts, there are trained professionals who know and care about children with disabilities. Give them a chance before you jump in their face. Hear them out. Ultimately, you have to follow your best judgment about your child, and if your judgment differs from that of your school, stick to your guns. The law gives you the right to protest and appeal if you're not satisfied with your child's education. But give the special educators a chance.

If at any time parents disagree with the evaluation, diagnosis or placement of their child, they can invoke what is called "due process," that is, they can ask for a hearing to try to change the decision they don't agree with. In many states, the matter will be referred to a mediator. If the parents and educators can't reach agreement, it will go to a more formal hearing. If the parents still aren't satisfied, they can appeal the decision to state or federal court. A few of these cases have even gone to the U.S. Supreme Court.

It might be helpful to pause and consider the legal rights that parents can exercise under the IDEA. These include:

- Parents must give written consent for the first evaluation and testing, and for the initial special education placement. Some states give parents the right to approve any change in placement or any private school placement.

- Parents must receive written notice, in the parents' dominant language, of any proposal to initiate or change special education placement, and notice of IEP meetings.

- Parents have the right to full participation in the development of their child's educational plan.

- Parents can examine all records concerning their child, and challenge any they feel are misleading or inaccurate.

- Parents have the right to a full explanation of any step of the special education process.
- Parents can appeal any part of the process they don't agree with.

These rights, and the law that created them, have made a world of difference to countless thousands of children. But not enough. Special education teachers say too many parents still don't get involved enough in their children's education, don't always communicate with teachers, and sometimes don't even attend planning meetings. One of the biggest problems teachers cite are parents who won't allow children who clearly need the help to be evaluated or placed in special education classes. If parents refuse to participate, the law allows the school to override the refusal and initiate the process itself.

Sometimes, parents won't allow their children to be evaluated or placed in special education classes to avoid the stigma sometimes associated with special education. This is a genuine concern. When a parent raises the stigma objection, it is often helpful to bring in someone to counsel parents about the situation. This can be an educator, psychologist or a lawyer familiar with special education issues. Counselors often ask parents to weigh the alternatives. For example, children with some disabilities may be stigmatized by the other children anyway. The special educators may be able to design a program that will help resolve the problem, thus eliminating the stigma. Also, many special education students spend part of the day in the regular class, and part of the day in a resource room. This process doesn't have to be stigmatizing. Schools systems as a rule will do everything they can to minimize the stigma problem. School officials don't want to go through the time and trouble of fighting parents through formal hearings and court cases. They would rather work out a mutually acceptable program.

If the child isn't disruptive, it's almost always possible to find a plan acceptable to parents and to school officials. The battleground today is over children who disrupt their classes, in one way or another. Schools have to make an effort to educate disruptive youngsters in regular classes, but at the same time cannot let them compromise the educational opportunities of the other children in the class. These are the most difficult cases.

THE MAINSTREAM

One of the main principle thrusts of IDEA is called "mainstreaming" or "inclusion." This means that if all goes well, a child will stay in a regular class. The IDEA says children with special needs must be educated in the "least restrictive environment." This means, whenever possible, that children with disabilities should be in class with children without disabilities.

Courts and schools take this seriously, which is why you'll see disabled youngsters, sometimes accompanied by aides or even nurses, in regular classrooms all over the country.

How far does a school have to go to mainstream a child?

In a 1992 New Jersey case, the court held that the school must consider putting the child in a regular classroom, with supplementary aids and services, before trying any other kind of placement.[5] This case involved Rafael Oberti, a 7-year-old boy with Down Syndrome. His school's child study team recommended he be placed in a segregated special education class. His parents, who were actively involved in his education, wanted him in a regular kindergarten.

The previous year, Rafael had been in a developmental kindergarten, a special program for children with certain disabilities. His teacher wasn't trained in dealing with Down Syndrome children, and she received only periodic assistance from specialists. Rafael had had some behavioral problems.

But the court said this wasn't a good enough try at mainstreaming, and asked the school to try to work with Rafael in a regular classroom, with appropriate help, to see if it could be done.

Courts have also held that youngsters can't be kept out of regular classrooms just because they are handicapped. The test is whether they can, with the help of supplemental aids and services, receive a satisfactory education in a regular classroom. "Only if the child cannot receive a satisfactory education in a regular education class, even if appropriate services are offered, should the child be placed in a special education class."[6]

The message from these cases is that schools have to make a very serious effort to place youngsters with special needs in regular classrooms. Parents of all children should applaud this effort. The experience is usually very positive for the whole class.

But it doesn't always work. The courts have to balance the interests of the child with special needs with the needs of the rest of the class as well as the resources available to the school. A court in Utah in 1992 held that a youngster who needed a full-time nurse due to the constant possibility of a mucous plug in her tracheotomy tube could not be mainstreamed satisfactorily.[7] A court reached a similar conclusion in New York with a child who needed a specially trained nurse. The child was a respirator-dependent quadriplegic.[8] If there's a trend to be discerned, it is that courts are willing to agree that youngsters with dire handicaps who need constant specialized medical attention are difficult to mainstream.

Is mainstreaming the right thing for every child? A lot of parents don't think so. Lawyers who work in the special education field say as many parents try to get their children in more restrictive environments—usually special ed classes or even private schools—as try to get them into mainstream classes.

The parents who want their kids in special ed classes may have a point. Perhaps a youngster in the second grade who couldn't do what the other second graders can do might resent it, and that resentment could lead to other problems. Also, some research indicates youngsters with disabilities fail courses much more often in mainstream classes. Yet, some youngsters with disabilities thrive in regular classes. The fact is that every child has different needs. That's why it's necessary to carefully evaluate each child. The heart of IDEA is individual decision making. Also, it's important to remember that mainstreaming isn't a question of either/or. It's often a question of degree. Most children can be mainstreamed for some classes or subjects.

Mary Morningstar of the Beach Center on Families and Disability at the University of Kansas suggests parents think what being around nonhandicapped children can do for their child. For example, said Morningstar, let's say a child has a delay in speech development. Look at the benefit the child could receive from listening to children all day who don't have that problem.

She said, whenever possible, families should look for specialized services in an inclusive environment. A child with a mild attention problem, for example, may benefit from a behavior modification program in the classroom, which might consist of rewards for completing tasks on time. If a child has to be pulled out for a period of therapy, the therapist and teacher should work together so the regular class and the therapy complement one another and move toward the same educational goals.

If you feel your school isn't trying hard enough to mainstream your child, you can, as we said earlier, invoke due process. In some states the first step is a informal or formal mediation session. The federal IDEA doesn't have mediation as an option, but efforts are under way to include it.

If the mediation process fails, or if it is unavailable in your district, you can demand a hearing. Some states have a two-level hearing process. If that fails, you can take the complaint to state or federal court. Ultimately, you must live with the final decision, if you wish to keep your child in the school.

RELATED SERVICES

As we have seen in some cases, school districts have to provide many services youngsters need to get an education. The law says these include: "transportation and such developmental, corrective and other supportive services (including speech pathology and audiology, psychological services, physical and occupational therapy, recreation, and medical and counseling services, except that such medical services shall be for diagnostic and evaluation purposes only) as may be required to assist a handicapped child to benefit from special education, and includes the early identification and assessment of handicapping conditions in children."[9]

Many parents have gone to court to determine what exactly some of those terms mean. One of the best known cases involved an 8-year-old girl named Amber Tatro from Texas, who was born with the condition known as spina bifida. She suffered from orthopedic and speech impairments, and a neurogenic bladder, meaning that for her to stay in school all day, she had to have a catheter inserted into her urethra to drain her bladder every three or four hours.

Her school declined to provide someone to perform the catheterization. Amber's parents protested. The case was in court for several years. Finally, the Supreme Court held that, yes, such catheterization was a "related service" and should be provided by the school.[10]

Chief Justice Warren Burger said that in passing IDEA, Congress sought to make public education available to handicapped children, in a meaningful way. He said a service that enables a student to remain at school all day was related to that goal. However, it is important to note that courts have sometimes held that complex medical services are not considered a related service. But if you can make the case that the child needs the service to learn in school, it's probably covered by the rather vague term "related services."

Related services may be the make-or-break factor in deciding whether to mainstream your child. Much research indicates children with disabilities who have all the help they need do much better than children who have been mainstreamed without the specially trained teachers, aides and support services. Again, you can invoke due process to get the services. But you need to analyze the situation first. If your child is going into a badly overcrowded class, and the class already has a high number of special needs students, then you might want to think of other options.

WHAT IS "APPROPRIATE"?

The IDEA calls for a "free appropriate public education" for youngsters with special needs. What is appropriate? Does it mean the child must be given every possible service, to, as the old Army ad put it, be all they can be?

Not really. This can be inferred from a famous case involving little Amy Rowley, a deaf girl entering first grade in Peekskill, New York. As she went into kindergarten, Amy, an excellent lip reader, was provided with an FM hearing aid. She successfully completed kindergarten. An IEP was prepared for her first grade. She was to have instruction from a tutor for the deaf for one hour a day, and from a speech therapist three hours a week. Her parents wanted, in addition, a sign language interpreter for all her academic classes.

School officials said she didn't need an interpreter. She'd had one for two weeks in kindergarten and didn't appear to need him.

A lower court found Amy well adjusted and performing better than average in her class, but still not able to understand everything that was said in class, thus not learning as much as she could. The lower court felt she should have the interpreter to reach her full potential.

The Supreme Court disagreed.[11] The high court said "appropriate" meant the child was getting personalized instruction with sufficient support services to "benefit educationally." Deferring to the state's judgment, the court said Congress meant to provide a "basic floor of opportunity," and not the maximum possible educational opportunity.

A few states have found this standard unacceptable, and have set higher standards. Some states do require services that will provide a youngster with the best possible education. Hence it's critical for parents pursuing this question to consult the law in their state.

> Want to keep a solid relationship with educators at your child's school? After you meet with them about a problem or concern with your child, send them a thank-you note. It's a courtesy that most parents forget, yet one that is tremendously appreciated.

Who Pays?

With a couple of possible exceptions, the school district pays for special education.

One such situation is when parents move their child to a private school. If they go through all the due process steps, and the hearing officer finds that the public school program is inappropriate and the private school can meet the child's needs, then the district must pay for the private school placement. But if the parent moves the child before going through due process, and a hearing officer later finds the private school placement inappropriate, the parent could be required to pay for it.

Courts have held that school districts cannot refuse to pay the costs of such residential placements, if the placement is necessary to meet the child's education needs, even though the costs are high.[12]

Usually the district must pay. Does that mean the district has to pay all costs in a private facility? They are supposed to be relieved from the costs of medical services that aren't part of the educational costs. But it is often difficult to separate the two, and when that is the case, courts usually require the school district to pay. Services such as speech therapy, physical therapy, recreation and psychological counseling are considered part of the educational costs.

As we suggested earlier, parents can incur costs when they object to a placement or evaluation and, instead of waiting until the end of due process, pull their child out of his current placement and put him in a private school. They have a right to do this, but they might have to pay for it. Courts have several times held that a parent who unilaterally moves a child to a private school without going through the due process hearing procedures is not entitled to tuition reimbursement—unless they win the hearing. If officials decide the original placement was inappropriate and the private placement is appropriate, judges can order the school district to pay for the private schooling, even after the fact.[13]

The bottom line is that parents take a risk by moving their children before the due process procedures are completed. Check your state regulations. Most states have time limits for each step of the process so parents aren't put in this situation.

The IDEA, and other laws such as the Rehabilitation Act of 1973 and the Americans with Disabilities Act, have made a new and better life for countless American children. These laws have brought so much attention and so many resources to bear on children with disabilities that some parents and activists have made the same complaint about special education that they have made about gifted and talented programs—why can't all the kids in the middle get individual education plans and this much individual attention? And this is not the only complaint about special education programs.

The Controversy

For all its good intentions and results, special education programs have engendered considerable controversy in many districts around the country. Critics charge that countless thousands of youngsters, a disproportionate number of them members of minority groups, are mislabeled as "learning disabled" or "emotionally maladjusted" and shunted into dead-end classes from which few ever return. Many of these youngsters wouldn't be considered to have a disability outside of school. Many of these placements are made because the general education teacher, perhaps because of cultural reasons, cannot handle the children. In a provocative series in special education titled "A Class Apart," *New York Times* reporter Sam Dillon said the system actually encourages more and more special education placements. He said such placements mean a teacher can reduce class size and a principal improves his school's statistical profile on standardized tests. Also, school funding formulas make funding available for special education students, but not students who may need extra help in the classroom but haven't been labeled.[14] Many inner-city programs have grown. New York City's special education population has grown from 30,000 in 1974 to more than 130,000 in 1994.

Many parents and experts feel the way out of this is more pre-school counseling and enrichment that will help keep more students in regular classes.

Critics also charge that special education in many cities has become a huge and separate bureaucracy within the school system, not unlike what once existed for black students in some parts of the country. This special education bureaucracy employs numerous specialists who perform too many evaluations, some of marginal worth, at a staggering cost. Critics say classes for younger students with special education needs are often too large and poorly organized, and that some teachers aren't prepared to either teach children with disabilities or teach youngsters who have been mainstreamed.

The results of special education programs leave room for improvement. Only 57 percent graduate from high school with a diploma or certificate, and only 49 percent are employed two years later.

◆ Action Steps ◆

If you suspect your child has a disability that is impeding his or her education, you must do something. It may well be difficult to admit that the beautiful child to whom you have committed so much love may have a problem, but you are the parent.

Call the teacher. Discuss the problem. Bring in the school psychologist. Get their take on the problem. They may want to do tests. Have them explain the tests to you. Familiarize yourself with IDEA.

As the nature of the difficulty becomes clearer, read everything you can about it. Talk to people in your community who may be familiar with the problem. If you're not happy with tests done by the school, make arrangements to get a second opinion.

Check your family's health coverage. See what kinds of pediatric evaluations are available to you, should you need them.

Should your school present you with a plan, go over it closely. Ask your pediatrician to review it, if appropriate. Stay involved in the process, every step of the way. If you aren't happy with the plan, see if there's a middle ground on which to compromise. Often, there is. If not, invoke due process and go to a hearing. Ultimately, you're the parent, and have to fight for what you believe to be in your child's best interest.

You must continually ask, "Why?" Why is a child being sent to a self-contained class, or why is a child being mainstreamed? Is it in the best interest of the child, or is it because of teacher availability, cost or cultural differences?

◆ Selected Questions ◆

Can children in special education classes be sent to summer school?

Yes, in some circumstances. If it can be shown that a summer program would keep the child from regressing educationally, then the school district may have to provide a summer program.[15]

Can a special education student be evicted or suspended from school for inappropriate or antisocial behavior?

Yes, but only for short periods of time, 10 days, according to the leading case on the subject, *Honig* v. *Doe*.[16] In that case, two emotionally disturbed students were suspended indefinitely from a San Francisco school for violent and disruptive conduct related to their disabilities.

The IDEA says children must "stay put" in their current placements while any change is discussed. The Supreme Court said the law means what it says. The court said school officials can temporarily suspend a student who is an immediate danger to others for up to 10 days, but no more. During that time, the school can initiate proceedings to change the student's placement, if that is in the child's best interest. Many educators found the Honig decision unrealistic when dealing with particularly dangerous youngsters.

Is there any provision in the law for handicapped parents?

There may be. In a recent case, two deaf parents asked for a sign language interpreter so they could take part in their child's education. Citing the Americans With Disabilities Act, the court found the parents were entitled to an interpreter, but only for academic or disciplinary conferences, not for other activities (including graduation).[17]

Since we're talking about "special education," does the IDEA apply to gifted and talented children?

The federal IDEA does not apply to gifted children, but rather to children with disabilities.[18] However, a handful of states have included gifted and talented children in the state version of the IDEA. About half of the states have laws that provide some kinds of services for gifted and talented children. Note this: It is very possible for a child considered mentally gifted to also have a learning disability that qualifies the student for special education services. Some very well-known people, including Albert Einstein, Nelson Rockefeller, Cher, Robin Williams, and Tom Cruise, have overcome learning disabilities.

My child's special education class has the worst classroom and the worst facilities in the school. It makes me sick. Is this legal?

Absolutely not. In-school discrimination against a group of handicapped youngsters directly violates Section 504 of the Rehabilitation Act of 1973. If you bring it to your principal's attention and he fails to rectify the situation, you can file a complaint with the U.S. Department of Justice's Office of Civil Rights.

My daughter's teacher says she thinks Mary has Attention Deficit Disorder, and should be on medication. What should we do?

It's beyond the scope of this book to do an in-depth analysis of Attention Deficit Disorder (A.D.D.), but it seems to be quickly becoming the instant diagnosis of the 90s. The production of Ritalin, one of the drugs used to treat A.D.D., has increased 500 percent from 1990 to 1995. Yet some experts don't believe this is even a medical problem (see *The Myth of the A.D.D. Child,* Thomas Armstrong, Dutton Books). The first thing you should do is get another opinion, preferably from your pediatrician. Thoroughly explore all intermediate steps. Look for child psychologists and pediatricians in your community familiar with the problem. Learn everything you can about A.D.D.

FOR FURTHER INFORMATION

Beach Center of Families and Disability
University of Kansas
3111 Haworth Hall
Lawrence, KS 66045

Council for Exceptional Children
1920 Association Drive
Reston, VA 22091
703–620–3360

Disability Rights Education and Defense Fund
1633 Q Street NW Suite 220
Washington, DC 20009
202–986–0375

National Association of State Directors of Special Education
1800 Diagonal Road Suite 320
Alexandria, VA 22314
703–519–3800

SpecialNet
National Electronic Network for Special Education
GTE Educational Services, Inc.
1090 Vermont Avenue NW
Washington, DC 20005

NOTES

1. *Pennsylvania Association for Retarded Children* v. *Commonwealth of Pa.*, 334 F. Supp. 1257, 343 F. Supp. 279 (E.D. Pa. 1972).

2. Ibid.

3. *Mills* v. *Board of Education*, 348 F. Supp. 866 (D.D.C. 1972).

4. *Taylor* v. *Secretary of Department of Health and Human Services*, 24 Cl/ Ct. 433 (1991).

5. *Oberti* v. *Board of Education*, 789 F. Supp. 1322 (D.N.J. 1992).

6. *Board of Education, Sacramento Unified School Dist.* v. *Holland by and through Holland*, 786 F. Supp. 784 (E.D. Cal. 1992).

7. *Ellison* v. *Board of Education*, N.Y.A.D. 3 Dept., May 6, 1993.

8. *Granite School Dist.* v. *Shannon M. by Myrna M*, 787 F. Supp. 1020 (D. Utah 1992).

9. 20 USC 1401 (17).

10. *Irving Independent School District* v. *Tatro*, 104 S.Ct. 3371, 486 U.S. 883 (1983).

11. *Board of Education* v. *Rowley*, 102 S. Ct. 3034 (1982).

12. *D.S.* v. *Board of Education of the Town of East Brunswick*, 458 A. 2d 159 (1983).

13. *Timothy W.* v. *Rochester, N.H. School District*, 875 F. 2d 954 (1st Cir. 1989).

14. Sam Dillon, "A Class Apart," *The New York Times*, April 6–8, 1994.

15. *Yaris* v. *Special School District of St. Louis County*, 558 F. Supp. 545 (E.D. Mo. 1983).

16. *Honig* v. *Doe*, 98 L. Ed. 2d 686 (1988).

17. *Rothschild* v. *Grottenthaler*, 907 F. 2d 286 (2d Cir. 1990).

18. *Huldah A. by Anderson* v. *Easton Area School District*, 601 A 2d 860 (Pa. Cmwlth. 1992).

chapter 8

STUDENT RIGHTS AND DISCIPLINE

◆ INTRODUCTION ◆

Back in the spring of 1964, a young woman who was a junior in high school in Harrodsburg, Kentucky, got married. She was summarily bounced out of school. The rule was that if a student married, he or she had to leave school for a year, and could be reinstated in the following year only with the special permission of the principal.

That was how schools were run. It was considered a privilege, not a right, to attend school. Getting married, becoming pregnant, being seen smoking across town and other such offenses got you expelled, no questions asked.

But society was changing in the 1960s; people who had been denied civil rights were demanding them. That included students. Often, the point was fundamental fairness. For example, in many cases a pregnant girl would be forced to leave school, but the father could stay. Others couched it in terms of rights; that students were Americans who were protected, to some degree at least, by the Constitution.

139

Cases from the last three decades created the framework for the rules of school discipline today. We'll look at some of the major rulings in this chapter, to see how much school officials can control student conduct. Others issues we'll consider include:

- *Is corporal punishment legal?*
- *Can school officials control a student's personal appearance?*
- *Do Constitutional protections against illegal search and seizure apply to students?*
- *When can a student be suspended or expelled?*
- *Can grades be lowered to discipline a student?*

◆ DISCUSSION ◆

For years, as we said earlier, students went to school, did what they were told, and lived by the rules, whether the rules were fair or not. But in the 1960s, as Bob Dylan put it, the time's they were a changin'. The young woman from Kentucky went to court and won. The court held the school's rule was arbitrary, unreasonable and thus void.[1]

The big breakthrough, the major case on the subject of constitutional rights for students followed a Vietnam War protest that took place at a high school in Des Moines, Iowa. Some students planned to wear black armbands to protest America's involvement in the war. School officials found out about the protest and adopted a policy that prohibited wearing the armbands. Five students wore them anyway, and were suspended. They and their parents went to court.

The Supreme Court looked back over the previous half-century and found a few cases that indicated that neither "students nor teachers shed their constitutional rights at the schoolhouse gate."[2] They recalled a 1943 case, *West Virginia Board of Education* v. *Barnette* (319 U.S. 637), which held that students could not be compelled to salute the flag.

The court affirmed school officials' right to prescribe and control conduct, but said school officials don't have total control over students.

Freedom of expression is a precious freedom that must be protected. Students should be taught about the principles of our government in school. Schools should be, like society at large, a "marketplace of ideas," where "truth can be discovered from the robust exchange of ideas." American public schools "may not be enclaves of totalitarianism."

The court then balanced the right of school officials to control conduct with the students' right of free speech. The result was that if the speech was not likely to cause a substantial disruption or materially interfere with school activities, it was allowable.

The school had to do more than merely *suspect* disruption; there had to be a reasonable fear, supported by some evidence, of a substantial disruption.

Two years later, a federal court found an example of when a school might reasonably fear a substantial disruption. An inner-city high school in Cleveland had a history of disruption caused by the wearing of buttons or insignia, and so unofficially prohibited the wearing of those items. A young man was suspended for wearing an anti-war protest button. He went to court, and lost. The court said where such insignia, badges or buttons had caused strife before, the school had a legitimate right to curtail their use.[3]

Nonetheless, for almost two decades, the principle espoused in the *Tinker* case, as the Des Moines case is known, held considerable sway. Courts prohibited schools from keeping articles on controversial subjects out of school newspapers. School officials couldn't make a student change the quotation that went with her picture in a yearbook, because it expressed an ideological position.[4] In other words, considerable leeway was given to student expression.

But since 1986, the pendulum has begun to swing the other way. A high school student in Bethel, Washington, gave a nominating speech for a friend at a student government assembly. The speech was full of sophomoric, sexual innuendo. The boy was disciplined, with a three-day suspension and loss of the chance to be the commencement speaker. He sued and lost.

The court held that offensively lewd and indecent speech enjoyed no First Amendment protection, and that the school had a right to protect the captive audience in the student body from exposure to lewd and offensive speech.[5] What might be free speech for adults isn't necessarily free speech for students because of the sensibilities of fellow students. Also, the court said schools teach by example "the shared values of a civilized social order," and that these lessons cannot be taught by a school that tolerates lewd and offensive speech. The court also noted that the school board has the authority to determine what manner of speech is inappropriate.

In 1987 a federal court upheld a school's ban on T-shirts that showed caricatures of three school administrators drinking alcohol. The court said the robust exchange of ideas envisioned in the Tinker case can only happen "in a civilized context." Here, the court found the school doing its job by not tolerating the message on the T-shirts.[6]

The following year, the trend continued with a case involving a school newspaper. The principal pulled two stories, on the subjects of teen-age pregnancy and divorce, before they were published. He felt the stories didn't adequately protect the identities of three pregnant students who were interviewed, or the privacy of their families. He also felt the references to sexual activities and birth control were inappropriate for some younger students.

The U.S. Supreme Court upheld his action.[7] The court said student newspapers aren't a forum for public expression unless for some reason they have become newspapers for the general public. If not, newspapers are part of the educational curriculum and subject to the school's control as such.

The distinction the courts make in these cases is that where the school appears to give its approval to an activity, such as what happens in a student assembly or what is printed in a student newspaper, the school has the power to restrict the activity to ensure that it is consistent with the school's educational objectives. If the expression is purely personal, such as having a "Save the Whales" sticker on a knapsack, then the Tinker rule would seem to apply. But with anything that smacks of official expression, and the definition of this is fairly broad, it appears that the school's policy will prevail. Thus, schools now have more discretion in what speech they can censor. In recent cases, courts have generally deferred to school authorities on such subjects as inappropriate campaign speeches and questionable advertising in student newspapers.[8] Whether this conservative trend will inhibit the marketplace of ideas remains to be seen.

The bottom line—and we'll see this more as we look at student discipline—is that students have some constitutional rights, such as free expression, privacy, and due process. But for a variety of reasons, these rights aren't as extensive as those enjoyed by adults.

◆ ACTION STEPS ◆

Whatever the level of student rights, parents must be involved in all aspects of school discipline, says Joan First, co-director of the National Coalition of Advocates for Students of Cambridge, Massachusetts, which represents almost two dozen student advocacy groups. She said school policies should provide parental access to the disciplinary process, not build boundaries around it. Parent groups should work for such policies.

As for individual parents, First recommends:

- Read the district's disciplinary policy. Usually it can be found in the school handbook or the district handbook. One very good reason to read the disciplinary policy, First said, is that schools often violate their own policies. If you know what the policy is, you can most often stop the violation. Also, as we said earlier, kids do have rights, and parents should know what those rights are.

- Develop a strong and positive relationship with the teacher, and ask to be involved in any disciplinary measures involving your child. Emphasize that the teacher and parent are partners in the act of educating a child, and that you want to hold up your end of the partnership. School discipline really is a case where two heads are better than one. Parents and teachers working together can identify and solve problems, often before they became serious enough for formal discipline. Also, if the parent and teacher work together, the child will get a consistent message, at home and in school.

- If your child is sent to the principal's office, or anywhere else for disciplinary reasons, go along. Be there. You can help by providing background on your child, and your presence will help assure your child isn't subjected to arbitrary or unfair punishment.

- Talk to your child. If there has been an incident that may lead to school discipline, discuss it fully with your child. Find out what is going on and why. The teacher or school counselor may not have gotten to the bottom of it; there may be a reason everyone is unaware of.

In addition to these steps, First said parents groups can also help by clarifying language in school discipline policies. For example, some states and districts have "zero tolerance" policies regarding weapons in schools. No one wants unsafe schools, but some of these policies don't define what a weapon is. As a result, such things as pen knives, pens, hair picks and nail files have been defined as weapons. She said in a couple of instances, students in the fourth or fifth grade have been expelled for carrying—not brandishing—a nail file or small souvenir baseball bat to school.

A new federal law, the "gun-free school act," part of the Elementary and Secondary Education Act of 1994, threatens to withhold federal funds from schools that don't develop policies for excluding students who bring weapons to school. This law, however, defines a weapon as a gun. Also, it allows schools to develop their own policies, said Kathleen Boundy of the Center for Law and Education.

CORPORAL PUNISHMENT

The main authority figures for children are, of course, their parents. When a child is in school, courts have for centuries held that the teacher stands "in loco parentis," in the place of the parent. That means the teacher can exercise parental authority in controlling the conduct of the student. But this authority is not absolute. Everyone agrees a teacher can discipline a student. The question is how far the teacher can go.

The value of corporal punishment has been debated for centuries. Some parents insist no one touch their child, others follow the ancient adage, "Spare the rod and spoil the child." Whatever your opinion, corporal punishment is legal in the public schools of

23 states, mostly in the South and Midwest, and has been banned, either by law or regulation, in 27 states. According to the National Center for the Study of Corporal Punishment and Alternatives of Temple University in Philadelphia, the states that have banned corporal punishment are: Alaska, California, Connecticut, Hawaii, Illinois, Iowa, Maine, Massachusetts, Michigan, Minnesota, Montana, Nebraska, Nevada, New Hampshire, New Jersey, New York, North Dakota, New Jersey, Oregon, Rhode Island, South Dakota, Utah, Vermont, Virginia, Washington, West Virginia, and Wisconsin.

How much corporal punishment goes on? The Office of Civil Rights of the U.S. Department of Education periodically collects data on corporal punishment. In the 1991–92 school year, the last year the data was collected, 555,531 students were corporally punished at least once.

From the legal perspective, the question of corporal punishment has reached the U.S. Supreme Court a couple of times, most recently in 1977. That case involved two junior high school students in Dade County, Florida, who were paddled severely.[9] One received 20 licks, so hard that he suffered a hematoma and had to stay home for several days. The other student was struck twice on the arm, and didn't have full use of one arm for a week.

The students claimed the beatings violated the Eighth Amendment proscription against cruel and unusual punishment, and that they were denied due process.

Not so, the court ruled. It said the Eighth Amendment only applies to criminals in custody, not to kids in schools. As for due process, the court said it was impractical to hold a hearing every time a teacher wanted to spank a child. The judges said there weren't many abuses, that schools were open, and that teachers and other students were there to keep a watch on excessive force.

Teachers may impose "reasonable but not excessive force to discipline a child," the court said. What is reasonable depends on such things as the nature of the offense, the age and strength of the child, the availability of other means of discipline and the past behavior of the child. If the punishment is excessive, the court said, school officials may be liable for damages, or even subject to criminal penalties.

There haven't been many instances where a teacher has been found guilty of using excessive force, but there have been some. In those cases, teachers have sometimes beaten a child over a trivial matter, or used an instrument not usually used to administer corporal punishment (switches and paddles are apparently acceptable; baseball bats are not).

Corporal punishment is a very difficult issue, says Joan First, because in some parts of the country "there is a school of thought that says this is the way to raise children." She said some people consider corporal punishment an integral part of "in loco parentis" and hold it in high regard. "It's culturally acceptable," she said. Also, she will concede, corporal punishment usually stops the offending behavior for the moment by overpowering the child. What is wrong with corporal punishment? Plenty, says First. To wit:

- Children can get hurt. When parents administer corporal punishment, it is most often mitigated by the parent's affection for the child. That is not always the case with someone who has no such natural affection.

- Schools usually have rules about how corporal punishment is to be administered. The rules may require witnesses, for example, and only allow paddling on the backside. But, says First, schools often ignore these rules.

- A disproportionate amount of corporal punishment is meted out to minority youngsters. First said a survey showed 20 percent of the African-American students in Florida had received corporal punishment, a percentage much higher than given to white children. The problem is that adults make subjective judgments about dishing out corporal punishments, and these judgments can be affected by their attitudes toward minorities.

- The power to use corporal punishment can lead to extreme punishment for relatively little cause. For example, a teacher in Florida flew into a rage and broke a child's arm. Her offense? She spoke in Haitian Creole instead of English in school.

- Corporal punishment "models violence and the inappropriate use of power," First said. In other words, when we use violence, we teach children to use violence to solve problems. This comes at a time, First said, when the country is staggered by every kind of violence from domestic beatings to drive-by shootings; we should be thinking seriously about the causes of this epidemic.

• Finally, she said, recent research indicates that corporal punishment violates the psychological and physical boundaries of children. This may give them the sense that they cannot defend their boundaries, making them more likely to be victimized by violence or sexual abuse later in life.

Dr. Irwin Hyman, head of the National Center for the Study of Corporal Punishment, says corporal punishment can amount to public humiliation and intolerable psychological mistreatment. He is the author of *Reading, Writing and the Hickory Stick: The Appalling Story of Physical and Psychological Abuse in American Schools* (Lexington Books, 1990).

◆ ACTION STEPS ◆

If you object to corporal punishment, it's important to know your state law. Many of the states that allow corporal punishment don't have a law on the subject, which means they leave the decision up to the local school board. If that is the case, you and others who agree with you need to lobby your local school board to change the rule. If your state allows corporal punishment by state law, you need to write your local legislator, or a member of your state legislature's education committee, and urge that the law be changed. The more individuals and citizens groups you can get to join you, the better your chances are.

Sometimes local rules, or even state rules, ban corporal punishment for children under a certain age, and dictate how corporal punishment is to be administered. Also, some districts require parental permission to administer corporal punishment. If you don't want your child hit, don't give your permission. If you are worried about your school following its own rules about corporal punishment, ask to be present.

PERSONAL APPEARANCE: LONG HAIR AND SHORT SKIRTS

Blame the Beatles. Before the mopheaded Fab Four arrived in New York in 1963, most American schoolboys wore crew cuts and hair length wasn't much of an issue.

But by the late 1960s, many youngsters wanted to wear their hair long. Unfortunately, many of these lads were in schools with regulations against long hair.

It's next to impossible for those students of the 60s and 70s, who are today's parents, to explain how political the length of their hair was. After all, many of today's young men are wearing their hair short again, although perhaps with a pony tail.

But hundreds of cases went to court over hair length—yes, we tied up scores of judges and a fortune in court time to battle over the length of boys' hair. Cases were appealed to all 12 U.S. Circuit Courts of Appeals.

And for all of this effort, the federal courts could never reach a consensus. About half decided length of hair was a personal freedom protected by the Constitution, and the other half decided local school boards had the right to set school policies such as hair and dress codes, and that federal courts shouldn't interfere. The U.S. Supreme Court has declined to settle the matter, saying in effect it had better things to do than decide how long a boy's hair should be, so there we stand.

Here are some of the cases, pro and con.

A boy named Greg Carpenter from Indiana chose to violate his school's ban on long hair. He was taken out of class and told he couldn't go back until he got a haircut. His parents sued.

The school board presented no reason or purpose for the long hair rule. The court held in favor of young Carpenter, saying hair length is "an ingredient of personal freedom protected by the U.S. Constitution."[10] The court indicated the school board might limit that right, if it could provide some substantial reason for the long hair ban.

In a similar North Carolina case, the school board claimed a young man's long hair provoked "jest, disgust, and amusement."[11] These problems were minor and probably could have been avoided, the court said, adding that a student could exercise his rights to self-expression by growing his hair, as long as his mane wasn't unsafe, dirty, or indecent.

These decisions are typical of courts that have taken on the cases. They have found no reason for bans on long hair except adult taste and prejudice, or conformity for conformity's sake.

When federal courts uphold local bans against long hair, they usually do so by saying local school boards and not federal courts should be in the business of deciding local policy on hair.

For example, an Arapaho Indian family in Canton, Oklahoma, brought a suit because school officials ordered their fifth-grade son to cut his tribal braid, and didn't give the parents the right to a hearing.[12] The court said the parents should receive at least an informal hearing, because the penalty could be a suspension. But on the subject of the ban against long hair, the court said it was keeping its hands off.

"The Constitution does not impose on the federal courts the duty and responsibility of supervising the length of a student's hair," the court wrote.

In another case, a Pennsylvania high school athlete named Brent Zeller was not allowed on his soccer team because his hair was too long. The family sued, and lost. The judges of the 3rd U.S. Circuit Court of Appeals said courts can't redress every claim by students of violation of their personal liberty, and that local officials are better equipped than the federal court to make value judgments about hair length. "Student hair cases fall on the side where the wisdom and experience of school authorities must be deemed superior and preferable to the federal judiciary's."[13]

So where does this leave us? In about half the states—those in the Northeast and Midwest covered by the 1st, 2nd, 4th, 7th, and 8th U.S. Circuit Courts of Appeals—parents can challenge restrictions on students' hair length, and the federal court will see if the school board can offer a reasonable educational purpose for the restriction. In the rest of the country, the federal courts won't get involved. Of course, it's still possible to challenge the regulations in state court.

That's just hair. Then there's the issue of clothes. Schools have a right to regulate clothing, but courts hold that the regulations have to have some point, some educational purpose.

In a 1993 Massachusetts case, a federal judge rejected a request for a preliminary injunction from students who challenged a school policy that prohibited them from wearing certain T-shirts in school. The shirts in question read, "Coed Naked Band: Do It to the Rhythm," and, "See Dick Drink, See Dick Drive, See Dick Die. Don't Be A Dick."

The court said it was unlikely the students' First Amendment rights were violated in light of the school's goal of calming a sexually charged environment to enhance students' ability to learn.[14]

This is a fairly typical decision. If a school can offer a good reason for the rule, it will usually stand. For example, rules against short or excessively tight skirts or other immodest clothing are usually upheld, as are rules that encourage safety, such as no shirttails hanging out in shop class. Rules against T-shirts with vulgarities also usually stand up: A suspension for wearing one with "Drugs Suck" on it was recently upheld in Virginia.[15] Rules against wearing gang colors are almost always upheld. But rules that simply reflect taste—rules against pants for girls, or tie-dyed shirts, or jeans, are sometimes thrown out.[16]

Still, it's hard to make generalizations. Courts, as we have said, are increasingly giving deference to local school boards, so some fights over hair or clothing are going to have to be fought at the school board level. And though the long hair era is over (except for rock musicians and a couple of pro tennis players, for some reason), this generation may fight over earrings, ponytails, backward baseball caps indoors and who knows what. And there are some curious regulations out there.

In the Mesquite, Texas, Independent School District, for example, "Startling, unusual or immodest attire of any sort shall not be permitted. This includes fads in hair styles . . . " Who decides what is "startling"?

While hair and clothing aren't the most urgent issues in education, they raise interesting issues. Should conformity be encouraged? Are school officials improperly restricting students' freedoms? Should courts get involved?

◆ ACTION STEPS ◆

The time to challenge your school's hair or clothing policy is before your child decides to make a fashion statement. If you disagree with the policy, go before your school board and ask the board to change it. Approach this as you would any other issue; prepare a well-documented case, and get support from other parents and experts from your community such as child psychologists.

If your child decides to go to school with shocking pink hair, a T-shirt with a lewd slogan on it, or a see-through blouse, and school officials order your child to go home and change, you have two choices, says education lawyer and University of Connecticut law professor Thomas B. Mooney. You can comply with the school's order, or you can fight it.

If you choose to fight it, you may have to get a lawyer. By this point, there aren't any intermediate steps left. The school has ordered your child to do something, and he or she isn't doing it. The school will likely respond with a punishment. If that punishment is a suspension or expulsion, you'll be entitled to a hearing. You may consider getting a lawyer familiar with education law in your area. Ask other parents, or call your local bar association. If the situation has a First Amendment freedom of expression overtone, you might call your state's chapter of the American Civil Liberties Union (ACLU). The ACLU may take the case. But, Mooney warns, learn about the hearing process in your state. Some hearings offer no right of appeal unless a constitutional question is raised.

SEARCH AND SEIZURE

School officials have always had to go through students' pockets to remove slingshots or jackknives or candy bars stolen from the corner store. It was never a big deal. But with the tremendous and tragic increase in guns and drugs in schools in recent years, search and seizure has taken on a new importance. Again, courts have been forced to balance competing rights. The students have a right to privacy and a right under the Fourth Amendment to be protected from unreasonable search and seizure. School officials have a right and obligation to maintain order and protect students from themselves and others. How to accommodate both?

In the adult world, police have to prove to a judge they have "probable cause" before they can get a warrant to search someone's property. School officials are held to a lesser standard. What they have to have to justify a search is a "reasonable suspicion."

This means officials can't go on what judges sometimes call a "fishing expedition," looking for anything and everything. They probably can't, for example, have all the students in the school empty out their pockets. The suspicion has to be individualized and reasonably specific.

In a 1993 case, school officials strip-searched a 16-year-old student who was suspected of, to use an indelicate term used by school officials, "crotching" drugs.

The youth had been involved in several recent drug incidents, and teachers had noticed an unusual bulge in his crotch area.[17] The court held this created a reasonable suspicion to search him. Also, the search was done in the privacy of the boys' locker room, and the student was allowed to wear gym clothes while his clothes were searched.

In New York, a student placed his book bag on a cabinet and it made an unusual metal thud. A judge held it was reasonable for a school security guard to touch the outside of the bag to see if the metal object was a weapon.[18] In Oregon, a school official's search of a student's fanny pack was held to be reasonable when two reliable students told the official the student had been seen with a gun on campus, and had brought a gun to school before.[19]

One of the major cases in the field took place in New Jersey. Two girls were caught smoking in the girls' room, a violation of school rules, and were sent to the principal's office. Making what in retrospect seems at least a tactical error, one girl denied that she had been smoking. The principal asked to see her purse. He found a half-pack of cigarettes, and some rolling papers. Looking further, the principal found some marijuana, a wad of cash, and drug paraphernalia.

The high court held the search was reasonable. The search for cigarettes was reasonable, because the principal had the teacher's observation that the girl had been smoking, which was a violation of school rules. Discovering the rolling papers, which are often used to smoke marijuana, made further search of the purse reasonable.[20]

The same rules apply to searches of student lockers. The school owns the lockers and lets students use them with the tacit understanding they'll be used properly. If there is reasonable suspicion that lockers are being used to store contraband of one kind or another, school officials can search them.

In a Massachusetts case decided in 1992, a search of a locker was held to be reasonable when school officials were reliably told the student was selling marijuana from a book bag.[21] Although there are few cases on the subject, the same rules would appear to apply in searches of students' desks.

A point of disagreement among judges is whether sniffer dogs can be brought into schools for random drug searches. On the face of it, canine searches would seem to violate the precept that searches have to be individual and specific. Most courts have so held. But a few judges have allowed the sniffer searches, on the theory that the school's obligation to protect the student body outweighs the individual student's right of privacy.

Can searches go too far? Certainly. In one egregious case, school officials conducted a nude search of a 13-year-old girl for drugs, and a federal court found this outrageous. In granting her the right to sue for damages, the court said the girl was denied her "constitutional and basic human rights," and called the search "a humiliation."[22]

If school officials bring the police into a case, then the higher standard of probable cause should apply, and the officer should get a search warrant before searching a student. If the officer makes an illegal search, what he finds should not be admissible in a criminal case against the student.

◆ ACTION STEPS ◆

The oft-quoted sign on the ceiling of the wrestling room at the U.S. Military Academy at West Point says, "If You Can Read This, You Are in Trouble. Move!" If your child has a problem that involves bringing drugs or a weapon to school, you too have a major problem that needs your undivided attention. Move. Call the teacher or principal, and make arrangements to come to the school and learn all you can about the situation. Talk to your child. Talk to the school counselor. Call your lawyer, if it appears there will be major disciplinary action taken against your child. As we'll see in the next section, such action cannot be taken without a hearing. Assure your child of your support, be involved in the process, and try to find what caused the behavior. Also, if school officials searched your child's locker and found nothing, make some noise. Ask what the problem is, why the search was conducted, and what else the school is doing about it.

SUSPENSION AND EXPULSION

As another example of the balancing of rights that is involved in student discipline, let's look at the extreme disciplinary measures of removing the child from class or school.

Suspension is, and should be, a last-ditch disciplinary action. Most disciplinary measures run toward extra homework, detention, or conferences with parents. But suspension or expulsion has been used with unruly students for years. Why is that a problem? As we said earlier, students have a legal right to an education. If you take them out of school, aren't you violating that right?

It's not an easy question.

The big case in this area involved the suspension of nine high school students in Columbus, Ohio, during a period of unrest in the early 1970s.[23] The school rules at the time allowed the principal to suspend students for up to 10 days at his own initiative. All he had to do was notify the parents within 24 hours and tell them why the action was being taken. Parents of students being expelled for longer than 10 days had a right to appeal to the school board, and could be heard at a board meeting. If their arguments were persuasive, the board could reinstate the student.

No such right existed for students suspended for up to 10 days. The nine students argued they were being shortchanged. The court agreed.

The court said there was a property right, a thing of value, an entitlement, that couldn't be taken away without due process, in being able to attend school. Also, due process prohibits the arbitrary deprivation of liberty. Liberty includes a person's good name, which can be damaged by suspension from school. For these reasons, the court held that even for short-term suspensions, students at least should be given notice of the charges against them, and if they deny the charges, the right to present their side of the story. Today most districts still tend to provide more due process rights for longer suspensions or expulsions than for shorter ones.

In some states, expulsion has become a less severe threat. There, when a student is "expelled," the school is required to provide the student with an alternate education program, which may mean simply being sent to another school.

Courts are also reluctant to uphold suspensions of youngsters still within the age limits of mandatory education. Where courts uphold a suspension, it is usually when all other disciplinary means have been exhausted, and the school has considered the student's age, history of behavior and school performance and the disruptive effect of the student's conduct.[24]

Nonetheless, many school boards move for expulsion in cases where students bring weapons or drugs to school, or do bodily injury to other students, and these actions are upheld if proper procedures are used.[25]

Schools use different kinds of suspensions. Some schools suspend a student until the student's parents come to school. This is usually acceptable, unless the student has recalcitrant parents who won't come to school. After a few days the student is being punished for the parent's ineptitude, and that is unacceptable. Some schools use in-school suspensions, where a student is kept in school but not allowed in class for a certain period of time. State law usually dictates how often this tactic can be used in a school year. Obviously, if a student spends weeks or months sitting at a table in the cafeteria, the educational experience isn't what it should be.

When suspensions and other disciplinary measures don't seem to be working, it may be time to consider evaluation for learning disabilities or other problems.

◆ ACTION STEPS ◆

Note that for a suspension or expulsion, there should be a conference. Some parents groups, such as the Parents Union for Public Schools in Philadelphia, have an advocate who works with parents on suspensions or expulsions (any parents group in a district where many parents can't afford lawyers should consider such a position). Your parents group can hire an advocate, if you have the resources, or seek a volunteer. The person should have a background in youth work, and be familiar with the process. Obviously, you can hire a lawyer. If you cannot afford one, look for a "super-parent," a parent who is familiar with the process and is willing to help. Your school social worker may also be able to help. When a parent is faced with a suspension or expulsion hearing, the Parents Union recommends:

- Talk to the advocate before the hearing. You can bring the advocate, or anyone else, to the hearing.
- Bring your child to the hearing.
- You should expect that the school has thoroughly investigated the suspension and can provide you with specific details. What exactly did your child do? When? To whom?
- Ask questions. If the facts presented do not agree with the facts you collected from your child, try to settle this disagreement. In a longer suspension (more than three days in Philadelphia), you can cross-examine witnesses and bring witnesses of your own.
- Ask what school services were used to solve your child's problem before the suspension. If your child was promised help but never received it, point this out. You may object to any discussion of your home life, or anything else not pertinent to the incident.
- Don't agree to any recommendation that you don't understand, or that you don't want for your child. Don't sign anything until you have talked with the advocate.
- If the conference is more involved than you thought, or if communication is breaking down, end the meeting for a "cooling-off" time, and call the advocate for help.
- If a child is being repeatedly suspended, it usually indicates there are serious problems that need to be resolved.

GRADE LOWERING

Can schools lower grades for misbehavior or for absence? No and yes.

The trend is against lowering grades for misconduct or violation of most school rules. The theory is that grades are to reflect academic achievement, and there are other ways of dealing with misconduct. Also, schools can give a grade or make a notation on student records concerning conduct.

A major case in the area involved a Pennsylvania honor student who went to a party with her friends and drank a glass of wine. This violated school rules. Her punishment included being thrown off the cheerleading squad, bounced from the National Honor Society, suspended for five days, and given a grade reduction of 10 percent in each class.

She and her parents went to court to protest the grade reduction, and they won. The court said the grade reduction practice could misrepresent the girl's academic achievement, which would be wrong.[26]

On the other hand, courts have been more willing to allow school districts to reduce grades for unauthorized absences, especially when the report card indicates the grade has been reduced for that reason.

New Milford, Connecticut, had a policy in which no course credit was given when a student had more than 24 absences in a given year, and in which the grade was reduced five points for each unauthorized absence after the first such absence. A student challenged the grade reduction part of this policy, and lost.

The court said the school board had the authority to establish such a policy, and said it wasn't any more arbitrary than a teacher adjusting a grade for classroom participation.[27] Grades that had been reduced for unauthorized attendance were circled on report cards, so anyone reading the report card would have an idea of what the problem was.

The court said that using grade reduction in addition to some other punishment was probably wrong, as would be using the policy in an arbitrary or capricious manner, but said neither was the case here.

In cases where parents pull students from class for a family trip, parents are well advised to make informal arrangements with the school in advance, a common practice. Some districts have a policy prohibiting this practice more than once a year, so it is helpful to find out what the local rules are.

Many schools won't give credit for a course if the student misses too many classes for any reason. Courts usually uphold this rule. Absences are usually caused by sickness or injury, and are no one's fault. Unless the student has been able to study at home and can go in and ace the final exam, there's usually no alternative but to repeat the course.

◆ Action Steps ◆

If your child's teacher or your school has a policy of lowering grades for disciplinary reasons, fight it. Talk to the teacher, the principal and, if necessary, the school board. Academic grades that are lowered for disciplinary reasons present parents, students and future teachers with a confusing diagnostic picture of the student, and don't encourage getting at the root of whatever the disciplinary problem may be.

As for lowering grades for unauthorized absences, an active parent should be able to avoid this problem. First, if you are in touch regularly with all of your child's teachers, you should know whether or not your child is cutting classes or skipping school. What you don't want to do is create an unauthorized absence problem for your child. For example, if you plan to pull your child for a family trip, make informal arrangements with the school in advance. Some districts have a policy prohibiting this practice more than once a year, so it is helpful to know what the local rules are.

◆ Selected Questions ◆

Can students be denied the right to participate in extracurricular activities because of low grades?

Yes. A classic example is the state of Texas' "no pass, no play" rule, which came from an educational reform commission headed by Ross Perot. The rule is that students must have grades of 70 percent or "C" in order to take part in extracurriculars. It came as a shock in certain parts of the Lone Star State that academics were more important than football, but the rule has been upheld.[28] Many local districts have similar "C" rules. They are controversial—many parents feel the chance to play sports is a great motivator in keeping some youngsters in school—but they are legal.

Can students be disciplined in school for what they do off school grounds?

Yes, if the conduct has some connection to the school and its educational function. Thus, say professors Kern Alexander and M. David Alexander, schools have the responsibility to discipline students going to and from school, and in situations where off-campus activity has a direct bearing on the well-being of the school.[29] Thus, situations in which a violent bully hovered across the street from the school and preyed upon students leaving school, or in which a drug dealer did the same thing, the school would be within its rights to take action, because their activities obviously would be detrimental to the students' performance in school. In a 1993 Delaware case, the court upheld the suspension of a student for off-campus drug sales.[30]

My state does not allow corporal punishment. My son was in a tussle in school, and a teacher broke it up. When he did, he hurt my son's arm. Did the teacher violate state law?

Most likely not. State laws banning corporal punishment usually exclude using force for self-defense or to defend another student or staff member, to break up a fight or to restrain an unruly student who won't respond to oral requests to halt his behavior.

My son has a history of behavior problems, and his principal wants to send him to an alternative school. Should I go along with this?

Not without taking a very close look at the alternative school. Joan First says there's been a proliferation of "alternative schools" for children with behavioral and other problems. In many instances, she said, no one has examined these schools to see how well they are doing. You should demand to know if students do real work, whether or not teachers are certified, and how well graduates of the school are doing.

FOR FURTHER INFORMATION

National Center for the Study of Corporal Punishment and Alternatives
253 Ritter South
Temple University
Philadelphia, PA 19122
215–204–6091

Education Commission of the States
707 17th Street Suite 2700
Denver, CO 80202–3427
303–299–3600

Parents Union for Public Schools
311 S. Juniper Street Room 602
Philadelphia, PA 19107
215–546–1156

National Coalition of Advocates for Students
100 Boylston Street #731
Boston, MA 02116
617–357–8507

Center for Law and Education
955 Massachusetts Avenue
Cambridge, MA 02139
617–876–6611

NOTES

1. *Board of Education of Harrodsburg* v. *Bentley*, 383 S.W. 2d 677 (Ky. App. Ct. 1964).

2. *Tinker* v. *Des Moines Independent Community School District*, 393 U.S. 503 (1969).

3. *Guzick* v. *Drebus*, U.S. Circuit Court of Appeals, 431 F. 2d 594 (6th Cir. 1970).

4. *Stanton* v. *Brunswick School Dept.*, 577 F. Supp 1560 (D. Me. 1984).

5. *Bethel School Dist.* v. *Fraser*, 106 S. Ct. 3159 (1986).

6. *Gano* v. *School District 411 of Twin Falls City, Idaho.*, 674 F. Supp. 796 (d. Idaho 1987).

7. *Hazelwood School Dist.* v. *Kuhlmeier*, 98 L. Ed 2d 592 (1988).

8. See *Planned Parenthood* v. *Clark County School Dist.*, 887 F. 2d 935, 941 F. 2d 817, (9th Cir. 1991), and *Bull* v. *Dardanelle Public School Dist. No. 15*, 745 F. Supp. 755 (E.D. Ark. 1990).

9. *Ingraham* v. *Wright*, 430 U.S. 651 (1977).

10. *Arnold* v. *Carpenter*, 456 F. 2d 939 (7th Cir. 1972).

11. *Massie* v. *Henry*, 455 F. 2d 79 (4th Cir. 1972).

12. *Hatch* v. *Goerke*, 502 F. 2d 1189 (10th Cir. 1074).

13. *Zeller* v. *Donegal School District Board of Education*, 517 F. 2d 600 (3rd Cir. 1973).

14. *Pyle* v. *South Hadley School Committee*, D Mass. Civ. A No. 93-30102-F June 8, 1993.

15. *Brainard* v. *School Board of the City of Norfolk*, 801 F. Supp. 1526 (E.D. Va. 1992).

16. *Wallace* v. *Ford*, 346 F. Supp. 156 (E.D. Ark 1972).

17. *Cornfield by Lewis* v. *Consolidated High School Dist. No. 230*, (C.A. Ill) No. 92-1863 April 23, 1993.

18. Matter of Gregroy M., 585 N.Y.S. 2d 193 (1992).

19. *State ex.rel. Juvenile Department of Washington County* v. *DuBois*, 821 P. 2d 1124, 110 Or. App. 314 (1991).

20. *New Jersey* v. *T.L.O*, 83 L. Ed 2d 720 (1985).

21. *Com.* v. *Snyder*, 597 N.E. 2d 1363, 413 Mass. 521 (1992).

22. *Doe* v. *Renfrow*, 475 F. Supp. 1012 (N.D. Ind. 1979) 635 F. 2d 582 (7th Cir. 1980).

23. *Goss* v. *Lopez*, 95 S. Ct. 729 (1975).

24. *C.L.S.* v. *Hoover Bd. of Education*, 594 So. 2d 138 (Ala. Civ. App. 1991)

25. *Freemont Union High School Dist.* v. *Santa Clara County Board of Education*, 286 Cal. Rptr 915 (1991) and *Nicholas B.* v. *School Committee of Worchester*, 587 N.E. 2d 211 (Mass 1992).

26. *Katzman* v. *Cumberland Valley School District*, 479 A. 2d 671 (Pa. Cmwlth. Ct. 1984).

27. *Campbell* v. *Board of Education*, 193 Conn. 93 (1984).

28. *Spring Branch Independent School Dist.* v. *Stamas*, 695 S.W. 2d 556, (Tex. 1985).

29. Alexander and Alexander, *The Law of Schools, Students and Teachers in a Nutshell* (West Publishing Co., 1984).

30. *Howard* v. *Colonial School Dist.*, 621 A. 2d 362 (Del. Super. 1993).

STUDENT INJURIES AND SCHOOL RESPONSIBILITY

◆ INTRODUCTION ◆

A bully picks a fight with a smaller student in the cafeteria and breaks his jaw. Two students are "sword fighting" with pencils and one gets stuck in the eye. A student picks up a piece of debris in the school yard and throws it, striking a girl in the face. A teacher walks out of a shop class, leaving a table saw running, and a student is cut. A playground swing hits a kindergarten student in the back of the head, right in front of a teacher.

Are school officials responsible for these injuries? Are the students and their parents entitled to monetary damages?

Ideally, your child will sail through school with no more than the usual bumps and scrapes. But in case of a serious injury, it's helpful to know the rules courts use to determine liability. In this chapter we'll look at:

- *The elements of negligence*
- *The risk of sports injuries*

◆ Discussion ◆

A "tort" is a wrongful injury for which a civil lawsuit can be brought. There are two kinds of torts that might happen in a school, intentional and unintentional.

An intentional tort can happen when a teacher or other school official commits assault and battery on a child by dishing out excessive punishment. It doesn't happen often, but it happens. It is also possible for a teacher to commit other intentional torts such as defamation. But intentional torts are relatively rare. The vast majority are unintentional, which means they involve negligence.

For an educator to be held liable for negligence when a student is injured, the incident has to meet a four-part legal test. The four parts are:

1. *The teacher must have a duty to exercise reasonable care for students.* Teachers, standing in for parents, have to do what is reasonable to protect students. Note this distinction: Passers-by have no legal obligation to come to the aid of someone in distress. They may feel a moral obligation, when seeing someone drowning or being beaten, to jump in and help. But there is no legal obligation to try to make a rescue. A passer-by cannot in most circumstances be negligent by omission. But a teacher can. By nature of the quasi-parental relationship, teachers have an affirmative duty to try to protect students from harm. Also, that duty increases in proportion to the potential danger of a particular activity. There is a greater obligation for student safety when the teacher is supervising a tricky chemistry experiment than when the teacher is supervising a meeting of the stamp club.

2. *There must be a breach of that duty.* Let's say a teacher is supposed to monitor a hallway where there's been trouble in

the past. The teacher, for whatever reason, fails to do so one day. As a result, no one is monitoring the hallway. That is a breach of duty, a failure to use reasonable care. But that alone isn't enough to establish liability.

3. *The breach or failure of duty must be the cause of the injury.* Let's go back to our example of the teacher failing to monitor the hallway. That, arguably, is a breach of duty. Then let's say a tree falls through a window in the hallway and injures a student. The teacher's absence had nothing to do with the accident—and the teacher wouldn't have been able to stop the accident if he or she had been there. But change the situation. Instead of a tree falling, two unruly students walk down the hallway, notice there's no teacher present, and throw a rock at a girl walking by, injuring her. This time, the teacher's presence might well have stopped the injury, so the teacher's absence may well be viewed as the "proximate cause" of the injury.

4. *There must be a provable injury.* The teacher isn't going to be liable for damages unless the student can prove he or she actually suffered an injury or loss of some kind.

WHAT IS THE SCHOOL'S DUTY?

Many cases hinge on whether there was a duty of care in the given situation.

For example, two teachers in Chicago took 50 junior high school students on a field trip to a museum of natural history. While they were there, the students broke into small groups and were allowed to look at exhibits on their own. One boy wandered off by himself, ran into some bullies from another school, and was badly beaten.

His parents sued the teachers and the museum. The court found neither could be held responsible for the assault. In determining what level of duty exists, the key question in this case and many others is this: Was the danger foreseeable? Should the supervising authority, in this case the teachers and museum staff, have reasonably suspected that such an assault might happen? The museum often let groups of children walk around. The court could find no special circumstance "that would charge the museum with special knowledge of the potential danger of an assault."[1]

The court held that there was minimal risk that a 12-year-old boy would be assaulted in a museum. Because of this, the court said that constant surveillance by teachers wasn't required. If it were, teachers simply would never take children on field trips.

In Florida some high school students went to the roof of the school building to shoot pictures for the school yearbook. One teacher was monitoring more than two dozen students. The teacher gave a "general admonition to be careful." A girl fell through a skylight and was killed.

The court held that the general warning wasn't nearly enough. In this dangerous situation, the school had a duty to take "extraordinary precautions," such as giving explicit instructions on the layout of the roof, dangers of the roof and the skylight, and exact pro-cedures to be followed while on the roof. The school should have provided "intensive supervision."

The court said in this situation an accident was foreseeable, and the lack of proper precautions was the cause of the accident.[2]

How far do schools have to go in taking precautions?

A California student was shot by gang members as he stood in front of school after school hours. The school was aware of gang problems, and had taken precautions to minimize gang-related problems. The court said on the day of the shooting there was no advance warning of gang violence. To have stopped it, school officials would have had to have scouted the neighborhood for gang members and then waited until they were all gone before releasing the students. School officials weren't required to go this far, the court said.[3]

Now take a situation only slightly different. School officials told a fifth-grade student to wait in front of school at 6:15 A.M. for a bus to take her to a gifted class. Usually one of her parents waited with her, but one morning she was there alone, and was grabbed and sexually assaulted.

A lower court said the school wasn't liable for this assault, which took place before school was staffed or open. But an appeals court reversed the decision. The higher court said teachers and other school officials have a general duty to supervise the activity of students when the students are entrusted to their care.

Because the school directed the girl to wait in front of the school at a particular time, the school had a duty to provide her with adequate security, and breached this duty by not providing any security.[4]

In these two cases, students who were standing in front of the school building, one after school and one before school, were injured. The distinction is that the Florida girl was there under school instruction, as part of an official school program, so should have received school supervision and security. Both cases indicate that a school can be liable for student injuries that take place before or after school, if the injuries are somehow caused by the negligence of the school.

If a school is aware of a problem and has taken reasonable steps to solve or ameliorate it, courts generally don't find them liable. For example, a second-grader in North Carolina tripped over a tree root in the schoolyard and was injured. The parents sued. The court held the school had not breached its duty of care because school officials had taken reasonable steps to protect the youngsters, such as placing sand in the schoolyard, to mitigate any problems with the roots.[5]

Another frequent question in these cases is how much information do school officials need to be considered on notice that there may be a problem. If a youngster gets in one fight, does that put the school on notice that other students who are around this one must be protected?

Courts usually say no, one fight by itself isn't enough to mark a student as a source of future violent behavior.[6] But say a student has had one fight, but has also announced he's after a particular student. Does the school then have a duty to protect that student? If the school is on notice of the impending assault, someone would be wise to intervene.

As you doubtless suspect, many of these cases are close, tough calls. Most of the time, courts simply demand the teacher do what is reasonable, not what is ingenious or heroic.

CAUSATION

Let's say there's a duty, followed by a breach of duty. That still doesn't mean the case is won. The breach of duty has to be the "proximate cause" or "legal cause" or simply "cause" of the injury.

Let's look at a couple of cases. In a New York sixth grade, the teacher was out of the class. The classroom aide was monitoring two classes, so left to look in on the other class. There were no adults in the room. A boy pulled an old and stupid trick on another student, pulling his chair out from under him as he was sitting down. The student who was trying to sit fell and was injured. His family sued the school.

The court said the school may have been negligent in not supervising the room, but that wasn't the cause of the injuries. They were caused by a "sudden and unexpected prank that could not have been realistically anticipated or prevented."[7]

But look at a similar case. A third-grade girl was hit in the eye and injured when boys were throwing apples into the girls' restroom. A teacher was supposed to monitor the hallway outside the restroom because there had been trouble before. But that day the teacher who was supposed to be there wasn't. The court found the school negligent, saying that if the teacher had been there, the incident wouldn't have happened.[8]

What's the difference? Not much, except the seat-pulling case was so fast and unpredictable that the student might have done it with the same effect if an adult had been there. In the apples-in-the-bathroom case, the boys had to case the hallway, to make sure there was no teacher present. Hence, the teacher not being there was the cause of the incident, the court reasoned.

A Missouri girl named Buffy Dale was injured in her schoolyard when another student picked up a piece of debris and threw it. It hit Buffy in the eye. As it turned out, the schoolyard was littered with debris. For Buffy and her parents to win the case, they had to show:

- There was a dangerous condition on public property.
- The condition created a reasonably foreseeable risk of harm.
- The condition directly caused the injury.

- The condition was created by a public employee, or the employee had actual or constructive knowledge of it.

The key point in the case was "direct cause." If Buffy had slipped on a piece of debris, the outcome might have been different. But the student who picked up something and threw it changed the flow of direct causation and became what the court called an "intervening resulting cause."[9]

This seems like a harsh result. If you leave a schoolyard littered with dangerous debris, pieces of asphalt or trash, doesn't it figure that kids would play with it, and hurt themselves? Some courts might have held that way, but the case still illustrates the concept of causation. The breach of duty has to directly cause the problem.

✦ Action Steps ✦

Obviously, an ounce of prevention is worth a pound of legal documents. The best way to deal with lawsuits is to avoid them as best you can. That means eliminating, as much as possible, the conditions that might lead to student injuries.

We believe each school parents group should have an advisory school safety committee, to advise the administration on potential safety problems. Ultimately, the school must be responsible. But your parents group can help by:

- Listening to your children. Kids have a way of talking about things that are out of the ordinary, near-accidents, broken pieces of equipment. Listen to them.

- Walking through the building. Are the corridors monitored at proper times? Is there debris in the school yard? Are there any "attractive nuisances," such as ditches or pieces of machinery, in the schoolyard that might attract and injure curious children?

- Using your parent network. As we'll mention again in Chapter Eleven, we think each school should have a committee that works with the administration on the condition of the building and grounds. Such a committee can be most effective if its members know what they are talking about. So review your parents group. Do you have a structural engineer? A lawyer familiar with building safety? A building inspector? A real estate developer? Chances are you have someone with the expertise to work with the administration to improve the school building and assist with school safety by looking for potential safety problems in the building and on the grounds.

If your child has been injured at school, whether in sports or any other activity, immediately investigate the circumstances and gather all the facts you can. Start by talking to your child. If it's a playground injury, talk to the monitor and the building staff. Keep an open mind: Sometimes children exaggerate or leave out key details. Talk to other children who might have witnessed the accident. Examine any equipment that may have been involved in the accident. Talk to the principal and ask what steps the school has taken to correct the problem, if steps are necessary. Remember that sometimes children trip over their feet. But if you are convinced the school's negligence caused the injury, you then must make what is in essence a business decision. You must decide whether it is worth your while to hire a lawyer and pursue the matter. If you do, the chances are your lawyer will write what is called a "demand letter," stating that the injury was caused by the school's negligence and demanding compensation. Typically, the letter will offer the possibility of negotiating a settlement with the school's insurance carrier, and in many cases that is what happens.

THE RISK OF SPORTS

It is possible to get hurt playing sports in school, and it's also possible to have a bad sports program that doesn't teach anything. Let's look at the injury problem first.

Many student injuries happen when children are playing organized games. Does that mean their parents can sue the teacher and the school? Not necessarily. If youngsters have been coached, instructed, equipped, and supervised properly, and are still injured, they may well have assumed the risk inherent in playing the sport. Accidents happen.

"Assumption of the risk" is one of several possible defenses to tort cases, and it's one that is often raised in sports-related cases. Perhaps the best example of assumption of the risk involves foul balls at baseball games. Any baseball fan knows that players sometimes hit foul balls into the stands. And, they know that if they are sitting in the stands, they might get hit by a foul ball. But if they go and sit in the stands anyway, they are said to have assumed the risk of being beaned by a foul.

Courts have reached similar conclusions in other sports-related cases. A youngster went out for his high school football team as a freshman and made the team. He was running the ball late in a game, and gained quite a bit of yardage. Finally, he saw two tacklers in front of him. He knew his run was about over, so he put his head down and charged into the tacklers. They were bigger and older than he, and he injured his neck. His parents sued, saying a light, inexperienced freshman shouldn't have been playing against bigger, older players.

They lost. The court said the youngster was properly coached and equipped, could have gotten new equipment if he wanted it, that all freshmen are inexperienced to some degree, and that some football players are always bigger than others. Football is a contact sport. If you carry the ball, someone will try to tackle you. That is the nature of the game. If you get injured, it isn't anyone else's fault. The judge dismissed the case.[10]

But a student does not assume the risk of incompetent coaching, improper equipment, or improper medical treatment. If, for example, a student is injured, and the trainer or coach doesn't seek medical help, the school may be liable.[11]

A student, under the direction of a teacher, tried to lift 360 pounds in the weight-lifting maneuver known as squat-pressing. The teacher apparently didn't impart the technique as well as he might have; the student suffered serious back injuries. A court dismissed the case, but an appeals court sent it back for trial, to let the jury decide if the coaching was negligent.[12]

Children don't assume the risk of dangerous equipment. A group of kindergarten students were playing in the schoolyard under adult supervision. Among the equipment in the schoolyard was a 60-pound, two-person swing that was too big for kids to stop by putting their feet down. The swing struck and injured a youngster. The court held the swing created an unreasonable risk of harm to such small children.[13]

These are problems that can lead to physical injuries. Then there's the problem of weak, even counterproductive, sports programs. Sports, like all other school activities, should support the educational mission of the school. Indeed, many studies show children who participate in school activities have higher attendance, get better grades, and have more success in their adult lives. So kids should be learning something when they are on a sports team or there isn't much point to it. They should be learning sportsmanship, teamwork, self-discipline, and self-esteem. They should have fun, let's not forget, and should learn athletic skills. They should learn that hard work can have a reward—winning.

But some adults put too much emphasis on winning, and not enough on education. Some coaches, thankfully not the majority, push kids too far, show them no respect and encourage poor sportsmanship, cheating and anything else that will get them a win. As a parent, you should find such behavior unacceptable.

◆ Action Steps ◆

If you feel a coach or physical education teacher is pushing your child too much, or poking fun at your child, or even getting too involved with your child, go to the coach as you would any other teacher and say, "I think we have a concern here." Most difficulties can be straightened out this way. If the problem persists, call the principal or the district's athletic director. Some parents won't intervene for fear of hurting their child's playing time, or of being thought of as a nuisance. Nonsense. Your child's welfare is your main concern. If you have to make a pest of yourself, so be it.

If your child has suffered a sports injury, pursue it as you would any other injury. Gather the facts. Make particular note to inspect equipment. A surprising number of schools use faulty sports equipment, or sometimes not enough equipment. Also, determine if physical exams were given. When you have learned what you can about the circumstances of the injury, you must decide whether or not to pursue legal action. If your findings can help improve the school's sports program, by all means bring them to the attention of school officials.

You and your parents group should support a sports program that truly complements and supports your school's academic program. In other words, you want a program in which academics come first, and sports are kept in a proper perspective. A program with many of these ideal elements is offered at Edgemont Junior/Senior High School in Scarsdale, New York. Highlights from the Edgemont program include:

- In the 7th through 9th grades, "modified teams" are offered in basketball, football, soccer, and wrestling for boys and soccer, field hockey, and lacrosse for girls. For these teams, explained athletic director Jim San Marco, the rules of each sport are modified so there is more learning and less stress for the players. For example, there are five quarters instead of four in basketball, so more kids can play. In soccer the coach may be allowed on the field to give instruction. In football there is no kickoff, to reduce the chance of injury. Also, teams aren't allowed to play games on consecutive days, which gives the chance for more practice. In some communities, city recreation programs offer variations of modified teams for elementary school, middle school, junior high school, and high school youngsters.

- Students can only play after obtaining parental permission slips and undergoing sports physical examinations. Any youngster who wants to play well above his or her age group, say an 8th grader who wants to play with the high school junior varsity team, must undergo a maturation test and a state fitness test to determine if the student's body has reached the level of growth and maturity for the higher level of competition.

- Practices nearly always begin at 4 P.M., so students have time for after school academic programs. Students who need extra academic help are not only encouraged to get it but are required to get it.

- The district has a booster club and other activities for parents, and publishes a helpful "Introduction to Interscholastic Sports," which covers frequently asked questions about such subjects as practices, transportation to games, and who washes the uniforms.

San Marco reports that his program garners tremendous parental support and has for years. Would that all school sports programs were as comprehensive and educational.

A particular concern in recent years across the country has been the decline in sportsmanship. A national coaches organization, The National Federation of State High School Associations of Kansas City, Missouri, has made sportsmanship a priority in all 50 states. The federation formed a sportsmanship, ethics, and integrity committee in 1989 to improve sportsmanship in interscholastic competition.

The committee encourages school districts to adopt sportsmanship creeds and rules. The Central Lakes Conference in Minnesota has done so. Rules include:

- No throwing objects onto the playing surface.

- All signs and locations for signs must be approved by the home site supervisor. Only signs of a positive nature are permitted.

- No profane or abusive cheers or chanting is allowed, nor is spitting.

- Fighting is prohibited.

- Use of drugs or alcohol is prohibited.

- No noisemakers allowed. Full face painting is discouraged.

- Music is limited to timeouts, intermissions, and quarter breaks.

- Only official cheerleaders and mascots are allowed on the playing surface.

In addition, the conference encourages home cheerleaders to greet visiting cheerleaders, home security personnel to welcome and seat visiting fans, and athletes to congratulate one another after the games. Sportsmanship must also be on the agenda of every athletic directors and governance board meeting.

Your school should make sportsmanship a top priority as well. Ultimately it's not whether you win or lose. It really is how you play the game.

◆ Selected Questions ◆

How can I tell if my school's sports program is good for my child?

First, ask yourself what you and your child want to get out of sports. If it is simply to have fun, and learn the value of teamwork, discipline and sportsmanship, then you should proceed on those grounds, and see if those goals are being met. Talk to your child about a coach as you would about any other teacher. If there is a problem, approach it the same way you would with any other teacher. A frequent complaint in scholastic sports is that the coach doesn't have a good understanding of a child's temperament. If that is a problem, discuss it with the coach.

If you take sports more seriously, and see it as a possible vehicle for a college scholarship, even a professional career, for your child, first make sure you are being realistic about your child's abilities. Then take a hard look at programs. If a girl is a star basketball player and the school has a weak program, or if a boy is a hockey star and the school has no program, should you think about transferring? First, talk it over with your child and his or her coaches, and other parents who have been in the same situation. Transferring has become more common in recent years, but it needs to be completely researched.

If we rent our school gym to a group of adults, and one of them gets hurt playing basketball, is the school liable?

Usually not. If adults rent a school gym for basketball and someone is injured, courts will usually say the hoopster assumed the risk normally associated with playing basketball. However, it's possible the school could be liable if the injury was caused by a hidden defect in the gym, such as a faulty floor board.[14]

When I was growing up my school never had gym classes, and I turned out all right. Really, how important are gym classes for my kids?

We think they are very important, as does Charlene Burgeson, program director for physical education for the American Alliance for Health, Physical Education, Recreation and Dance, of Reston, Virginia. Burgeson said children should be physically educated to develop the motor skills they'll need for the physical activities they'll do in their lifetime, and the fitness skills they'll need to enjoy sports and stay in shape. Parents begin the process of teaching motor skills when they teach a child to walk, and perhaps to throw a ball. An elementary school physical education program builds on the base, teaching the proper ways to run, hit a ball, lift, march, dance, and climb. Then these skills are put together to learn fitness skills. In addition, gym classes can be great fun. They are also a rejuvenating physical break from the mental activity of school, and some research indicates kids who exercise regularly learn better. Good gym classes teach the rudiments of teamwork and sportsmanship, and can be the basis for a lifetime of regular physical activity. A good physical education program should involve daily exercise for all children, preferably in sports or activities they can continue well into their adult lives.

My son was cut from his junior high soccer team. Shouldn't every kid who wants to play be allowed to play?

We think so. Unfortunately some schools don't have the resources to keep every child who wants to play on every team. Also, while good coaches try to let as many players as possible play, most schools don't guarantee each player a certain amount of playing time. Short of getting more resources into school sports programs, the best solution may be city recreational leagues, which often embrace the philosophy of keeping everyone on the team and letting everyone play.

_____

My son wants to play football in junior high and high school. I think it's a dumb and dangerous game. How can I talk him out of this?

It depends entirely on your son. Through the eye of adult logic, football has a lot of risk for questionable reward. Most players don't play organized football beyond high school. On the other hand, sports such as tennis, running, golf, baseball, and soccer are played much longer, so it could be argued the time would be better spent learning these "lifetime sports."

But some kids just love football. Some kids stay in school and keep their grades up because of football. It provides a sense of accomplishment and bonding, and can be a vent for youthful aggression. It may also offer memories that get more spectacular with the passing years. Talk it out with your son. Lay out the pros and cons, and let him make the decision.

FOR FURTHER INFORMATION

National Federation of State High School Associations
P.O. Box 20626
Kansas City, MO 64195–0626
816–464–5400

American Alliance for Health, Physical Education, Recreation and Dance
1900 Association Drive
Reston, VA 22091
703–476–3400

American Civil Liberties Union
132 W. 43rd Street
New York, NY 10036
212–944–9800

National School Boards Association
1680 Duke Street
Alexandria, VA 22314
703–838–6722

American Bar Association
750 N. Lake Shore Drive
Chicago, IL 60611
312–988–5000

NOTES

1. *Mancha* v. *Field Museum of Natural History,* 283 N.E. 2d 956 (1972).
2. *Dade County School Board* v. *Guitierrez,* 592 So. 2d 259 (1991).
3. *Brownell* v. *Los Angeles Unified School District,* 5 Cal. Rptr. 2d 756 (1992)
4. *O'Campo* v. *School Board of Dade County,* 589 So. 2d 383 (Fla. App. 3 Dist. 1991).
5. *Waltz* v. *Wake County Bd. of Ed.,* 409 S.E. 2d 106, 104 N.C. App. 302, review denied 412 S.E. 2d 96 (N.C. App. 1991)
6. *Coleman* v. *Joyner,* 593 So. 2d 451, writ denied So.2d 657 (La 1992).
7. *Tomlinson* v. *Board of Education of the City of Elmira,* 583 N.Y.S. 2d 664 (1992).
8. *Carson* v. *Orleans Parish School Board,* 432 So. 2d 956 (La. App. 1983).
9. *Dale By and Through Dale* v. *Edmunds,* 819 S.W. 2d 388, (Mo. App. 1991).
10. *Vendrell* v. *School District 26 Malheur County,* 376 P. 2d 406 (Ore. 1962).
11. *Jarreau* v. *Orleans Parish School Board,* 600 So. 2d 1389 (La. App. 4 Cir. 1992).
12. *Koch* v. *Billings School District No. 2,* 833 P. 2d 181 (Mont. 1992).
13. *Glankler* v. *Rapides County School Board,* La. App. 3rd Cir. No. 91-239 (Dec. 1, 1992).
14. *Yarber* v. *Oakland Unified School District,* 6 Cal. Rptr. 2d 437 (Cal. App. 1 Dist. 1992)

HEALTH AND SAFETY

◆ INTRODUCTION ◆

Most of us remember the kindly school nurse, who put Mercurochrome on skinned knees, handed out polio vaccine, and took temperatures.

The school nurse was an important part of the school staff, because children must be in good health to learn. That's a point worth mentioning again. If a child is listless, not able to pay attention, or not completing work, the problem may have to do with the child's health. Also, bad health habits developed in childhood will become adult health problems.

Experts now believe we ought to pay considerably more attention to school health, to help children be better prepared to learn, to cut down on adult diseases, and deflate the national crisis in health care. This chapter will discuss comprehensive school health education, and also cover other health and related safety issues, including:

- *Do school sex education programs work?*

- *Is it safe for my child to go to school with a child who has AIDS, and what should schools be teaching about AIDS?*

- *If you are what you eat, will better nutrition make for better students?*

- *Should schools teach students not to smoke?*

- *Are bullies an overlooked school health problem?*
- *With the increases in school violence, how can we create safe schools?*
- *How prevalent is teen suicide, and what are the warning signs?*

◆ DISCUSSION ◆

If you have followed the ongoing debate on health care, you know we're spending a whopping 13 percent of our gross national product on health care, and the figure could be as high as 32 percent by the year 2020 if nothing is done.

Can this enormous cost be lessened by better health education and disease prevention programs in the schools? Dr. Lloyd Kolbe, head of the Division of Adolescent and School Health of the U.S. Centers for Disease Control and Prevention (CDC) of Atlanta, thinks so. He makes a compelling argument.

Traditionally, the school nurse provided a school's health services and health education. That's pretty much the way things remain in a majority of the country's schools. Although laws differ from state to state, typically schools have access to a nurse, aide, or nurse practitioner who provides an array of services.

These may include such things as vision, hearing and postural screenings, immunization checks, direct medical services, dispensing of medications, physical exams, health education and counseling.

However, because the nurse-to-student ratio is often very high, it becomes extremely difficult for the nurse to provide a thorough and comprehensive health education and prevention program. At present, 28 states require some level of health education, but these programs vary in quality and thoroughness.

In the past decade, school-based health clinics have been created, mostly in poorer urban schools where many youngsters don't otherwise have access to medical care. These have been a boon to the schools that have them, but less than one-twentieth of the country's schools do. Experts such as Dr. Howard L. Taras of San Diego, California, author of the American Academy of Pediatrics' guidelines on school health, thinks school-based clinics are the wave of the past, that budget cuts will reduce, rather than increase, the number of such facilities. He and other experts think it's time to concentrate on education and prevention.

Kolbe says six categories of behavior are responsible for most of the country's major health problems: irresponsible sexual behavior, drug and alcohol abuse, behaviors such as fighting that cause injuries, tobacco use, inadequate physical activity, and improper diet. Most of these behaviors are established in youth. Given that, he believes school health programs could be the most efficient way to modify these behaviors. He believes such programs would improve learning, reduce health costs and thus improve overall economic productivity.[1]

Kolbe envisions a national, comprehensive, kindergarten-to-12th-grade health education program to combat the behaviors that make our country sick.

With such a program of prevention and intervention, including counseling, social and psychological services, better diet, improved physical education, and consistent health education, many diseases could be stopped before they start and others could be caught in their early stages, when they are more easily treatable, he said.

Education and prevention make sense from both quality of life and economic points of view. Tobacco use, for example, is linked to 400,000 deaths a year and billions of dollars in health costs. Our prisons are full of drug addicts. According to Advocates for Youth, formerly The Center for Population Options, the more than 1 million live births to teenage mothers each year cost taxpayers more than $25 million in just food stamps, Medicaid, and welfare costs, and often relegates the mother to a life of welfare and the child to a life without much hope. Yet teen pregnancy remains a problem of epidemic proportion.

Federal support for increased school health education increased in the late 1980s. Congress approved about $500 million a year for the U.S. Department of Education to help schools provide drug abuse information. Also, Congress provided $4 million a year for the education department to support health education demonstration projects. Finally, Congress gave the Centers for Disease Control and Prevention $40 million to help schools provide HIV education.

However, another bill, the Healthy Students-Healthy Schools Act, would have authorized $500 million for the CDC to realize Kolbe's vision and establish and maintain comprehensive health education programs in our nation's schools, but it has yet to win Congressional approval.

Nonetheless, it's possible for states, counties, school districts, and individual schools to design comprehensive health programs for themselves. What does such a program look like?

One of the best such programs in the country is West Virginia's, designed by the state Department of Education, the American School Health Association and the CDC. The Mountaineer State was chosen for this model program because it had among the worst health statistics in the country, said Lenore K. Zedosky, executive director of the state education department's Office of Healthy Schools. She said the state had the highest incidence of heart disease, the highest per capita use of cigarettes, and second highest use of smokeless tobacco. With cutbacks in mining, much of the state's population had become sedentary.

In 1990 Governor Gaston Caperton appointed a 28-member blue ribbon task force to develop a statewide, school health program. The result is an eight-part program that includes: Health education, health services, a healthy environment, physical education, food service, counseling and psychological services, teacher/staff wellness, and community involvement.

Nearly all of the state's schools now make time each week for health education. In the early grades, the emphasis is on such subjects as basic hygiene and health practices, the relationship between food choices and exercise and health, the major parts and functions of the body's major systems, good touching versus bad touching and the need to report child abuse, and the difference between the use of drugs for medicinal purposes and unlawful drug use.

In the middle-school years, children learn healthy behaviors that can prevent lifestyle diseases such as AIDS, other sexually transmitted diseases, diabetes, cardiovascular diseases, and cancer. The youngsters learn to reject pressures to engage in risk behaviors such as drug, tobacco and alcohol use, and sexual activity. They also learn coping skills in peer, social, and family relationships that enhance mental health.

In adolescence, avoiding risk behaviors is emphasized, along with other skills necessary to make healthy decisions as adults. In addition, teens are taught the responsibilities of parenthood, along with such things as an understanding of health care costs and basic first aid.

In addition, the state has made all 55 county boards of education tobacco-free. This means no smoking or chewing in any school, school grounds, or other school facility. Also, faculty and staffers are prohibited from using tobacco at school functions away from the school. Students are instructed in the dangers of tobacco use.

In physical education, the goal is age-appropriate physical activity at least three times a week in every grade. The emphasis is on lifetime physical activities. The results so far are promising. In one county, the number of eighth-graders passing the President's Physical Fitness Test rose from 4 to 25 percent, Zedosky said.

In the nutrition area, which we'll look at in more detail later in this chapter, the state has become one of the first in the nation to require that schools meet USDA Dietary Guidelines for Americans, which call for limits in the fat and sodium content of food and increased amounts of fiber. The guidelines encourage consumption of fruit, vegetables and other healthy foods.

West Virginia has also initiated programs to improve staff wellness, counseling and social services, health delivery services, and community involvement in school health programs.

In addition, teachers are being trained to integrate health concepts into other areas of instruction. For example, math problems may involve calculating the amount of fat in food at home. Finally, Zedosky said, the comprehensive school health program has been accompanied by a state marketing program to emphasize outdoor tourism activities.

◆ Action Steps ◆

What you need to do in this area depends greatly on what's already been done. If your school happens to be a West Virginia school that has just added these excellent programs, then perhaps your energy might better be applied somewhere else. But if your school is one of the thousands with no health education program and only rudimentary health programs in other areas, then it's a different story.

Kolbe said the most important first step is an education program to give parents an understanding of the problem. "Parents and school officials are rightfully concerned. Health is a basic prerequisite for academic and economic success," he said. He said many schools have school health councils, which include parents. The council could be the leader of this effort.

Council members should create a partnership with school health professionals and child health specialists from local hospitals or universities, along with health officials from your city, county, and state governments. This partnership should study the types of health problems facing the community, as the West Virginia task force did for the entire state. They should then look at other programs to see what a modern health education program looks like. "Note that it includes lifetime exercise plans, nutrition, that sort of thing," Kolbe said. From this overview, the council can then develop a game plan, tailored to the school, for its own program. Kolbe stressed the importance of a broad, strategic plan that meets the long-term needs of the students, and doesn't respond only to the "disease of the month" that everyone just read about in the newspaper.

Funding is a concern. The West Virginia legislature appropriated $1.5 million to start its program. Some states may not be as generous. Once you've settled on a plan, you should pursue funding from both public and private sources. Many local and regional foundations make children a priority, and will look kindly on a well-prepared grant application for school health programs. Your school administration should have someone with grant writing experience; if not, your parent skill pool may well have a grantsman or grantswoman.

SEX EDUCATION

Education about sexuality has been with us since the early 1900s, when educators and parents, worried about young people engaging in premarital sex, began teaching about the dangers of venereal disease. Many more schools began offering programs to address adolescent sexuality in the 1970s, when unintended pregnancy and sexually transmitted diseases (STDs) became increasingly serious problems. These classes, sometimes called family life classes, increased in the 1980s, spurred by the AIDS epidemic. Many of the classes have multiple goals; instead of just reducing teen pregnancy and STDs, the programs seek to enhance self-esteem and nurturing, and promote respect for different types of families.

Now, 17 states require comprehensive sex education, and 29 more states either mandate or encourage sex education. The classes have sometimes been challenged as violating the parents' right of religious liberty, or their right to privacy.

However, courts have continually upheld the schools' right to offer such classes because of the state's interest in the health and well-being of children.

"The prevailing view appears to be that sex education can be constitutionally defended as a required course of study," say professors Kern Alexander and M. David Alexander.[2] Nonetheless, there is some sentiment that making such courses mandatory might in some instances violate a student's right to privacy or religious liberty. To make absolutely certain that sex education laws withstand judicial scrutiny, and to accommodate parents' wishes, most states either make their courses noncompulsory, or allow parents to remove students from any portion of the course they find objectionable.

A federal court noted that a 1979 New Jersey state regulation calling for the establishment of family-life education courses in each school did not violate a student's right to religious freedom. A key factor in the decision was the state's excusal clause, which allows parents to remove a student from any portion of the class they found objectionable.[3]

Thus, family-life classes go on at most of the nation's schools, usually without incident. The more controversial issue about sex education is not whether it is legal, but whether or not it works. Critics such as Douglas Besharov of the American Enterprise Institute in Washington, DC, an authority on teen pregnancy, say that many sex education classes inadvertently encourage the onset of sex. He says the courses are taught in the following manner: "It is your body, you do not have to have sex if you don't want to. It is for you to decide when you are ready to have sex." The implicit message to many students, he said, is that if you are not having sex, you must be immature. In a highly controversial lead article in the October 1994 issue of *The Atlantic Monthly,* Barbara Dafoe Whitehead of the Institute for American Values in New York City called comprehensive sex education a failure. Many disagree.

Do sex education programs work? Perhaps the most extensive analysis of school sex education programs was that done by a team headed by Dr. Douglas Kirby, director of research for ETR Associates of Scotts Valley, California. They reviewed 23 programs, to see if the programs reduced sexual risk-taking behavior.

Kirby's team found, in essence, that some programs worked, and some didn't. They did an analysis of the characteristics of successful programs, and found:

- Effective programs focus narrowly on the behaviors the program is trying to encourage, notably delaying the initiation of intercourse or using protection. These programs don't spend a lot of time on other sexuality issues, such as gender roles, dating, and parenthood. Programs that stressed more abstract skills such as decision-making also weren't effective. In other words, the way to get children not to have sex is to teach them not to have sex.

- Effective programs use social learning theories. For example, the programs help young people understand the social pressures on them to have sex, and show them how to resist these pressures. The programs review "lines" used to get someone to have sex, and offer rejoinders to those lines. The successful programs focus on values and norms that lead to responsible sexual behavior.

- Effective programs provide accurate information about the risks of unprotected intercourse, and used personalized methods to transmit this information. Instead of lectures, successful programs use small group discussions, simulations or games, role-playing, rehearsal, coaching, visiting family planning clinics, and interviewing parents.

- Effective programs include activities that deal with media influences on sexual behavior. These programs explain how sex is used to sell products, and how television shows suggest that characters have unprotected sex, but don't explain the consequences.

- Effective programs reinforce clear and appropriate group values to strengthen individual values against unprotected sex. The norms of postponing sex and avoiding unprotected sex worked best when offered to age- and experience-appropriate students. Programs aimed only at abstinence didn't work well with high school students who had already initiated intercourse, while programs that stressed use of contraceptives worked better with this group.

- Effective programs provided skills in communication and negotiation.

Kirby and his team stress that their work isn't definitive and that more research must be done. Nonetheless, their findings strongly suggest that quality programs can reduce sexual risk-taking behaviors. For one thing, good sexuality education programs apparently do not cause young people to initiate sexual intercourse, a sometime complaint against the programs.

Also, despite what many people thought, abstinence may have a future. One program Kirby praises is called Postponing Sexual Involvement, developed at Grady Memorial Hospital in Atlanta, Georgia. The goal of the program is to help middle-school boys and girls resist pressures to engage in sex. It focuses specifically on that goal. Popular older teens teach the classes. Eighth-graders perform skits in which they practice refusing to engage in intercourse. The students aren't allowed to come up with their own endings. The ending must be refusal.

So far, so good. After ninth grade, only 24 percent of the program group had tried sex, as opposed to 39 percent in a nonprogram group. Among those who did try sex, half used contraception, while only a third in a group that didn't take the program used contraception. Along with the Atlanta program, other programs the Kirby team found effective in reducing sexual risk-taking behavior included Reducing the Risk, the Schinke-Blythe-Gilchrest curriculum and AIDS Prevention for Adolescents in School.

CONDOM DISTRIBUTION

One aspect of school policy toward sexual behavior that raises the ire of many parents is the distribution of condoms. Condoms are being handed out in about 400 schools around the country, the majority in large urban districts such as New York, Chicago and Los Angeles. Advocates say the distribution is to stop the spread of AIDS and other sexually transmitted diseases, and to slow the nation's epidemic of teen pregnancy.

They offer a compelling statistical argument. According to national CDC surveys in 1991, 1993 and 1995, the percentage of high school students who are sexually experienced is holding steady at about 53 percent. The median age of first intercourse is 16.1 for males and 16.9 for females. The health consequences of this activity are fearsome. The U.S. has the highest rate of teen pregnancy of any developed nation, more than 1 million pregnancies a year. School-aged youth account for a fourth of the 12 million STD cases reported each year; one in four adolescents acquire an STD before graduating from high school. Teens are more likely to have asymptomatic infections, which lead to a variety of lifetime health problems. On the AIDS front, the number of infected teenagers is steadily rising. According to one estimate, the number of teenagers infected with the HIV virus is doubling every 14 months. A CDC study found the number of teenagers with AIDS increased by 30 percent from June 1993 to June 1994. AIDS is now the sixth leading cause of death for 13- to 24-year-olds, but the leading cause of death for 25- to 44-year-olds.

One of the principle reasons these numbers are as bad as they are is that the majority of teenagers aren't using contraception. The CDC study found that 49 percent of males and 40 percent of females reported using condoms in their last coitus. Other studies put the number of teens using condoms as low as 38 percent. Advocates say if more youths used contraceptives, fewer would become pregnant or get sick.

Proponents such as Claudia Page of Advocates for Youth say one reason so many teenagers don't use effective contraceptives, such as latex condoms, is that they don't have access to them. She said studies show contraceptive availability doesn't increase sexual activity, and that surveys show a majority of the public supports contraceptive availability.

Most proponents of condom use to curtail AIDS and other STDs and teen pregnancy don't make it an either/or situation. The American Academy of Pediatrics, for example, urges abstinence first, because it is the surest way to avoid sexual risks. But for sexually active youngsters, the academy asks pediatricians to support the use of condoms, and to emphasize the responsibility of males as well as females in the prevention of unwanted pregnancies and STDs.

Opponents of condom distribution don't see it this way. They say distribution encourages sexual activity for teens, which in turn encourages teens to seek sexual gratification without commitment or intimacy. This can leave them psychologically dysfunctional, and make it difficult for them to keep a marriage together as adults, says Dr. Paul Atmajian of the Yale-New Haven Hospital in New Haven, Connecticut. Atmajian and many others believe parents should be the ones who deal with their children's sexual discipline.

Opponents say distribution of condoms sends a mixed message at best, that it confuses teens when they are told to abstain from sex, but are also told that condoms are available. Some parents say the distribution of condoms not only undermines parental authority but interferes with religious beliefs. The legal battles over condom distribution have involved giving parents the right to "opt-out" of the program, and parents have won this right in New York, Philadelphia and other cities. Page said 1 to 5 percent of parents have chosen not to allow their children to participate in the New York and Philadelphia programs. The issue remains one of the most emotional and highly controversial health issues involving young people today, one that requires parental involvement. Several experts, as well as the American Academy of Pediatrics' position paper on condom availability, stress that to be optimally effective, condom availability should be developed through a collaborative community process and be part of a comprehensive sexuality education program.

◆ ACTION STEPS ◆

What action you take depends almost entirely on where you come down on the issue. If you wish to start a condom distribution program in your high school—or stop a program already in existence— follow these steps:

- Talk to other parents to build support.
- Talk to health professionals in your school and gauge their support.
- Bring the request to the school health council or school health advisory council, or whatever body advises the school on health matters. Ask the council to prepare a recommendation for the school board.
- Perhaps most importantly, get students involved. The condom distribution plan in Cambridge, Massachusetts, was going nowhere until students started circulating petitions, making signs and attending meetings. Then it passed almost immediately.
- The easiest way to run a distribution plan is through a school clinic. If the school has no clinic, find a faculty member sympathetic with the program to run it.

AIDS

The AIDS epidemic has posed several health questions for school officials. Is it legal for a child with AIDS to go to a regular class? Is it safe?

After a short but explosive series of vigilante incidents and court decisions in the 1980s, it is now established that children with the HIV virus or with AIDS can go to school with other children.

When the AIDS tragedy started in the 80s, there was considerable misinformation about how the disease was transmitted. Some thought it was spread like a cold, through droplets in the air, by mere skin contact, or by such things as touching urine while changing diapers.

Fear led to violence in some parts of the country, as parents tried to prevent children with the disease from being in the same room with their own children. A house was firebombed in Arcadia, Florida, in an attempt to keep a child with AIDS out of school. Some youngsters were placed in glass cases in schools. Some teachers were harassed and even fired.

But some of these youngsters who were kept out of school went to court. Fortunately, this was at the time scientists determined that the AIDS virus wasn't spread by casual contact, but rather by the exchange of blood, semen or vaginal fluid. With this information, judges found it very difficult to keep children with AIDS out of school.

Ryan Thomas, a youngster who got AIDS from a transfusion of contaminated blood, was being kept out of regular school classes in California. He and his parents went to court. The judge found the boy was "handicapped" under Sec. 504 of the Rehabilitation Act of 1973. Under this law, handicapped children are to be placed in a regular educational environment unless it can be shown that "education can't be achieved in this environment." The court said with the risk of transmission of the disease so minimal, Ryan should go to school.[4]

Eliana Martinez was a mentally retarded girl who also had AIDS. Her Florida school wanted to put her in a separate classroom, and a lower court agreed. But the 11th Circuit Court of Appeals disagreed. The appeals court said if the girl didn't have AIDS, she would have been placed in a regular classroom, and said the possibility of transmission of the disease was so "remote and theoretical" that it wasn't enough to keep the child out of a regular classroom.[5] "Parents really need have no concern if their child is going to school with an HIV-positive child," said Devon Davidson of the National Coalition of Advocates for Students, a Boston umbrella organization that has done considerable research on AIDS in schools. She said AIDS is transmitted through blood to blood contact or unprotected sex, two activities that most definitely aren't supposed to be happening in schools.

Indeed, she said, children are much more at risk from other flus and viruses. Hepatitus B, much more contagious than AIDS, can be fatal, she said; hence, it is important that schools have good routine procedures for sanitation and hygiene in the handling of bodily fluids. Such procedures should include:

- The use of disposable rubber gloves during care, treatment and clean-up
- Discarding disposable items such as bandages and diapers in plastic bags that won't be reused
- The use of paper towels to pick up or discard any solid waste materials, such as vomit or feces
- Washing hands thoroughly with soap and warm water after any contact with bodily fluids
- The use of disinfectants to clean washable surfaces, such as tables and floors

A question that sometimes comes up is whether AIDS is transmitted by biting. We contacted more than a half dozen AIDS and school health organizations, and none could confirm an incident of AIDS transmittal by biting. Davidson knew of one unconfirmed instance of a biting transmittal. There have also been at least a few incidents in which AIDS wasn't transmitted when an infected student bit another student, Davidson said, perhaps because bites don't usually result in blood to blood contact. While it's safe to say that biting transmittal is an infinitesimal risk, biting itself is still an antisocial and problem behavior that teachers must attend to immediately.

As for teaching about AIDS, every state either requires it or encourages it. The CDC, working with several government agencies and major education groups, has produced "Guidelines for Effective School Health Education to Prevent the Spread of AIDS," a blueprint for a successful AIDS education program from elementary school through high school. A successful program is one that leads to the prevention of HIV infection. The guidelines call for school officials, teachers, parents, and the local medical community to develop such a program for the community, and stress careful preparation of the program and quality teacher training.

As for the content of the program, the guidelines suggest that in the early grades, students be taught that AIDS is a disease making many adults very sick, that it usually doesn't affect children, and that it's very hard to get. In middle schools, students should be taught about the nature of viruses, and how they sometimes cause diseases. In high school, the program should focus on the ways AIDS is transmitted: sexual contact with an infected person; use of needles or other injection equipment an infected person has used; from an infected mother to her infant before or during birth. The guidelines say facts about AIDS are best taught in the context of a comprehensive sexuality education program.

◆ ACTION STEPS ◆

As a first step, parents have to realize that sexuality and sex education are important, and can be a matter of life and death. When a gang of white suburban high school males was found preying on younger girls in a well-off California community in the early 90s, many of their parents couldn't have cared less. "I was always trying to score when I was a teenager, too," one father was quoted as saying.

This wrong-headed attitude fuels the problem. Putting aside the tremendous psychological and emotional damage that sexual assault can cause, consensual teen sex is fraught with danger. The numbers on STDs and AIDS are staggering. For girls, teen pregnancy is the end of adolescence.

Who should be the primary sexuality educators of children? Parents. Parents need to talk to children about anatomy, puberty, sexual behavior, love, relationships and other concerns that relate to human sexuality. Parents who accept this duty and want reading materials should contact the Sexuality Information and Education Council of the United States (SIECUS), 130 W. 42nd Street, New York, New York 10036–7802, and ask for the SIECUS annotated bibliography for parents. This contains some of the best books available on how parents can talk to their children about sexuality.

Some parents feel they should be their children's only teachers about sexuality. Nearly all schools accommodate these parents by allowing them to "opt out," or remove their children from sexuality education programs. The majority of parents, however, feel they should work in concert with their school's sexuality program. The thing to do then is to make sure your school has a quality program. SIECUS offers some tips:

- Find out what sexuality programs are offered in your schools. If you are not familiar with them, ask to see course materials.

- Find out what committees exist to review and recommend curricula. If you would like to serve on the committee, tell whomever appoints the committee.

- Join or develop a coalition of parents and health professionals (and go to the meetings).

- Attend school board and curriculum committee meetings whenever possible, and get to know your administrators and board members.

- Critique your school's sexuality program. If it's good, tell the school board and the administration. If it isn't, point out the flaws. Frequently, parents say yes, their school has a sexuality program, but the program is weak. Using information from organizations such as SIECUS and the CDC, suggest better programs. Also, examine the level of teacher training. Is your school's program being taught by a properly trained teacher, or the gym teacher with a pamphlet? If you don't have a qualified teacher, lobby for one.

- If you are the parent of an HIV-positive student, you will have to face the question of whether to disclose the illness to school officials. Some states require public health officials to notify school officials if they are aware that a student is HIV-positive. This isn't a good policy. it doesn't guarantee that other students will be protected from the virus, because many students don't know they are infected. Better for the school to enforce infection-control guidelines all the time, and let the parent and physician make the decision on who should know about the infection. Often it's wise for the principal and school nurse to know, for purposes of medi-cation, or to keep the child from receiving improper im-munization. The best policy is for the parent to confer with the child's doctor, decide who absolutely needs to know, and inform those people only. If some families wish to go further and make a public announcement, that is their decision.

- Finally, remember that your children's health and happiness are important, and that you can play a vital role in seeing that they grow up to be sexually responsible adults.

THE CAFETERIA

Parents may remember the school cafeteria as the place where the school's social strata was established, or where Crazy Freddy started a food fight. But the biggest problem today in many school cafeterias is not who sits with whom, or the occasional flying bologna sandwich. The biggest problem is what the kids are eating.

Take a look at the menu your child brings home. Chances are it's loaded with pizza, cheese dogs, fried chicken nuggets, cheeseburgers, macaroni and cheese, and other high-fat, high-calorie foods. The seriousness of the situation was well described in a speech by Ellen Haas, longtime child nutrition advocate who is now assistant secretary for food and consumer services of the U.S. Department of Agriculture. She said: "School-age children get too many of their calories from fat. Both the American Academy of Pediatrics and the [Agriculture Department's] Dietary Guidelines recommend children get only 30 percent of their calories from fat. Studies show the figure is much higher. In a survey by the USDA . . . 35 percent of the children ate no fruit on the day of the survey. (Guidelines call for 2–4 servings of fruit daily.) A large proportion of the vegetables children eat are potatoes, most of them fried."

The problems with this are plentiful, she said. There's "no longer any question that diet is related to chronic disease." Also, "There are indications poor nutrition leads to learning problems," and "there is growing evidence children are suffering obesity, high cholesterol, and high blood pressure."

The problem of poor school nutrition is particularly severe for many low-income children, who get their best meal of the day at school. The USDA is the key player in what millions of children eat at school. The department runs the National School Lunch Program, which provides federally assisted lunches to about 25 million youngsters a day, 59 percent of the public school population. The program also provides breakfasts to millions of youngsters. It's administered by state education agencies, who work with local school districts.

The USDA has developed a variety of programs to lower the amount of sugar, salt, and fat in school lunches. In 1985 the department, along with experts from the Department of Health and Human Services, developed Dietary Guidelines for Americans. Both departments updated the guidelines in 1990, this time setting numerical limits on fat content of school menus. Among the key recommendations are that students get no more than 30 percent of their calories from fat, and no more than 10 percent of calories from saturated fat. The guidelines also call for certain numbers of servings of fruit, vegetables, and grains per meal. Lunches also must meet a third of Recommended Dietary Allowances (RDAs) for certain nutrients, while breakfasts must meet one-fourth of RDAs.

Some states, including California and West Virginia, have adopted laws or policies requiring their schools to meet the guidelines. They were ahead of the curve. In 1994 Congress passed the Healthy Meals for Healthy Americans Act, which requires all the country's schools to meet the guidelines by the 1996–97 school years. The USDA will develop a database to help schools analyze the nutrition content of their meals, and will offer technical assistance to schools as they work to meet the new guidelines. Schools won't be required to make every meal a perfect nutritional masterpiece, but rather will be asked to make their weekly meal cycles meet the guidelines.

Awareness of the school nutrition problem is spreading around the country. Many parents groups have investigated their school cafeterias and urged the introduction of more nutritious meals. They sometimes run into the response, "But the kids won't eat it." But they might, depending on how the meal is made, and how it is presented.

Several groups, the USDA, the Henry J. Kaiser Foundation, the American Cancer Society, and others, have taken the cheese, so to speak, and accepted the challenge to create healthy school lunch menus of familiar foods that kids like. In pilot projects in cities around the country, these groups showed that traditional food could be both healthy and tasty. Some tips:

- Instead of beef hot-dogs, use turkey dogs.
- Instead of fried chicken nuggets, use baked chicken.
- Make pizza with low fat cheese and whole wheat crust, and add more vegetable toppings.
- Puree broccoli and add it to chili.

These may seem like slipping your child a nutritional mickey, but fair is fair. They had to be conditioned to eat high-fat, high-sugar foods, now you are just bringing them more into balance. "Slowly, we're spreading the good nutrition gospel," said Phil Shonholtzer of the USDA's Food and Consumer Service division.

◆ ACTION STEPS ◆

Your school health council or parents group should review your school's food operation, with the goal of meeting the Dietary Guidelines for Americans. If your school system has a dietitian, you can form a partnership, which can include local medical and diet specialists, as well as specialists from your county or state education or health departments. An excellent source of low-fat menu ideas is the American Cancer Society's Cook Book, available from the society's offices in all 50 states. To get the address of your state chapter, you can call the national headquarters in Atlanta at 404–320–3333.

In addition to a healthy menu, your parents group can initiate other steps toward better nutrition, including:

- Have your school remove snack vending machines that sell high-sugar and high-fat snacks.
- Make sure your cafeteria makes provision for students with special nutritional needs, such as obese students or handicapped students.

- Make sure students have enough time to eat. Some schools, often schools that are overcrowded, try to race the students through lunch periods too quickly.

- Make sure professionals responsible for health instruction have at least three credit hours of classwork in nutrition. Ask the instructors, or the principal. If they aren't trained, your parents group and the school health council should initiate such training.

- Use the school cafeteria as a laboratory and classroom for instruction in home lunch preparation. Thus far we have spoken about lunches served at school. But millions of youngsters bring their lunches to school, and many of these are laden with sugar and fat. "What's coming from home is far worse than what is served in school," said Lenore K. Zedosky of the West Virginia Department of Education. She said cafeteria programs for parents on how to prepare healthier lunches have been both popular and effective in getting children to eat more nutritious meals.

- Finally, visit the cafeteria frequently, and make sure it is inspected regularly by your local or state health department. Periodically, inspectors find a school cafeteria serving old, moldy, dirty food. That's inexcusable, and can be avoided.

TOBACCO

Nothing is quite as depressing as seeing a bright and healthy teenager pull out a cigarette and light it up. The jury is in on this. Tobacco is linked to almost 400,000 deaths a year in this country, and may be killing as much as a tenth of the population of the world. The financial costs in health care and loss of productivity are in the tens of billions annually. As the Surgeon General has pointed out in reports over the past three decades, smoking causes heart disease, vascular disease, obstructive pulmonary diseases, and any number of cancers. Tobacco use is the leading cause of preventable death in this country. According to the Centers for Disease Control and Prevention, 82 percent of daily smokers started smoking before the age of 18. Of these, 18 percent started smoking in elementary school and 30 percent

198 · SCHOOL RIGHTS

started by the ninth grade. According to the CDC's research, 3,000 young people start smoking every day.

Because the vast majority of smokers start while they are in school, it follows that school programs could be the most effective way to reduce tobacco use. It is critically important that schools do all they can to keep youngsters from starting, because nicotine is extremely addictive, and the majority of youngsters who start can't stop. Three of four teenagers who smoke have made at least one major but unsuccessful effort to quit. The earlier youngsters start smoking, the harder it is for them to stop. For more bad news, about 29 percent of high school seniors smoke, the same number as in 1980. The good news is that school health programs aimed at the prevention of tobacco use work, and contribute to the prevention of the use of illicit drugs as well.

◆ ACTION STEPS ◆

The CDC has compiled an excellent series of recommendations for school programs to prevent tobacco use and addiction. In short, the recommendations call for:

- A school tobacco policy that, among other things, prohibits tobacco use by anyone on school property, in school vehicles and at school-sponsored events away from school property.
- Instruction in the short- and long-term negative effects of tobacco use, including social influences on tobacco use, peer norms and refusal skills.
- Prevention education for kindergarten through the 12th grade.
- Specific instruction for teachers, and involvement of parents in support of the school program.
- The support of cessation efforts by faculty, staff and students.

To get a copy of the guidelines, called "Guidelines for School Health Programs to Prevent Tobacco Use and Addiction," you may contact the Superintendent of Documents, U.S. Government Printing Office, Washington, DC, 20402–9325, or call 202–783–3238.

To institute the guidelines in your school, talk to your school health professionals and your health advisory council. Prepare a plan to implement the guidelines. Get student support. Present the plan to your school board.

BULLIES

Nathan Faris, a seventh-grader in Dekalb, Missouri, had been picked on for four years. Students had nothing against him, he was just, as one student said, "someone to pick on." Faris came to school on March 2, 1987, with a gun. He shot another student, then shot himself.

The point of relating this gruesome story is this: Bullying is a very serious and often underrated problem in schools. Some principals will dismiss the subject by saying that bullies have always been with us. That may be, but they're still causing serious problems. According to Dr. Dan Olweus, one of the leading researchers on the subject, one in ten students is regularly harassed or attacked by bullies, and 15 percent of school children are involved in bullying incidents, either as bully or victim.[6] In one survey, 25 percent of students reported one of their main concerns in school was fear of bullies.

The problem, obviously, is difficult for victims. They can suffer serious physical injury, loss of self-esteem at a critical developmental period, withdrawal from school activities, lower grades and clinical depression. Victims of bullies will remember the degrading experience all their lives.

But the harm and damage to the bullies is also vastly significant. Bullies as young as 8 years old who aren't taught to cope with frustration are likely headed for lifetimes of failure. Bullies have a one in four chance of having a criminal record by the age of 30. For other children, the odds are 1 in 20.

There is also a legal aspect to the bully problem. Victims and their parents have begun suing schools, and courts have shown some sympathy to their actions. A New York youngster and his parents sued after 17 incidents of physical and verbal bullying. The school asked that the case be thrown out. The question was whether the school owed students a duty to protect them from each other. The court held there was "some duty of care" when school officials were aware of the problem, had said they would do something about it, and didn't. Such behavior by school officials "may rise to the level of deliberate indifference," the court said, in refusing to dismiss the case.[7]

Other cases have reiterated the point that a duty to protect a victim won't arise unless school officials are aware of the specific problem.[8] The point can't be emphasized enough. Remember, the doctrine of government immunity is still lurking around, waiting to protect public employees from simple negligence. To overcome the immunity doctrine, it's often necessary to prove willful or wanton neglect. It's almost impossible to do that without showing school officials were aware of a serious, imminent danger, and did nothing about it.

So for both legal reasons, and to protect your child, it's imperative that parents of victims notify school officials if they even suspect there's a bullying problem. The signs to look for are unexplained injuries, withdrawn behavior, loss of lunch or lunch money, truancy, lower grades, and general anxiety.

The bullying problem is so serious and pervasive that a conference was held at Harvard University in 1987. The experts asked school administrators to consider five central ideas about bullying:

1. Bullying is a serious problem.

2. Fear and suffering are part of the everyday lives of victims, causing them to avoid certain areas of school, stay home from school altogether, and in isolated cases, commit suicide.

3. Early prevention and intervention can stop bullying and save the bully, the victim, and society from years of tragic problems.

4. Kids fighting each other isn't normal aggressive behavior.

5. The U.S. should follow Japan and Scandinavia and create national prevention and intervention programs.

◆ ACTION STEPS ◆

The first step, as with other health problems, is to realize that bullying is a serious school health problem. Your school health council or parents group can raise the subject with the administration, and it can be a subject of in-service training. Bring it up. Ask what your school is doing about it.

The Harvard conferees recommended that parents and school officials first need to assess the bully problem in their schools. In other words, they need to find out if kids are being bullied. Some schools have chosen to do this with confidential questionnaires or surveys. Sage Park Middle School in Windsor, Connecticut, came up with another method. In January 1995 school officials learned that three older students were beating up nine or ten younger students and stealing their lunch money. The bullies were doing this every day. What concerned school officials was that the behavior had been going on since school started in September, and they didn't find out about it until January. To avoid such a lapse in the future, school officials started a mentoring program. Each adult staff member became the personal mentor of a group of students. The adult will regularly meet with each student, one-to-one. The idea is that they will develop enough trust so that if there is a bullying problem at the school, a child will tell a mentor about it.

Secondly, the conferees said, school officials must communicate clear and consistently enforced behavior standards and closely monitor playground activity. Parents can help school officials monitor hallways or restrooms, says Ronald D. Stephens, executive director of the National School Safety Center at Pepperdine University in California.

Finally, it's essential that the school have some kind of intervention program, and many schools across the country have such programs. A key to many programs is a partnership with mental health professionals in your community. At English High School in Boston, bullies are warned and suspended, then they are counseled by doctoral candidates in psychology at nearby Harvard University. The most serious candidates are referred to school psychologists. Other school systems use such measures as group counseling to deal with bullies. Student mediation is an increasingly popular way to deal with bullying problems. If your school has no intervention program, lobby for one. Bring the subject up at a parents meeting. Suggest it as a topic for in-service training. Ask your health advisory council to recommend to the principal that the school create an intervention program.

Mary Joan Parks, a mediation consultant to schools in the Washington, DC area, suggests bringing the bully and victim together, and asking each to tell a third party what his problem is with the other child, and what he perceives the other's problem is with him. They then must come up with a solution that is mutually acceptable.

As for victims, they should make a stand when confronting bullies, but not necessarily fight them, and leave the field with dignity, says Dr. Nathaniel Lloyd, a New York researcher and expert on the bully problem. This obviously is easier said than done, and Lloyd teaches victims how to do this in group counseling and role-playing sessions.

Lloyd, Stephens, and other experts say parents should teach children, starting in the toddler years, to talk and act assertively. Author Kathleen McGinnis says children as young as 2 can be taught to let another child know when that child is doing something they don't like. She recommends that youngsters not only tell what they don't like, but why they don't like it ("I don't like it when you push me. It hurts").

Sometimes ignoring a bully will make the bully go away. If your child reports an incident that he extricated himself from, and it doesn't bother him, leave it alone. Sometimes a joke or a question will distract a bully, and he'll give up the pursuit. Bullies expect physical confrontation, and can be disoriented when they don't get it.

But sometimes a child needs to look the bully in the eye and talk tough. Bullies like to pick on the weak and vulnerable, and will most often stay away from a child that projects assertive self-confidence. Some parents have signed their children for defense-oriented martial arts programs, to bolster self-confidence and self-protection skills.

If your child reports a bullying incident, or shows the signs of being picked on, talk it over. Unless your child vehemently objects, talk it over with the teacher as soon as possible. If your child is being victimized by a bully, it must be stopped.

What if the bully is armed? A victim in this hideous situation needs to do whatever it takes to get out of it. If running is an option, run. Talk if you can't run. A young person with a gun or knife is a troubled young person, and it's imperative the incident be reported as quickly and forcefully as possible.

SAFE SCHOOLS

Bullying is part of a bigger problem of school safety. Each year, 3 million children are attacked at school, said Ron Stephens of the National School Safety Center. In addition, he and other experts said, schools face a host of other safety problems. According to studies made public in 1989–90:

- Nearly 3 million thefts and violent crimes occur on or near school grounds every year.

- Each day, 10 Americans aged 19 or younger are killed in homicides, suicides or gun accidents.

- One in 11 students reports being the victim of a crime, and one in 12 stayed home at least once during the year for fear of crime.

- In a one-month period, one of every five high school students carried a weapon, although not always in school. Also, thousands of guns make their way into schools every year; in 1990–91, New York City had 131 gun incidents in and around schools, in which 34 people were shot and four killed.

- Fifteen percent of the country's high school students report gang activity in their schools, and a third of the students who report the presence of the gangs are afraid of being attacked in schools.

Don't think school safety is a problem only in the inner cities. Gangs and guns are getting into nice suburban schools as well. Assaults on teachers are up. Younger students are committing more dangerous crimes in schools. It's now reached the point where some youngsters claim they bring guns to school for self-defense. This is a big problem. Where to start solving it?

For openers, it's essential to keep guns out of schools. Penalties for possession or use of a firearm in school vary around the country. In some districts, it's an automatic 60-day suspension. In others, it's immediate suspension, with a hearing and recommendation for expulsion. In still others, it's expulsion for the remainder of that academic year and all of the next one. Punishment has to be swift and sure. Guns in school are unacceptable.

Courts seem willing to back up schools when it comes to stopping the flow of weapons. Recently a girl going into a New York school triggered the metal detector. She was searched and was found carrying a switchblade knife. She was charged with criminal possession of a weapon. She claimed in court that the procedure was intrusive and violated her Fourth Amendment rights against unreasonable search and seizure.

The judge didn't agree. He said it was no more intrusive than the government interest underlying the need for it, and likened it to metal detectors used in courthouses and spot-checks for drunk drivers. The court said it was a shame schools had to resort to such measures, but acknowledged the danger called for such steps.[9]

It's probably inevitable that we have a school gun problem; guns are out of control in this country. We have an estimated 200 million guns, almost one for every person. Gang counselors report some youngsters, who have been raised almost entirely on violent television shows, don't think bullets actually cause pain, and are surprised to learn that they do, often too late. It's important for parents to talk to youngsters about the consequences of gun use. If you keep guns in your house, at least lock them up. Some parents won't allow their children to play in homes where guns are stored because there have been so many accidents.

◆ ACTION STEPS ◆

Ron Stephens, who many consider the guru of school safety, is a major advocate of parental involvement to make schools safer. First, he tells parents, reassess your parenting skills. Make sure you spend time with your child, set limits, praise effort and accomplishments, monitor television viewing, and set a good example.

Having done that, Stephens recommends that parents get actively involved in the school's safety program. Steps can include:

- Helping to supervise the school grounds and routes to school before and after school, and corridors and restrooms during passing periods

- Organizing or joining a safe school planning task force. The task force can work on a wide variety of safety issues, from securing and supervising grounds to transportation safety, child pick-up, building security and crossing guard training.

- Helping to plan a violence-prevention curriculum in the school, as well as a school-mediation program, to teach youngsters to resolve disputes without resorting to violence

- Helping to clean up and repair the school grounds

- Chaperoning school trips

- Sharing any special expertise you may have regarding career opportunities; kids are less likely to get in trouble if they're excited about a personal goal or a school project.

The bottom line is that parents have to communicate to school officials that crime and violence in schools are unacceptable.

TEEN SUICIDE

Every community has been visited by the problem: A healthy, successful, good-looking teenager with a seemingly bright future suddenly commits suicide. Family and friends are stunned and saddened, and no one can explain it. We had better start looking for answers, because suicide by young people is a larger problem than most people think it is. According to a 1993 national survey by the CDC, 24 percent of the nation's high school students thought seriously about committing suicide in the year before the survey, and 19 percent made an actual plan to take their own lives. Of those, 8.6 percent actually attempted suicide.

Obviously, some did take their lives. The CDC estimates that suicide is now the fourth leading cause of death among people aged 5 to 24, claiming 11 percent of the victims. A rash of teen suicides in the late 1980s prompted a brief national examination of the issue, but it didn't last and the problem continues.

◆ Action Steps ◆

Be aware of the following signs that a young person is contemplating suicide:

- Family history of suicide
- The recent suicide of a friend or relative
- Withdrawal from family and friends
- Expressing suicidal thoughts
- Major changes in personality, habits, or appearance
- Running away
- Poor school performance
- Giving away personal possessions, or selling them for nominal prices

If your teenager exhibits one or more of these signs, you must speak to the child immediately. Learn what you can. Then speak to the youngster's guidance counselor, physician, or school psychologist as soon as possible. The sooner you act, the better your chances of getting the child through the crisis.

You should also contact your school's health advisory council, to explore ways of getting information about suicide to parents.

If a student at your school commits suicide, urge your principal to bring in counselors right away to work with the youngster's friends and classmates.

◆ Selected Questions ◆

Can I withdraw my child from school if the school is unsafe?

The cases indicate you can if the danger is real and immediate, and not merely hypothetical or rumored.[10] Of course, you can always move your child to a private or parochial school, if you can afford it. Hopefully, parental involvement can keep things from getting that bad.

Is "hazing" legal?

Hazing, the practice of initiating someone into a group or team with injury, humiliation, or ridicule, is illegal when it involves injury. It's also stupid. Most states have specific anti-hazing laws that create a category of crime for those who injure someone in a hazing incident.

Despite this, it seems every year we read about a coach somewhere who condoned a hazing in which someone was injured or killed.

Here's what can happen. A couple of years ago, lacrosse players at Western Illinois University held an initiation for new players that involved the consumption of significant amounts of alcohol. One student died of alcohol poisoning. The students who ran the affair were charged under the state's anti-hazing law. A lower court threw out the case, saying the law was too broad and vague. But the state Supreme Court reversed the decision, saying the law was constitutional, sufficiently clear and gave fair warning to anyone considering such behavior. The court said the law, passed in 1901, was to deter behavior that causes needless injuries.[11]

If parents hear that hazing incidents are planned, they would do well to remind the principal, in writing, that the school may well be breaking the law and inviting trouble.

Do teachers have to report child abuse that takes place at home?

Yes. All states have laws against child abuse and neglect. Teachers are required, at the risk of criminal penalty in most states, to report evidence of abuse or neglect. Teachers are protected from liability if their reports are in error, as long as the reports are made in good faith.

Does smoking lead to use of harder drugs by students?

According to the CDC, many students who smoke never progress to harder drugs, but among those who do, there is a sequence of use that most often starts with tobacco and alcohol. This is another reason parents need to be relentless in discouraging the use of tobacco in any form.

Our district recently decided to do away with guidance counselors. Is this any great loss?

It certainly can be. While some parents can recall schools without counselors, or with weak counselors who may have been kicked upstairs because they had lost it as teachers, that was then. Now, virtually all districts require professional certified counselors who not only help students with education and career development goals, but also with social development and self-understanding. Countless millions of students have received great help from school counselors. Fight to keep them, but work with your principal to make sure your counselors are properly certified and aren't swamped with so much paperwork that they can't see students.

You don't hear as much about drugs anymore. Have we won the war on drugs, or are drugs still a problem in schools?

Drugs remain a matter of concern in schools. According to the 1992 National Education Goals Report, marijuana use among high school seniors dropped from 34 percent in 1980 to 14 percent, and cocaine use dropped from 2 to 1 percent. However, since then there are some indications that marijuana use is rising again. Also, alcohol abuse remains the country's worst drug problem. Almost 88 percent of high school seniors have tried alcohol, according to the CDC's 1993 survey, and 30 percent of all high school students engage in episodic heavy drinking.

Drug education still should be a part of any comprehensive health education curriculum, particularly between the ages of 10 and 13, so youngsters will be ready to handle peer pressure to experiment with drugs. While drugs are everywhere, the problem is most severe in urban centers with high unemployment and large populations living in poverty. This is one of many reasons urban schools need all the support our society can give them.

FOR FURTHER INFORMATION

Centers for Disease Control and Prevention
Division of Adolescent and School Health
4770 Buford Highway N.E.
Atlanta, GA 30341–3724
404–488–5314

USDA Food and Nutrition Service
Child Nutrition Division
3101 Park Center Drive
Alexandria, VA 22302
202–720–3100

National School Safety Center
Pepperdine University
Malibu, CA 90263
818–377–6200

National Association of State Boards of Education
1012 Cameron Street
Alexandria, VA 22314
703–684–4000

National Coalition of Advocates for Students
100 Bolyston Street Suite 737
Boston, MA 02116
617–357–8507

American Alliance for Health, Physical Education and Dance
1900 Association Drive
Reston, VA 22091
703–476–3400

American Foundation for AIDS Research
733 3rd Ave. 12th Floor
New York, NY 10017
212–682–7440

Alan Guttmacher Institute
111 Fifth Avenue
New York, NY 10003–1089
212–254–5656

National Federation of Parents for Drug-Free Youth
8730 Georgia Avenue Suite 200
Silver Spring, MD 20910
1–800–554–KIDS

Sexuality Information and Education
Council of the United States
130 W. 42nd Street Suite 350
New York, NY 10036–7802
212–819–9770

National Center for Health Education
72 Spring Street Suite 208
New York, NY 10012
212–334–9470

National School Health Education Coalition
1400 I Street NW Suite 520
Washington, DC 20005
202–408–0222

Association for the Advancement of Health Education
1900 Association Drive
Reston, VA 22091
703–476–3441

Advocates for Youth
1025 Vermont Avenue NW Suite 200
Washington, DC 20005
202–347–5700

NOTES

1. Lloyd J. Kolbe, lecture, "An Essential Strategy to Improve the Health and Education of Americans," presented at the American Academy of Pediatrics Annual Meeting, San Francisco, Oct. 13, 1992.

2. Alexander and Alexander, *The Law of Schools, Students and Teachers* (West Publishing Co., 1984) p. 48.

3. *Smith* v. *Ricci,* 89 N.J. 514, 446 A. 2d 501 (1982).

4. *Thomas* v. *Atascadero Unified School District,* 662 F. Supp. 376 (1987).

5. *Martinez* v. *School Board of Hillsborough County, Fla.,* 861 F. 2d 1502 (1988).

6. "School Bullying and Victimization," resource paper, National School Safety Center, Pepperdine University, Malibu, Calif., 1993.

7. *Pagano* v. *Massapequa Public Schools,* 714 F. Supp. 641 (EDNY 1989).

8. *Russell* v. *Kansas City School District,* 784 F. Supp. 1576 (1992).

9. *People* v. *Dukes,* 580 N.Y.S. 2d 850 (1992).

10. *Zebra* v. *School District of the City of Pittsburgh,* 296 A 2d 748 (Pa. 1972).

11. *People* v. *Anderson,* 591 N.E. 2d 461 (Ill. 1992).

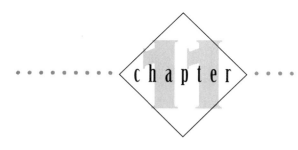

chapter

FUNDING
AND FACILITIES

◆ INTRODUCTION ◆

In the summer of 1993 Michigan's state legislature took a step that will long be remembered in educational circles. After two decades of arguing the pros and cons of supporting education mostly by property taxes, lawmakers simply eliminated the property tax.

Poof! They nuked it. They took a tax that produced $6.8 billion a year, 65 percent of the state's education expenditure, and made it go away. Without an immediate replacement. "They couldn't fix school finance, so they blew it up," said Dr. Mike Addonizio of the state's Department of Education. Officials were faced with something of an emergency. Such was the dissatisfaction with the property tax system that the school district in rural Kalkaska, Michigan, had to close three months early that year, after voters three times rejected property tax increases for schools.

In March 1994 voters in the Wolverine State-approved Proposal A, which replaced much of the lost local revenue with an increase in the sales tax from 4 to 6 percent, and increased other taxes such as the liquor and commercial forest taxes. The new plan also included a statewide property tax. One of the key elements of the plan is to reduce the spending gap between rich and poor school districts, by providing each district with a guaranteed minimum of $4,200 per student, which is $1,000 more than the poorest districts received under the old system.

If this plan works, Michigan may solve a puzzle that has bedeviled almost every other state in the past 30 years—how to provide equitable and adequate funding for public schools. The Michigan situation typified what is becoming a national conundrum in school funding. In the postwar period, America has consistently committed more dollars to education. The inflation-adjusted cost of a average year of public education more than tripled between 1960 and 1990. In each decade starting in 1960, per pupil dollars rose significantly; 69 percent in the 1960s, 22 percent in the 1970s and 48 percent in the 1980s. Even in the 1990s, education spending is staying slightly ahead of inflation. How long this will continue is the question.

Today activists from poorer districts want equitable funding as well as school reform. Parents, politicians and business leaders want better schools that produce smarter graduates. But faced with a sluggish economy and growing distaste with taxes, particularly property taxes, government officials at all levels aren't always eager to provide the money educators say they need to make significant improvements. This chapter looks at school funding issues, specifically:

- *Where do schools funds come from?*
- *Why have most of the states had to undergo lengthy and expensive school funding lawsuits?*
- *What kind of state funding system will withstand legal scrutiny?*
- *Does more money make a difference in academic achievement?*
- *How can parents lobby for more money for their school and augment their school's budget with outside fundraising?*
- *What can parents do about deteriorating school buildings?*

◆ DISCUSSION ◆

There are four potential sources of funds for your child's public school:

- Federal funds
- State funds
- Local funds
- Privately raised funds

Of these, state and local monies are the main sources of school funding. Traditionally, local property taxes were the mainstay of public schools. In 1972–73, local funds accounted for 51 percent of school funding across the country, with state revenues making up 41 percent and federal dollars 8 percent. By 1990 the state share was up to 50 percent, the local contribution down to 44 percent and the federal share had dropped to 6 percent.

To fund schools with local property taxes, school districts need property to tax. Some districts have vast taxable property; some have very little. That, in essence, is why almost every state has had a major lawsuit over school funding. Lawsuits over school funding have been decided in at least 27 states, and are pending or threatened in 20 more states. Between 1970 and 1985, 35 states changed their education aid programs when faced with real or threatened legal action, reports Paul Barton, director of the Policy Information Center of the Educational Testing Service of Princeton, New Jersey.

But, as Barton reports in an ETS policy report titled, "The State of Inequality," there are still huge differences in school spending between states, among school districts within states and even among schools within districts. For example, he said, New Jersey spends well over $8,000 per pupil, more than triple what Utah spends. Adjusted for inflation, New York spends two and a half times what Utah spends. Taken as a percentage of personal income, Wyoming spends two and a half times the 3 percent the citizens of New Hampshire expend. On the district level, the highest spending districts in Texas and Ohio spend nearly three times the amount per pupil as the lowest spending districts. He cited studies that found poorer schools in the New York and Detroit districts getting fewer resources than schools in wealthier parts of town.

These discrepancies exist despite long and costly lawsuits in almost every state. The first wave of school funding cases began in the late 1960s with suits filed in Texas, New Jersey and California. In Texas, a sheet metal worker named Demetrio P. Rodriguez, whose children attended inner-city Edgewood High School in San Antonio, and others filed state and federal lawsuits over the disparities between rich and poor school districts. They claimed the funding disparities violated the equal protection clause of the U.S. Constitution.

The U.S. Supreme Court decided in 1973 that the funding system didn't violate federal equal protection. The court said education was not a "fundamental right" granted by the Constitution, and hence not subject to equal protection guarantees.

The court also said Texas had a "foundation system" that attempted to equalize spending between rich and poor districts. "In sum, to the extent that the Texas system of school financing results in unequal expenditures between children who happen to reside in different districts, we cannot say such disparities are the product of a system that is so irrational as to be invidiously discriminatory."[1]

For advocates of financing reform, the *Rodriguez* decision seemed to cut off the federal courts as avenues of redress. They went to state court, looking for remedies in state constitutions. The Texans did somewhat better in state court, in a case known as *Edgewood Independent School District* v. *Kirby.* In this case, 68 school districts, along with students and parents, claimed the disparity in wealth among Texas school districts violated the state constitution. The State Supreme Court agreed. The court said, interestingly, that funding disparities were not unconstitutional per se, and only became unconstitutional when "excessive." An excessive disparity, the court said, was when a district installed a high tax rate and still couldn't garner enough money to meet minimum educational standards in its schools. The court also said its decision didn't preclude wealthier districts from augmenting a basic funding allotment.

The court ordered the state to prepare a new funding mechanism that would allow districts to have "substantially equal access to similar revenues per pupil at similar levels of tax effort."[2]

The state has had a great deal of difficulty coming up with a new funding mechanism that satisfies both the courts and the voters. A two-tier funding system was knocked down by a district court in 1990, and a plan that involved "recapture" of funds from wealthier districts was turned down by voters in 1993. In 1994 the legislature created an "Equalized Funding System" that offered five different ways to equalize funding between property-rich districts and property-poor districts. Under the new system: wealthy districts can consolidate with poorer districts or form tax bases with poorer districts; wealthy districts can pay for students from poorer districts, either directly or through a tax credit system; or wealthy districts can detach some of their property and let the tax it produces go to poorer districts. "We're waiting to see if this will work," said Deana Culbertson of the Texas Department of Education.

The *Edgewood* case has been settled and reopened a half dozen times, and has been a cross for five governors to bear. And still, the wealthiest district spent $73,000 per student in 1993, while the poorest district spent $1,897.

At about the time Mr. Rodriguez began his fight in San Antonio (he's still active, by the way), a Los Angeles parent named John Serrano demanded better services in his son's school. When told he'd have to move to a wealthier district for such services, he sued in state court. He won. The state Supreme Court held the disparities between rich and poor districts violated the equal protection standards of the state constitution and ordered fair funding standards to be in place by 1980.[3]

The California situation made a fairly dramatic case for the proposition that school funding was inequitable. Testimony indicated the state's wealthiest district had $952,156 of taxable property per pupil, while the poorest district had only $103 in taxable property per student, a ratio of almost 1 to 10,000. The court in essence ruled that a state must fund its public schools based on the wealth of the state, not the wealth of individual school districts.

Since then, 27 more states have have argued the same question, with the results about evenly divided. Some 14 financing systems have been upheld, while 13 have been struck down as unconstitutional. These cases have come in two waves, the first in the late 1960s to early 1970s, with the second wave beginning in the late 1980s. As we'll see, some of the second wave cases resulted in the states such as Kentucky and Alabama not only throwing out their school funding systems, but also radically restructuring their whole school systems.

Typically, school finance cases are brought by lawyers for students or parents from one or more school districts who believe their districts are getting significantly fewer resources than other districts. Sometimes the poor districts themselves are the plaintiffs. The defendants are usually the state officials who represent the state and its education funding mechanism. Sometimes wealthier school districts intervene to represent their interests.

The plaintiffs usually claim that fewer resources translate to larger class sizes, a less-experienced staff, fewer extracurriculars, fewer course offerings—in general, an inferior education. The defendants often counter by saying there's no correlation between money and educational achievement. We'll talk about this issue in a moment.

The legal difference in whether these cases win or lose seems to be whether the state Supreme Court views education as a fundamental right. The courts that take the U.S. Supreme Court's view in the Rodriguez case, that education isn't a fundamental right, tend to find that inequitable local systems aren't unconstitutional. Courts that follow California's reasoning in the Serrano case, that education is a fundamental right, look much more closely at the fairness of state funding and have found their systems unconstitutional.

One of the big problems with these lawsuits is the amount of time they consume. This New Jersey case is an example of how long and complicated these cases can be. Here is a brief chronology:

- In 1970 a lawsuit known as *Robinson* v. *Cahill* charged that the state's method of funding local schools discriminated against poorer school districts. The plaintiff was a Jersey City student named Kenneth Robinson, and he was joined by the cities of Jersey City, Paterson, East Orange, and Plainfield.

- In 1973 the state Supreme Court agreed that the system was discriminatory.

- In 1975 the state legislature created a new formula for school funding, but didn't raise taxes to pay for it.

- In 1976 the legislature missed a June 30 deadline to raise the funds, and the Supreme Court closed the public schools, locking out 100,000 summer school students. A week later, legislators passed a new state income tax to pay for the new school formula, which increased the state's expenditures from 28 to 40 percent. The court reopened the schools.

- In 1981 another suit, *Abbott* v. *Burke,* was filed on behalf of 20 children attending schools in Irvington, Camden, East Orange, and Jersey City, claiming that the new system didn't work, that it caused significant disparities between poor urban and wealthier suburban districts, and left the urban districts unable to meet the needs of their students.

- In 1990 the state Supreme Court again ruled the school funding plan was unconstitutional because it didn't provide poorer districts with enough money to meet the state constitution's requirement that each student receive a "thorough and efficient education." The poorer the district, the less money available, the court said. The court ordered the state to come up with another plan. Officials produced the Quality Education Act, which raised taxes by $1.1 billion, increased aid to poorer and mid-income districts, and reduced or eliminated aid to wealthier districts. The plan was widely praised, although a year later $300 million was diverted from school funding for property tax relief.

- In 1992 another suit was filed, claiming the new law wasn't doing the job.

- In the summer of 1993, the new system was declared unconstitutional. The court said the state still had not closed the gap between rich and poor districts. Officials are working on a new plan.

IS MONEY THE ANSWER?

A basic question raised by all of these cases is whether, beyond a certain basic level, more funding actually makes any difference. Some researchers, such as University of Rochester economist Eric Hanushek, say no, that it's never been proven that greater per-pupil spending or higher teacher salaries leads to greater learning.

But others, such as University of Wisconsin law professor William H. Clune, say there is a "modest, positive link" between spending and student achievement.[4]

That there's only a modest link between spending and increased learning is enough to merit equal spending, says Clune. Here's why.

There is only a modest connection between additional funding and more learning because some schools don't use the money wisely. For example, teacher salary increases for seniority alone aren't likely to improve learning. Salary increases for successful, innovative teachers would more likely improve learning.

But at least with the extra money, children have the opportunity for improved learning. Clune and other experts feel they should have that opportunity. Jonathan Kozol, the writer, often quotes a judge who said if more money doesn't make a difference in their educations, poor children should have an equal right to be dissappointed.

As these cases indicate, school funding battles are long, bitter and costly. Is there such a thing as a perfect system?

WHAT WORKS AND WHAT DOESN'T

As an activist parent, you will undoubtedly confront the issue of school funding. Your school and district parents groups can influence your state's funding system by opening a dialogue with your local legislators and members of your legislature's education committee. But what kind of system should you promote?

Some experts feel the states should simply assume the full cost of education and do away with heavy reliance on the local property tax. They make persuasive arguments for this. The property tax was invented to pay the costs incident to property, not education costs. Despite all the lawsuits, property-tax systems still result in spending disparities in many states.

The percentage of state spending has been creeping up anyway and is now at about 50 percent. Why not go all the way? Hawaii has "full-state assumption," and New Mexico just about has it. California went a long way toward state assumption after a constitutional amendment severely limited the property tax. Some of the more recent lawsuits have nudged states toward assuming the cost of education.

On the other hand, state assumption is a hard sell politically. People from the wealthier districts, who tend to be the politically powerful, often don't like or trust a state system. Plus, there's a long tradition of local financing, which many confuse with local control, to deal with. Also, state assumption of school financing usually results in higher taxes, and many states today aren't in the mood. Many states are trying to limit state expenditures, says Allen Odden, a professor at the University of Wisconsin and one of the nation's leading experts in school funding. He thinks the states' share of school funding is beginning to fall. Also, said Odden, a constant complaint in states that have assumed most or all of the cost of school funding is that the level of funding reaching local schools is too low.

Without state assumption, the next tried-and-true method is a grant-in-aid program, in which a state gives grants to needy districts to make up for their lack of wealth. But these grants have become increasingly expensive; most states also give some money to wealthy districts in order to win their political support, then a lot more money to the poor districts. The result is a program that is increasingly difficult to finance. For example, if Texas were to bring spending in all districts up to that of the wealthiest districts, it would require a school budget four times the size of the current state budget.

Some states have tried to "cap" the spending increases of wealthier districts to let the poorer districts catch up; others have tried to "recapture," or transfer, funds from wealthier districts to poorer ones. These steps, as one might imagine, are vastly unpopular with wealthier districts. They say such measures hurt the students in the wealthier districts by "dumbing down" good schools, suppressing a source of educational innovation and removing an upward pressure on the entire state budget.

So what do you do?

◆ ACTION STEPS ◆

Parents and parents groups should get involved in designing a fair and effective funding system in their state. If you want a system that can withstand a lawsuit, design it so that it is NOT based on a district's wealth, advises John Augenblick, a Denver-based education consultant. Augenblick says states should attribute school spending to such factors as a district's size, enrollment, rate of growth, cost of living, and teacher training and experience.

Also, experts say, other steps should be considered. These include:

- *Redraw school taxing districts to equalize property tax availability.* Such redistricting doesn't have to mean a loss of local control over schools, it just changes the funding scheme.

- *Look more closely at where the money is going.* Education spending in this country rose by 25 percent from 1983 to 1992, without a concurrent rise in school quality. If the money we are spending were used wisely, we would be in much better shape. Parents should urge school officials to look at what's working and what isn't, and stop paying for what isn't.

- *Focus grants to lower-income school districts based on each district's needs.* A district may not need more money for senior teachers, but may need money for a preschool program for at-risk youngsters. In other words, broaden the equality question to programs as well as money, and see if smaller but better-focused uses of money can improve the quality of the schools.

- *Compromise.* Colorado wanted to cap spending in wealthy districts to equalize spending, but faced political opposition. The result was a compromise, a cap that allows a district to spend no more than 7.5 percent more than its state-assigned local funding level.

- *Refocus spending on core academic subjects.* Research by Jeffrey Mirel of Northern Illinois University and David Angus of the University of Michigan indicates that one reason that test scores aren't higher is that school spending has increasingly gone to the "social component" of schooling, such as athletics and health clinics.

- *Build school funding from many income sources.* Property ownership isn't an exact determinant of wealth and ability to pay: it is only one factor. Personal and corporate income is another, as are sales, lottery revenue and special resources. These should all be used in a fair and balanced manner to pay for the school system, a resource that benefits the entire state.

- *Use fiscal incentives for schools to improve.* Most people respond to fiscal incentives; it's human nature. If schools know they'll get more money for improved performance, they'll try to improve performance.

Odden goes a bit further. He says schools must begin restructuring their financing systems to link finance structure to student achievement results. To do this, he recommends a basic four-step process:

1. Set clear performance standards at the top of the system.
2. Flatten the organizational structure.
3. Move decision-making down to work teams actually providing the service.
4. Hold them accountable for results.

Under Odden's proposed system, states would send block grants to schools, not school districts. The schools would set high-quality curriculum standards, and have assessment tools that can measure whether students are meeting these standards. Management over budget and personnel would be at the school level. Teacher compensation could be restructured to focus on results rather than credentials and more resouces could be applied to teacher training. He says such a system would provide fiscal equity at the district and school level and improve the productivity.

Massachusetts took a step in this direction with a new law that attempts to raise achievement by imposing a core curriculum with higher standards. Under the law, each 10th grader will have to pass an "initial mastery test" to move on. Schools with students who fail must help them learn enough to retake and pass the test. Low-performing schools would get help from a team of experienced educators. If a low-performing school doesn't improve, the state would have the right to remove the principal and teachers and rebuild the whole school. The first test will be given in 1997.

REFORM

Parents and legislators should know that changing the funding system presents an opportunity for systemic, statewide school reform. That's what happened in Kentucky, after the state Supreme Court threw out the whole state education system. Kentucky had struggled with its property-tax-based system for funding public schools (still called "common schools" in the Bluegrass State) for several years. The state had struggled with the schools in general; the system was considered one of the worst in the country. Finally, 66 poor districts brought suit in 1985.

It took four years for the suit to work its way through the state court system. In 1989 the Kentucky Supreme Court ruled that the state's "entire system of common schools is unconstitutional." Thus, the court threw out both the financing system and the administration.[5]

In response, the state in 1990 passed a comprehensive school reform package that increased income, sales, corporate, and property taxes enough to raise an additional $400 million for educational spending. The law radically changed the finances, curriculum and governance of the state's schools. The new system features school-based management by councils of educators and parents; preschool programs for all at-risk children; a statewide performance assessment system; rewards and sanctions tied to school performance; funding for a longer school day, longer school week and longer school year; family resource and youth service centers; and a mechanism to equalize spending in rich and poor districts.

Whatever form it may take, it's important that parents be aware of school funding problems and inequities. In too many parts of the country, children in poor school districts aren't getting the resources they need. As Jonathan Kozol put it in his penetrating book on school finance, *Savage Inequalities* (Crown, 1991), "Surely there is enough for everyone . . . all our children ought to be allowed a stake in the richness of America."

◆ ACTION STEPS ◆

In addition to influencing state school funding policies, parents can fight for more resources for their local school. Professor Gary Natriello of Columbia University, a leading expert on school funding, said activist parents and parent groups should view school funding as a process and be involved in the issue on a continuing basis.

"Ask the principal and the teachers if they have what they need. Ask what they don't have that would be useful. Ask if there is anything that is eating up a lot of money without much of a return," he said.

Natriello says it is very difficult, even for financial people, to tell if a school or a district isn't getting a fair share of resources. He said many schools and districts have begun comparing the amount of money they spend with the amount others spend for the various components of education. Let's say you discover that your school is spending $300,000 on administration, while the school across town is spending $400,000. The flaw in this methodology is that you don't know if the other school is spending the right amount, or you are.

Still, Natriello finds it helpful to break down school spending into categories such as:

- Cost of staff
- Pupil and instructional services, which includes teaching assistants, medical consultants and others not on the school district payroll
- Textbooks and instructional supplies
- Library books and periodicals
- Equipment
- Tuition, which includes payments to other educational agencies or schools for services to students within the district
- Plant operation
- Transportation
- Purchased services, including such things as insurance
- Other resources

This helps everyone see where the money is going and not going. It may also present an argument for better funding from local or state sources. For example, a school district may have a high per-pupil expenditure level. But much of this money may go to, say, special education and bilingual students, as well as salaries. This may not leave enough money for school supplies or building maintenance. Now you know what you need money for. Remember that parity and equity aren't the same thing. Two schools may both be getting, say, $5,000 per student. It might be fine for one, and not nearly enough for the other.

Natriello and other experts suggest parent groups do the following, working with the administration:

- Talk to teachers and administrators, and analyze the budget to see what you need. See if resources can be switched from other programs.

- Study what other schools are spending for the same things. It isn't certain they are spending the right amount, but at least it's a starting point. And as Natriello says, most state education departments make all these budget numbers available.

- Hold public meetings to explain the budget. These are extremely important. Many opponents of school budgets, including taxpayer associations, don't have a specific complaint about the budget, just that it is too high. Many people don't understand how costs have risen since their children were in school. Explain it to them.

- Anticipate obvious questions. For example, a standard complaint is that administrative costs are too high. That notion may well have outlived the data. Researchers now think most school administrative costs aren't particularly high when compared to organizations of similar size and complexity. Find similarly sized organizations in your area and make comparisons, Natriello suggests.

- Use the media. If parents feel their children aren't getting the resources they need, it is a story. Notify the media before a meeting in which school funding will be discussed. Prepare a press release with all relevant data and get it to the newspaper, radio and television reporters before the meeting.

- Make the wheel squeak. As you learn about the school funding process in your area, you'll learn your budget cycle, when the budget is prepared, and when you can make a case for more funding before city or county officials. Bring lots of parents, bring children, make signs, get across the point that educating children is local government's most important responsibility.

- Finally, make sure you are getting a fair shake from your local government. When Kentucky began to look at its school system, officials found that several communities weren't collecting all the taxes they should be because of fraud in the tax assessment process. If you suspect your community has the same problem, ask a lawyer or accountant in your parents group to look into it.

Raise Your Own Money

These are, as we said, difficult times to squeeze money from the public till. Despite your best efforts, your school may well not have all the money for all the programs and equipment you would like to have. So now what?

Many parents groups are raising money themselves. This, of course, isn't new. For as long as most of us can remember, PTAs, PTOs, and other nonprofit parents groups have held bake sales, auctions, dances, and raffles to raise money for new playground equipment, class trips, computers, or whatever. What is different now is that parents are raising money for such things as librarians' salaries, school writing paper, and alarm systems, things that are not frills or extras.

If the school needs the paper or the alarm system, and there's no other way of getting it, then what is the problem? There may indeed be no other way of raising money in the short term, but there are problems with parents paying basic expenses of public schools. The first is that it lets the public off the hook. Public schools benefit society as a whole, and society as a whole has agreed to pay for them. When society fails in this responsibility, it should be held accountable.

Secondly, parents in effect paying tuition at public schools widens the gap between the haves and have-nots, the schools that serve well-off neighborhoods and those that serve poorer neighborhoods. To take one fairly dramatic example, parents at a public elementary school in the well-off Upper West Side of Manhattan in New York City in 1995 held a concert, closed a street for an Oktoberfest, and held a telethon to solicit donations from parents and alumni. They raised about $200,000. Across the river in a poor neighborhood in Brooklyn, a school held a candy sale and sponsored school photos. They raised less then $4,000. Guess which school has the most computers, the most library books, the neatest class trips?

If parents are going to raise money for local schools, how can they get the best bang for their buck? How about using the money to reform the school system. In almost 60 communities in 26 states, parents and local officials have formed what are called "local education funds." These are nonprofit groups, independent of the school district, that raise money from local and national sources and use it to improve and reform their local school systems. These funds have initiated a number of innovative programs around the country.

> Local education funds are doing remarkable things to improve and reform the education system:
>
> - The Los Angeles Education Partnership has developed a program called "Family Care," in which school readiness centers help day-care providers, connect education with health and social services, and provide parent education.
> - In Worchester, Massachusetts, the Alliance for Education has started a program that offers professional development and training to school principals.
> - The Cleveland Education Fund brings teachers together with university professors and corporate leaders to develop new teaching ideas.
> - The Washington Parents Group Fund has a program that trains parents how to be advocates for their children.

One of the most dramatic involvements of a fund is in Chattanooga, Tennessee, where the Public Education Foundation is designing an entirely new school system. The foundation was created in the late 1980s. It initially raised a $6 million endowment, mostly from local foundations and corporations. It first emphasized professional development, with innovative programs for teachers and administrators. "We felt you changed schools by changing the adults in schools," said Steve Prigohzy, the foundation's executive director.

The foundation developed a good enough reputation that, after voters decided in 1994 to merge what had been separate city and county school systems in Chattanooga, it was asked to plan the region's new school system.

Local education funds are coordinated by the Public Education Fund Network in Washington, DC. The network provides members with information not only on fundraising, but on a broad array of issues including curriculum and assessment, governance, educational leadership, and building community support for education. "We bring them into the policy arena," said network official Amanda Broun. She said new or existing parents groups can join and become a local education fund. It's a serious undertaking that entails a lot of work, but all parents groups should consider this option. In this era of budget strain, parents with the money for new programs are the ones who are going to see new programs. Contact the network if you are interested in starting a fund in your community.

THE OLD SCHOOL HOUSE

In 1861 President Abraham Lincoln stopped at the Burnett School in Newark, New Jersey, to give a speech on the school lawn. The Burnett School is still open. That a building almost a century and a half old is still in use underscores one of the growing problems in American education—the condition of school buildings and other facilities.[6]

A report by the U.S. General Accounting Office (GAO) in February 1995 titled,"School Facilities: The Condition of America's Schools," documented what many educators already suspected. One-third of the nation's 80,000 public schools have at least one building in need of extensive repair or replacement. These buildings house 14 million students. In addition, 60 percent of the country's schools have at least one major building feature, such as plumbing or heating, in disrepair. The price tag to bring these buildings back to an acceptable condition is $112 billion, which is roughly four times the annual budget of the U.S. Department of Education.

Some of the individual conditions GAO inspectors found were appalling. They include:

- In New Orleans, Formosan termites have eaten away much of the structures of many school buildings. In one school, the termites ate the books off the library shelves, then ate the shelves.

- In Montgomery County, Alabama, a ceiling weakened by extensive water damage collapsed 40 minutes after children left the room.
- In Ramona, California, one school is made up entirely of portable classrooms. It has no auditorium or cafeteria.
- In New York City, a school built a century ago for 400 students now has almost 600. The school has no ventilation, yet the windows don't open. It is unbearably hot in the summer and cold in the winter unless someone stokes the coal furnace by hand.

The main culprit for these disasters is lack of funds, which causes administrators to defer maintenance and repairs. This, the report says, has a domino effect. Lack of repair leads to faster deterioration of a building. Don't fix the roof, and incoming water will damage the walls and floors. In New York, a typical roof repair costs $600, while a full roof replacement costs $300,000. But school administrators say they can't get the money for repairs because of anti-tax sentiment among voters or reductions in school funding because of property tax limitations, the report says. Also, some administrators said they had to use their meagre repair dollars on unfunded state and federal mandates, such as making all buildings accessible to handicapped students or removing asbestos.

Some communities are facing a double-barrelled problem of having older and newer school buildings all falling apart at the same time. Schools such as Burnett and others of its generation were solidly built. Of course, they weren't built to host the heavy-duty utilities that a modern school needs to run labs and computer centers. Buildings such as Burnett were built to be lit by gas. Some of the newer schools built after World War II were erected quickly by the same developer who built the surrounding tract houses, using leftover materials and with no thought for energy efficiency. Now, many of them are falling apart. At the same time, older schools have reached the end of their useful lives.

While the GAO report doesn't mention this, another reason some schools are in bad shape is corruption. For example, New York City's Division of School Facilities, responsible for the maintenance of 1,069 public schools, is one of the sorriest excuses for a school bureaucracy in history. The division has been wracked with bribery and kickback scandals, with almost 30 employees indicted in 1986–87. It was so inefficient and incompetent that it took 19 months to respond to a request for routine classroom maintenance, such as fixing a window, according to a 1984 study.

◆ ACTION STEPS ◆

There is no excuse for sending children into a building that is dangerous or unsafe. As a parent, you need to know if there's a problem with your school building. You can often tell by looking at it or walking through it. Bring the subject up with teachers and administrators. If anyone believes there's a problem, your parents group can and should get involved.

What characterizes a decent school? A West Virginia court said such schools are structurally safe and in good repair. They should have:

- Fire safety measures
- Sufficient exits
- An adequate and safe water supply
- An adequate sewage disposal system
- Sufficient and sanitary toilet facilities and plumbing fixtures
- Adequate storage
- Adequate light
- Acoustics for noise control

If your building doesn't measure up, it's time for action. Edna Salzman, who headed the team that did the GAO report, and other experts suggest the following:

- School buildings are subject to building codes, covering such things as plumbing, electrical, fire, and sanitation. Your district should have an engineer or inspector who inspects the buildings. Ask to see the inspection report, to see if the problem you believe exists has been detected by a professional. If there is no report, ask for an inspection.

- After you have identified the problem, the next step is to get it fixed. As a first step, find out who is responsible. This isn't always easy. In some states, the school board is in charge of repairs, while school building committees have the responsibility for capital improvements such as new buildings.

- Go to the proper authority and ask that they take take care of the problem. Often, they will. Also, as Saltzman found, community pressure often results in schools being kept in good repair.

- Problems arise when the school board or building committee says it cannot make needed repairs or replacements, usually because of lack of funds. If your board will not repair a code violation, you should make an administrative appeal to your state department of education. If this fails, you should at least consider a lawsuit.

- Lawsuits should be a remedy of last resort because they take time and money. The better tactic is to develop community support for your school. How to do that? Saltzman said one of the best things to do is get the community into the school, make it a community school. Let community groups use the gym or auditorium. Have evening adult education classes. If the community feels it owns the building, it will be much more inclined to fix it.

- Remind your school board that inadequate facilities can jeopardize a high school's accreditation. Accreditation is a voluntary measure in which many secondary schools and colleges agree to meet certain standards they themselves set for such things as curriculum, faculty and staff, student services, school climate, and philosophical outlook. Among the criteria is school facilities.

   The site, plant, and equipment must be maintained to support "all educational aspects" of the school and to "insure the safety and health" of all occupants, said Joseph Daisy, deputy director of the New England Association of Secondary Schools and Colleges of Boston, one of six regional accrediting agencies in the country. A school that fails to maintain its buildings properly could lose, or fail to gain, accreditation. There is no legal penalty for losing accreditation (it is voluntary), but it would be a public-relations black eye for any school.

- It might help to see if your state law is working against the repair of school buildings. In some states, the state will reimburse the cost of capital expenditures but not operating expenses. In other words, they'll pay most of the cost for new schools, but not a nickel for school repairs. What happens? Some hard-pressed school districts stop paying for repairs, let school buildings go to pot, then apply for funds to build new buildings. If you're faced with this situation, write to your state legislators and see if you can enlist their aid in getting the law changed.

- A few cities that need new school buildings and can't get the funding have looked to an alternative—available office space, said Allen Odden. Many cities have a glut of Class-A office space, which often can be converted to classroom use. It isn't the best alternative in the world, but it's better than a building that's just been eaten by Formosan termites.

- Finally, you can do it yourself. Saltzman found schools in Chicago where parents were heading in every weekend to paint and perform other repairs. It's also possible to get volunteers from nearby colleges to help with such work, or to have a neighboring corporation "adopt" your school and provide volunteers and materials. If your parents group is blessed with persons in the construction or property management businesses, they can be of great help.

◆ SELECTED QUESTIONS ◆

Our school is about to spend a fortune on computers. Are they worth it?

Some educators view computers as essential to the future of education. Others do not. Author Clifford Stoll argues that computers are no substitute for creative teaching. He said schools face serious problems of overcrowding, teacher incompetence and lack of security, and computers don't solve these problems. "They're expensive, quickly become obsolete and drain scarce capital budgets," Stoll says. Others critize the instructional materials used in many school computers, saying they aren't much different from those in older workbooks. Also, teachers often aren't trained to get the most out of computers.

Obviously, if your school buys computers and they just gather dust, you have wasted a small fortune. It costs $50,000 to $100,000 just to wire an older school building for full computer service. Before you spend this kind of money, develop a plan for what you're going to do with the computers and how teachers will use them. The plan should cover teacher training. Evaluate the plan. If it makes sense, then go ahead.

Has Congress taken any action to provide funds for rebuilding American schools?

Barely. In 1995 an Education Infrastructure Act was proposed to provide $100 million for school repair and replacement. This is considerably less than the $112 billion the GAO deems necessary for the job. But when Congress passed the act, less than $8 million was actually appropriated.

Are American schools ready for the 21st century?

Many are not. Another survey by the GAO found that while three-quarters of schools reported having enough televisions and computers, most said they didn't have the system or building infrastructure to fully use this equipment. For example, many computers are not connected to other computers in the school or to the outside "information superhighway."

FOR MORE INFORMATION

U.S. General Accounting Office
P.O. Box 6015
Gaithersburg, MD 20884–6015
202–512–6000

Public Education Fund Network
601 13th Street NW, Suite 290 North
Washington, DC 20005
202–628–7460

Policy Information Center
Educational Testing Service
Princeton, NJ 08541
609–734–5694

Equity Center
400 W. 15th Street, Suite 404
Austin, TX 78701

Education Commission of the States
707 17th Street
Denver, CO 80202
303–299–3600

Center for Research in Education Finance
Wisconsin Center for Education Research
1025 W. Johnson Street, 7th Floor
Madison, WI 53706–1796
608–263–4260

Kentucky Department of Education
500 Mero Street
Frankfurt, KY 40601
502–564–3421

NOTES

1. *San Antonio Independent School District* v. *Rodriguez,* 411 U.S. 1 (1973).

2. *Edgewood Independent School District* v. *Kirby,* 777 S.W. 2d 391 (1989).

3. *Serrano* v. *Priest* (ii), 18 Cal 3d 728, 557 P 2d 929, 135 Cal Rptr 345, cert. denied, 432 U.S. 907 (1977).

4. Clune, William H., "School Finance Reform: The Role of the Courts," Consortium for Policy Research in Education's Finance Briefs, Feb. 3, 1993.

5. *The Council for Better Education* v. *Rose,* 790 W.W. 2d 186 (1989).

6. King, Wayne, "Repairs Soar in New Jersey's Baby-Boom Schools," *The New York Times,* Feb. 19, 1993.

SEXUAL
DISCRIMINATION

♦ INTRODUCTION ♦

Ronald W. Price's resume said he was a social studies teacher, girls' softball coach, and drama club advisor at a high school in suburban Anne Arundel County, Maryland.

Not on the resume was this: In his 24-year teaching career, Price had sexual relations with at least seven students, some as young as 14.

For at least seven years, complaints to school officials went unheeded. Finally, in 1993 Price was arrested on three counts of child sexual abuse. After a state investigation that found the school negligent, two more teachers were arrested on similar charges, two more were disciplined for sexual harassment, and two assistant principals were transferred.[1]

The case drew national attention. Price detailed his exploits on the TV show A Current Affair *and on the* Geraldo *show as well. Price claimed he sought sex with the students because he had some kind of illness. The judge didn't buy it. On October 14, 1993, Price was sentenced to 26 years in prison.*

Price's case was outrageous for any number of reasons. He took advantage of the trust students had in him, he got away with it, and the school did nothing to stop him. What is worse is that Price's case isn't particularly unusual; there are stories like it all over the country. Whether it is sexual intercourse, grabbing, pinching, groping, or name-calling, sexual harassment is rampant in this country's schools.

This chapter looks at sexual harassment and what can be done about it. It also looks at other issues of gender equity including:

- *Classroom bias*
- *Rules and admissions*
- *Athletic teams*

◆ DISCUSSION ◆

Many parents don't realize sexual harassment is a major problem. It is. "Sexual harassment . . . is part of the daily fabric of school life," said Dr. Nan Stein, director of the Sexual Harassment in Schools project at Wellesley College. According to polls by Louis Harris & Associates, Wellesley and the National Organization for Women (NOW), 85 to 89 percent of school-age girls have been sexually harassed, and almost 40 percent report being harassed on a daily basis.

As a rule, the harassment is done in public and most often comes from fellow students, according to the Wellesley-NOW poll, published in *Seventeen* magazine in 1993. Only 8 percent of the 2,000 respondents said their schools had and enforced a policy on sexual harassment.

As many of the nation's major newspapers have reported, many boys think it's a right of passage to manhood to "dis," or show disrespect for, girls. We are talking about everything from lewd remarks and "flip-up days," where boys try to flip up girls' skirts, to grabbing girls by the breasts or buttocks, and groping for girls' genitals in swimming pools.

Gary Peller, a Georgetown University law professor writing in *The Washington Post,* said he was appalled at the sexual harassment his daughter and her friends were subjected to in a suburban Washington high school. It included a steady stream of verbal abuse, such as being called "bitches" and "whores," being grabbed, and having boys push up against them. "An atmosphere demeaning to females pervades the school," he concluded.

"As a father, I was saddened they had become so accustomed to harassment and so convinced of their powerlessness to stop it that until recently they didn't even think to mention it to anyone—it was just part of going to school," Peller wrote.

Helen Neuborne, former executive director of the NOW Legal Defense and Education Fund, said a large part of the problem is that many boys simply don't understand that what they're doing is wrong, and neither do many adult teachers, who often seem to reward such behavior. She said the country made an attitudinal change in racial discrimination and must now do the same with sexual discrimination. That change is further along in the workplace than it is in schools.

Teachers and administrators, as well as boys, have to realize that harassment isn't harmless fun. "Whether it's pinching or lifting skirts, or some more subtle form of harassment, harassment often makes girls back off and drop out. That makes them victims of discrimination," Neuborne said. She said such harassment can exact a terrible toll on many girls.

There are three reasons to end sexual harassment in schools. First, it is wrong. Second, it is against the law. Third, it is starting to cost schools an awful lot of money.

In 1981 the U.S. Department of Education issued a memo stating sexual harassment in schools was a violation of Title IX of the Educational Amendments of 1972, that prohibits all forms of sexual discrimination in educational programs receiving federal funds. The memo defined sexual harassment as: " . . . verbal or physical contact of a sexual nature, imposed on the basis of sex" that violates Title IX rights.

In addition, many states have passed state laws specifically prohibiting gender discrimination and sexual harassment in schools. Until recently, the courts hadn't been much help in stopping sexual harassment in schools. But a 1992 decision has changed that, in a big way.

THE *FRANKLIN* V. *GWINNETT COUNTY* CASE

Christine Franklin was a student at North Gwinnett High School in Gwinnett County, Georgia. According to her complaint, she was subjected to continual sexual harassment, starting in her sophomore year, from Andrew Hill, a teacher and coach at the school. Franklin said the harassment started with suggestive conversations and escalated to forced kissing, then to forced sexual intercourse. She said school officials were aware of the problem, but took no action to stop it and discouraged her from filing a complaint against Hill. Finally, Hill resigned, on the condition that all matters pending against him be dropped. The school then closed its investigation.

Franklin brought an action for damages against the school under Title IX of the Education Amendments of 1972, which prohibits discrimination based on gender in any educational programs or activities receiving federal funds. Lower courts dismissed her claim, saying Title IX doesn't authorize an award of damages. Previously, victims of intentional gender discrimination had only been entitled to injunctive relief, such as an order to cease the improper conduct.

But the Supreme Court reasoned that if that's all Christine Franklin received, it would be meaningless, because the offending teacher had already resigned. The high court reversed the lower court's decision and said a victim of intentional sexual harassment could receive monetary damages.[2]

Since then, plaintiffs from Brooklyn, New York, to Petaluma, California, have gone to court asking for money damages for sexual harassment, and some of these cases have been settled for as much as $800,000. While it's still not clear what each school's legal obligations will be, it's clearly in everyone's best interest to halt sexual harassment in schools. Parents and students can take the lead in this effort.

◆ ACTION STEPS ◆

Experts such as Stein and Neuborne offer these tips to students and their parents:

- If you are the victim of sexual harassment, don't ignore it, it won't go away. If it makes you feel scared or uncomfortable, resolve to do something about it. Most harassment goes unreported.

Parents must urge their daughters to come forward and report harassment.

- Keep a written record of all harassment incidents.
- Try to tell the harasser to stop, if you feel comfortable doing so. A supportive adult may be able to help you write a letter to this effect. If you are ready to make a complaint, try to go through an adult at the school whom you trust.
- If the problem continues, make a complaint to the principal. If your school has an anti-harassment policy, the policy will dictate the form of the complaint. If there's no policy, include all salient points of the harassment, such as dates, times, number of occurrences and efforts you have made to stop it, in your letter to the principal.
- Don't blame yourself. It isn't your fault; it's a problem the school has to solve.
- If the school won't deal with the problem, file a complaint with your state department of education. If the state doesn't have a procedure, you can file a complaint with the U.S. Department of Education's Civil Rights Division, which is headquartered in Washington, DC (see end of chapter for address) and has 10 regional offices around the country. If the incident involves physical contact, you should also file a complaint with the police.

Above are steps to follow if sexual harassment has taken place. There are other steps that can and should be taken to prevent harassment, to stop it before it happens. These include:

- Middle schools and high schools should have an effective policy for dealing with sexual harassment. Parents should insist there be such a policy. The policy should be easily understood and widely distributed and should clearly explain how to file a complaint and with whom to file it. There should be provisions for speedy, confidential investigations and appropriate punishments, and there should be provisions against retaliation for filing a complaint. Teachers and staff should have special training that raises their awareness of this subject and teaches them how to deal with it. For a sample policy, plus an excellent Legal

Resource Kit on sexual harassment, write or call the NOW Legal Defense and Education Fund (see end of chapter for address).

- Parents should encourage students to start a peer group to address harassment.
- Parents and students should hold an assembly on harassment with a knowledgeable local speaker.
- The school library should have materials on sexual harassment. To raise consciousness, put up flyers about sexual harassment.
- Curriculum at all levels should discuss respect for others, sexual harassment, and violence. Students should be taught the proper way to treat other students and how to deal with harassment aimed at them.
- If your principal won't take the subject of sexual harassment seriously, make a presentation before the school board.

Of all the steps students and parents should take, none is as important as reporting any incident of harassment. School officials can't correct a problem they aren't aware of, nor can they be held responsible for it. If you are a bona fide victim of harassment and end up in court, you'll have great difficulty winning damages if you never notified the school of the problem.

CLASSROOM BIAS

Sexual harassment isn't the only type of gender bias out there. A year-long, 116-page study, "How Schools Shortchange Girls," by the American Association of University Women (AAUW) Educational Foundation in 1992 (released as a paperback book under the same title by Marlowe & Co. in 1995) found the following:

- Teachers spend significantly more time in class with boys than with girls. Boys answer as much as eight times more than girls in class. Also, teachers tend to ask boys more probing questions after they answer in class.
- Textbooks and other curriculum materials ignore women's issues and often ignore women's contributions. The materials often stereotype women as well.

- Standardized tests often contain some elements of gender bias.
- Science classes enroll fewer girls than boys.
- In vocational programs, girls still enroll primarily in office work training programs, while boys enroll in trade programs that lead to higher paying jobs.
- In 1990 women comprised 72 percent of teachers, 28 percent of school principals and 5 percent of district superintendents.

All the findings weren't as dismal. For example, the gender gap in math was small and shrinking. And, curiously, twice as many boys were in special education classes as girls, even though learning disabilities occur with the same frequency in boys and girls. This may mean some boys are being inappropriately enrolled in special ed classes or that some girls are being denied needed education services, the report suggests. Also, boys are reprimanded more often than girls, although this may also give the message that boys get more attention than girls.

◆ Action Steps ◆

The message is clear—parents need to pay attention to the education their daughters are receiving. How to do it? Jillian Ray of the AAUW offers the following tips:

- Videotape or observe classrooms to see how often teachers call on boys and girls. Ask teachers to keep a log of how often they call on boys and how often they call on girls. Listen for gender differences in the feedback children receive on their work. Are boys and girls held to the same standard? Form a partnership with teachers and meet with them to discuss these issues.
- Assess the content of textbooks and other materials and watch for messages that stereotype girls and women. See if assignments stereotype women. For example, said Ray, if the assignment is to write a paper about physicists and all the physicists mentioned are men, call the teacher and see if female physicists can't be included in the assignment.

- Talk to girls about gender stereotypes and assumptions, and how they create obstacles for women.

- Start a mentor program using women in science, mathematics and technological fields to encourage girls to pursue studies in these areas. Mentors can give presentations and sponsor field trips as well as mentor individual students. A parents group can start such a program by holding a brainstorming session, writing down all the names of women they know who might qualify and be interested. Then ask these women, and any others they can think of, to come to a planning meeting.

- Motivate your daughter to take risks, prove her abilities, and earn recognition for her talents—not her appearance. Encourage her to manage her own bank account, participate in sports and all-girl activities, take part in dinner conversations, and do math puzzles instead of watching television.

- Encourage a local woman-owned business to adopt your daughter's school. Not only can this mean more resources for the school, it can expand girls' awareness of careers for women.

- It may be difficult for you, a parent, to ask a teacher to keep a log on how many times they call on boys and girls. Ask the AAUW to do it. The organization has 150,000 members in 1,650 chapters, all committed to ending gender bias in schools. Your local AAUW chapter will be happy to come into schools, meet with school administrators and teachers, and discuss all of the gender bias issues raised in their report. To locate the nearest AAUW chapter, call 1–800–326–AAUW, Ext. 1.

There is good news. Since the AAUW made its report public, the organization has seen improvements in almost every area of classroom gender bias, Ray said.

RULES AND ADMISSIONS

When public schools started in this country women weren't even allowed in many of them. Over the 19th and 20th centuries, stereotypes evolved about the roles of male and female children. Girls were supposed to watch and boys were supposed to play. Boys were supposed to be better at math and science and girls were supposed to be better at languages.

The women's movement has done much to dispel these stereotypes, with the help of laws such as Title VI and Title IX of the Civil Rights Act of 1964. Victories have been won, but problems persist. One battle that was joined in the 1970s concerned rules and admissions.

Boston Latin School, the nation's oldest public high school, started in the 17th century as an all-boys school. It had since been joined by Girls Latin, a sister school for girls. Both were prestigious academic schools.

In the early 1970s the boys' school had room for 3,000 students, while the girls' school could hold only 1,500. Because the schools could accommodate more boys than girls, there were more spots and less competition for boys, so the boys didn't have to score as high on the entrance exam. In 1970 girls had to score at least 133 out of a possible 200 to gain admission, while boys only had to score 120.

Parents of girls who scored over 120 but less than 133 sued. The court held that the different admission standard was a violation of the equal protection clause of the 14th Amendment and that the girls had been illegally discriminated against.[3] Right after the decision, the state passed a law prohibiting any discrimination in the admission to public schools based on sex, race, color, religion, or national origin. Both of the Boston high schools are now coed and continue to be regarded as outstanding schools.

Shortly thereafter, a similar quota case was decided from San Francisco. The standards for admission to prestigious Lowell High School were different for boys than for girls. Girls needed a 3.25 grade point average, while boys got in with a 3.0.

The apparent purpose of this disparity was to have an even number of boys and girls in the school, but the court said no evidence was put forth that a balance of the sexes furthered the goal of a better academic education. The court said such a disparity in entrance standards was unconstitutional.[4]

However, a Pennsylvania court has held that the battle against gender discrimination doesn't require every public high school to become coeducational. Separate high schools for males and females can be maintained, as long as they are of equal quality. The case involved a girl who wished to go to Central High School in Philadelphia, a prestigious, academic school that was all-male. The court said equally prestigious Girls High School was available to her.

The court said single-sex schools were a "respected educational methodology" and that it wasn't the court's business to pass judgment on the wisdom of single-sex schools. Since the educational opportunities were equal, the schools were constitutional.[5] (Curiously, Central High School has since become coed, while Girls High School is still only for girls.)

Single-sex schools are allowed, but they must offer programs and facilities for the girls that are as good as the ones for the boys. If not, they'll likely run into the problems Detroit educators faced when they tried to start three elementary schools only for black males, with an Afro-centric curriculum. There was no immediate plan to start academies for girls.

The court said classification by sex violated equal protection unless it served some important government objective. The court could find no compelling reason that boys had to be schooled in an all-male atmosphere, getting services not available to girls.[6]

For all the battles over coed schools, many educators are beginning to think that single-sex schools, and single-sex classes, weren't such a bad idea after all, and can be a help to many youngsters of both sexes. Some all-women colleges boast that their graduates are 30 percent more likely to serve on corporate boards of directors as graduates of coed colleges. This may be because at all-women's schools, the student leaders are all women. Also, advocates for single-sex classes say that girls tend to do better in math and science classes when they are single-sex—maybe because there's less pressure and competition. They also seem to be a way to get more women to take math and science classes. Indeed, many schools are experimenting with all-girl math and science classes. Single-sex classes certainly offer fewer distractions for adolescents of both sexes.

◆ Action Steps ◆

The main goal of school is education, the best education possible. Parents should follow the research and monitor any local experiments with single-sex schools or classes. Find out how they're doing, if students like them, and what the test scores show. But remember that single-sex schools or classes have to offer equal resources to boys and girls. If they don't, if members of one sex are getting programs and services that are being denied members of the other sex, there's most likely a Title IX violation. If your school won't correct the problem, you can file a complaint with your state education department or with the Civil Rights Division of the U.S. Department of Education in Washington.

Athletic Teams

Prior to the passage of Title IX in 1972, the athletic opportunities available to girls in most of this country ranged from nonexistent to pathetic. Many high schools had football, basketball, baseball, and track for boys, and cheerleading for girls. There were exceptions—the wonderful girls' basketball tradition in Iowa, the great swimmers in California—but in general, girls weren't getting anywhere near a fair shake.

That has changed, thanks largely to Title IX. From 1972 when the law was passed to 1978, participation in girls' organized high school sports increased from 295,000 to 2,063,000, an increase of more than 600 percent.[7] Title IX demands that athletic opportunities, if they are offered, be available to all on reasonably equal terms. Title IX didn't change the world overnight. A few heads had to be banged.

Some outstanding female athletes led the way, such as Minnesota's Peggy Brenden, the state's top teen-age tennis player, and Toni St. Pierre, a first-class runner and skier. Minnesota had a rule prohibiting girls from playing on or against boys' sports teams. They challenged the rule and won, the court saying there was no evidence either would be damaged by competing against boys, nor was there any evidence the boys would be damaged.[8]

Ohio had a rule that girls couldn't compete with boys in contact sports such as basketball. Two girls in Yellow Springs, Ohio, made the boys' basketball team, but weren't allow to play. Not allowed on one court, they went to the other, and won big.

The U.S. District Court held that while some women may not be able to compete against men, it doesn't follow that all women can't. "School girls must given the opportunity to compete with boys in interscholastic contact sports if they are physically qualified," the court found.[9]

Although there have been a variety of rulings on girls participating in contact sports, most courts allow it, even in football.[10] By most estimates, more than 150 girls are playing high school football across the country, although most are playing in the ninth grade and most of the varsity players are kickers.

It is, of course, possible to go too far. Recently, a girl who was injured playing high school football in Baltimore announced she was going to sue the school for $1.5 million, claiming no one warned her how dangerous football could be.[11] While it's a shame she was injured, she shouldn't win this suit. Schools can't be put in the position of being charged with discrimination if they don't let women play and then paying damages if they do.

The rules now are:

- Schools may operate separate teams for boys and girls. This gives more youngsters the chance to compete.

- Where schools only offer teams for boys in noncontact sports, girls must be allowed to try out for the teams. If girls can't make the teams, but there are enough girls to form a girls' team, the school must offer to start a girls' team.

- If a school has a boys' and a girls' team in the same noncontact sport, some states, such as Michigan and New York, allow a girl to try out for the boys' team. Many states and school districts do not. Some schools allow the boys to try out for the girls' team, but the prevailing attitude is to keep the boys on the boys' teams.

- Title IX doesn't require an exactly equal expenditure of funds for boys' and girls' sports, but adequate funding is one criteria that can be used to determine whether or not a school is offering equality of opportunity.

Sometimes boys want to try out for a sport only offered to girls. Title IX doesn't demand schools allow this, unless the entire athletic program is deficient with regard to boys, and this is a rarity. When boys are interested in a sport offered only to girls, such as volleyball, school officials, such as Harry Tischler, a lawyer for the Philadelphia school board, say they try to find enough interested boys to start a boys' team. However, one state, Massachusetts, has allowed coed volleyball, based on the state's Equal Rights Amendment.

◆ Action Steps ◆

That girls and young women have made progress in gaining equal access to organized athletics is undeniable. For example, in 1972, the year Title IX was passed, the University of Connecticut had no women's basketball team. In 1995 the women's team won the NCAA championship. But despite victories such as this, the fight continues. The kinds of battles now being fought are what Helen Neuborne calls "second-generation discrimination," and are over such things as equal pay for coaches, equal facilities, and equal access to other resources.

Typical complaints now might be that boys' basketball practice always takes place after school, while girls' practice always starts at dinner time. Or that the boys' tennis teams plays 20 matches and the girls play 5. Or that the girls' basketball coach makes half of what the boys' coach makes. Or that the girls' locker room is inadequate. These are all violations of Title IX. Here are some steps for parents to take:

- Bring the problem to the attention of the principal and the athletic director.
- If it is not promptly corrected, bring it to the attention of the school board.
- If it is still not taken care of, contact your state department of education.
- If the problem persists, file a complaint with the Civil Rights Division of the U.S. Department of Education.

Attorney Jeanette Lim, head of the office of program enforcement and policy services of the Civil Rights Division, encourages students and parents with problems such as these to use the complaint process. "It works. We can work with school officials, we can change schedules," she says.

Although the struggle continues, Title IX has left a powerful legacy in athletics. Literally millions more women are participating in sports, setting new records and drawing countless millions of spectators each year.

◆ SELECTED QUESTIONS ◆

Can schools expel married or pregnant students?

They once did, but today nearly all schools do not exclude married or pregnant students. Many schools have special programs for students who have or are about to have children. Many educators feel if pregnant teens stay in school and graduate, they're more likely to go to college or get a decent job and not be relegated to a life on welfare.

My ninth-grade daughter plays field hockey. The equipment she's been assigned is 10 to 12 years old, worn out, and in dangerous condition. Needless to say, the boys football team has newer equipment. Is this a Title IX violation?

Almost assuredly. Go to the principal and athletic director and demand the situation be corrected immediately. If it isn't, file a complaint with the Civil Rights Division. When you file the complaint, call your local print and broadcast journalists who cover education. From the cases such as these that we researched, your complaint will come out as an ominous-sounding "civil rights lawsuit" in the paper. Most schools won't want the bad publicity and will quickly find the money for new helmets.

My daughter is in first grade and about to start a youth soccer program. In our town the girls have a choice at this age of playing on mixed teams or all-girl teams. Which is better?

You can come down on either side of this one. If your daughter shows promise of first-rate athletic ability, she may benefit from a mixed league. In some mixed leagues at this age, the kids alternately chase the ball, talk, and watch the grass grow, so it doesn't matter much. On the other hand, sometimes boys try to take over. If you can, take your daughter and look at both leagues. Ask which one she would like to play in. If you can't, and want a general rule, pick the all-girl league. In a few years your daughter will be playing in an all-girl league anyway, in all likelihood.

My daughter is in 2nd grade. In her gym class, the teacher only has the boys do the rope climb. While they're climbing, the girls jump rope. Is this a violation of Title IX?

Quite possibly. Talk to the teacher and get the reason. Rope-climbing is a good upper body exercise. We know of no reason to prohibit girls from getting the benefits of climbing. If the teacher can't give you a reason for this policy, ask him to change it. If he doesn't, go to the principal. Interestingly, jumping rope is probably the better of the two exercises, so the boys in this case may be getting shortchanged.

FOR FURTHER INFORMATION

American Association of University Women
1111 16 Street NW
Washington, DC 20036–4873
1–800–326–AAUW

NOW Legal Defense and Education Fund
99 Hudson Street
New York, NY 10013–2871
212–925–6635

Center for Research on Women/ Sexual Harassment in Schools Project
Wellesley College
106 Central Street
Wellesley, MA 02181–8259
617–283–2500

Equity Center
Council of Chief State School Officers
1 Massachusetts Avenue NW #700
Washington, DC 20001
202–408–8072

FairTest (research on gender bias in testing)
342 Broadway
Cambridge, MA 02139
617–864–4810

NOTES

1. Chen, Fern, "How Sex Abuse in High School Went Unchecked; Attitudes in Md. Community Partly to Blame, Some Say," *The Washington Post,* Aug. 23, 1993.

2. *Franklin v. Gwinnett County Public Schools,* 112 S. Ct. 1228 (1992).

3. *Bray v. Lee,* 337 F. Supp. 934 (D. Mass. 1972).

4. *Berkelman v. San Francisco Unified School District,* 501 F. 2d 1254 (9th Circ. 1974).

5. *Vorchheimer v. School District of Philadelphia,* 532 F. 2d 880 (3rd Circ. 1976), cert. denied, 430 U.S. 703 (1977).

6. *Garrett v. Board of Education of the School District of the City of Detroit,* 775 F. Supp. 1004 (1991).

7. Federal Register, Vo. 44, No. 239, Dec. 11, 1979.

8. *Brenden v. Independent School District,* 742 477 F. 2d 1292 (8th Cir. 1973).

9. *Yellow Springs Exempted Village School District Board of Education v. Ohio School Athletic Association,* 443 F. Supp. 753 (S.D. Ohio 1978).

10. *Larity v. Ambach,* 620 F. Supp. 663 (1985).

11. Barringer, Felicity, "Fullback Sues School Over Her Injury," *The New York Times,* Aug. 18, 1993.

THE ROLE
OF RELIGION

◆ INTRODUCTION ◆

Religion has become one of the hottest topics in American education today. It seems there's a story every other day about prayer in schools, prayer at graduation, religious groups meeting in schools, religious clubs in schools, or religious groups handing out flyers in schools. We pay more attention to these issues than you might think. Of the numerous educational issues reviewed by the U.S. Supreme Court, none has been taken up more often than questions of religion in schools. In virtually every term, the high court struggles with school prayer or some other aspect of the religion-in-schools issue. As a parent, you may be drawn into a school-religion issue. This chapter will examine:

- *How public money can and cannot be used in private/parochial schools*
- *Whether prayer is allowed in public schools*
- *Whether schools can host religious meetings*

◆ DISCUSSION ◆

We have debates about religion in schools, in part, because our public schools began as religious schools. The schools in colonial times were extensions of the "established" church, the Congregational Church in many colonies, that also ran the civil government. In other words, the minister was also the mayor and the schools were heavily oriented toward the Protestant tradition.

When 19th-century reformers such as Horace Mann, Caleb Mills, and Henry Barnard began the public schools we know today, their biggest opponents were ministers trying to stop them from creating what they considered godless institutions. Protestants gained control of the New York public schools in the 19th century and used them to promote the scriptures as revealed in the King James version of the Bible. Catholics, claiming the public schools were sectarian, began forming their own schools.

The fights between Protestants and Catholics became national battles. Sometimes gangs of Protestants burned Catholic schools. The Know-Nothing Party's presidential candidate, running on a platform of daily Bible reading and anti-Catholicism, carried three states in 1854. The Catholic schools, and those of other dissenting religions, tried to get the King James version banned from public schools and tried to get public funds for their schools.

In the early 20th century, the two sides reached an accommodation.[1] Religious instruction was taken out of public schools, and the use of public funds to support religious schools was banned. This seemed to agree with the First Amendment, which says "Congress shall make no law respecting an establishment of religion, or prohibiting the free exercise thereof . . ." and with Thomas Jefferson's dream that there be a "wall of separation" between church and state.

But the warp and woof of politics upset that equilibrium. Parents who sent their children to private school also paid taxes to support public schools, and some politicians felt they should receive some of the benefits that public school students receive. If it weren't for private schools, public school costs would be higher in most communities. But how could the government give aid to private schools, most of which have some religious affiliation, without violating the "establishment of religion" clause of the First Amendment?

The trick, lawmakers found, was to give aid to the student rather than the school.

WHAT THE GOVERNMENT CAN PAY FOR

In 1947 the Supreme Court upheld a state law that reimbursed parents of parochial school children for the costs of school bus transportation.[2] The court said the children, not the school, were the main beneficiaries of the service. Now, public busing of private school students is allowed and, indeed, in many states mandatory.

In 1968 the court upheld a New York program that furnished secular textbooks to parochial school students.[3] The court said the teaching of secular, religiously neutral subjects, such as math and science, and the teaching of religion were not intertwined; in other words, secular textbooks would not be instrumental in the teaching of religion. The loan or provision of secular, nonideological textbooks by public schools to nonpublic schools has been allowed ever since; in many states it's up to the local district. The government may also provide school lunches and public health services for private school students.

Beyond this, drawing the line at what benefits the student and what benefits the school has not been easy. The cases get so confusing they recall the alleged debates among medieval philosophers over how many angels could dance on the head of a pin. How can you tell if a particular program crosses the line, proselytizes religion and violates the Constitution?

In 1975 the Supreme Court developed a three-part test known as the Lemon Test, after the name of the case *Lemon* v. *Kurtzman,* to determine if a statute regarding aid to private schools is constitutional.[4] To pass the test, such a law must:

- Have a secular legislative purpose.
- Have a principle or primary effect that neither advances nor inhibits religion.
- Not foster an excessive government entanglement with religion.

Using this test, the court found two programs unconstitutional. One was a Rhode Island statute authorizing the state to supplement the salaries of teachers who taught secular subjects in nonpublic elementary schools. The other was a Pennsylvania program in which the state bought certain secular educational services from private schools. The court said both programs presented a grave danger of excessive government entanglement with religion. Hence, teacher salary subsidies and purchase of service agreements are not allowed.

For real confusion, no case quite matches an analysis the court did in 1975 of an Ohio plan to provide a number of services to private schools.[5] The court held that the state could provide textbooks to students in private schools at public expense. But the state could not provide other instructional materials, such as films or videos, lab equipment, or computers. So the state can provide a parochial student with a chemistry book but not a chemistry video. The court also said state funds could be used for school transportation but not for transportation on field trips. This means the state will pay to send students to a parochial school but not to a museum or art gallery.

Cases from Grand Rapids, Michigan,[6] and New York City[7] sent the message that public school educators were not allowed to work with parochial school children in parochial school buildings. The New York case was particularly difficult, because it involved the federally funded Title I program. Children in the parochial school were eligible for the remedial instruction, guidance and clinical services provided by Title I. But the teachers who provide these services weren't allowed in the parochial school. Some districts around the country dealt with this by parking vans near parochial schools, and serving the parochial school children in the vans.

These cases continue. A recent one suggests the court may be moving toward allowing more public programs in nonpublic schools. A deaf youngster at a Catholic high school in Arizona asked for a sign interpreter from the local school system to sit with him in class. The interpreter would be paid for with public funds. The request was denied, and the boy's family sued. A lower court found for the school district. It followed the Grand Rapids thinking, and said the placing of a public employee in the classroom would be promoting religion.[8]

But the U.S. Supreme Court disagreed, ruling 5–4 that the Constitution allows government money to pay for a sign interpreter in this case. The high court said a sign interpreter in a private classroom was different from a teacher. The interpreter couldn't add to the religious environment or initiate anything to influence the student toward religion; the interpreter merely repeated what was being given to the class as a whole.

The court said this was a neutral, nonreligious service to benefit the student and if the school received an "attenuated benefit" as well, that was all right. Churches do receive some government benefits, such as police and fire protection. Here, the court said, the state was merely offering a nonreligious service to a student with a disability.

So a public school staffer can go into a nonpublic school, despite the Grand Rapids and New York holdings, but not as a teacher. As we have said, few areas of the law offer such a rich legacy of legal hair-splitting.

PRAYER IN SCHOOL?

Most of us have probably forgotten, but for most of the 20th century, the public school day in many states began with a prayer or reading from the Bible. That changed in the early 1960s.

The New York Board of Regents had composed a prayer they recommended be used at the beginning of the school day. The prayer was: "Almighty God, we acknowledge our dependence on Thee, and we beg Thy blessings upon us, our parents, our teachers and our Country." The Supreme Court ruled that the prayer violated the establishment clause.[9]

The court said the government cannot use its power or prestige to support or influence religion. Even though this prayer was "denominationally neutral" and participation was voluntary, the First Amendment still meant the government shouldn't be in the business of composing official prayers.

A year later, the justices again invalidated government-sponsored prayer in public schools, this time in Pennsylvania and Maryland. There, students began the day with Bible readings or the Lord's Prayer or both. The court said these opening ceremonies were in effect government-sponsored religious ceremonies. When the government sponsors prayers, there's a risk of indirect coercion, meaning people of other faiths might be influenced toward the Christian faith. Because the court held the effect of prayer was the advancement of religion, the readings and prayers violated the establishment clause. The court did say it was okay to study the Bible or religion, in a secular, objective sense, but not to promote a particular religion.[10]

These controversial decisions greatly reduced prayer in public schools. But some states wanted to keep prayer in schools, and in order to do so they passed laws authorizing moments of silence at the beginning of the school day. One such law was New Mexico's, which said the period could be used for "contemplation, meditation or prayer, provided silence is maintained and no activities are undertaken." The law was declared unconstitutional, as promoting prayer in school.[11]

Some other "moment of silence" statutes have been upheld, as long as they don't mention the word "prayer." That seems to be the state of the law now: Schools can have a moment of silence at the beginning of the school day, and students can say a prayer during the moment of silence, but the law can't use the word "prayer" in their definition of the moment of silence.

Other prayer-in-school issues persist, and recent decisions suggest the courts are split on whether to allow prayer in school. Providence, Rhode Island, had a policy that allowed school officials to invite a clergyman to graduation to offer a nondenominational invocation and benediction. In 1989 the principal of Nathan Bishop Middle School invited a rabbi to give the invocation.

A student and her parents objected. The First U.S. Circuit Court of Appeals found that because school officials orchestrate the graduation, the prayer ceremony is a state-sponsored and state-directed religious ceremony, in violation of the establishment clause. The U.S. Supreme Court concurred.[12]

But two newer cases, from Texas and Idaho,[13] say if students freely vote to chose a nonsectarian, nonprosletyzing prayer at graduation, it's okay—it doesn't violate the establishment clause. The difference between these decisions and the Rhode Island case is that school officials invited the clergyman to give the invocation in Rhode Island, while in the Texas and Idaho cases, the students themselves chose whether or not to have an invocation.

If school officials run the show, and include a prayer, that is unacceptable. If students have the choice and vote to include a prayer, that may be acceptable, because, to summarize a lengthy argument, it is protected by the free speech and free exercise clauses of the First Amendment. The result is that the courts may allow some prayer at school graduations. Time will tell whether this signifies a movement toward more prayer in public schools.

RELIGIOUS MEETINGS

If public officials such as school principals can't support religion, as many cases have held, then what about public school buildings being used by students or community groups for religious meetings?

In the early 1980s, in response to the growing number of court decisions limiting religious activities in public schools, many principals forbade the use of buildings by groups such as student Bible clubs or by church groups in the community. On the other side of the coin, some school boards specifically passed ordinances allowing religious meetings in their schools. Inevitably, many of these meeting rules ended up in court, with mixed results.[14] Some decisions supported a ban against religious meetings, others said such meetings should be allowed.

In 1984 Congress passed the Equal Access Act (20 USC #4071-4074), which makes it illegal for public high schools to disallow student meetings based on what might be said at the meeting. In other words, if you allow the chess club or the stamp club to meet, you must allow the Bible club to meet. To qualify under the act, the meetings have to be voluntary and student-initiated, held during noninstructional times and not sponsored or controlled by school officials.

The law was tested in a case from Omaha, Nebraska. Some students at Westside High School wanted to form a Christian club, but they were turned down. School officials cited the establishment clause. The students sued, claiming the school's refusal to allow their club to meet violated the Equal Access Act. The case went to the Supreme Court. The first question was whether the school allowed other noncurricular clubs to meet. If it did, the school became what the act calls a "limited open forum," and must let other groups meet. Because the chess club, scuba club, and service club for special education all met, and because the subject matter of these clubs wasn't directly related to the curriculum, the court considered them noncurricular. If these clubs were allowed to meet, the court reasoned that the Christian club should also be allowed to meet. The court applied the three-part Lemon Test to the act, and said it didn't violate the establishment clause.[15]

This case applied to a student group. More recently, the court ruled that a school that opened its doors to community groups couldn't discriminate based on the particular group's point of view. In this case, the school allowed civic, social, and recreation groups to use the building, but prohibited religious groups from using it. An evangelistic church group wanted to use the building to show a film series on family values and child rearing.

They were turned down and sued. They won. The court held that if a civic group had wanted to show the films, they would have been allowed. The result was that the school was discriminating against a particular point of view, which was a violation of the free speech clause.[16] So the rule now seems to be this: You don't have to allow meetings in your school building, but if you do, you can't pick and choose who you let in.

◆ ACTION STEPS ◆

If students in your child's class vote to have a religious speech, a prayer or invocation at a school function and you and your child disagree with this decision, take action.

First, write to the principal and the head of the school board stating your opposition to the proposed religious speech, and that you believe it violates the First Amendment. State clearly that if the speech isn't stopped immediately, you will go to federal court to seek a temporary restraining order against the school, and will ask the school pay your attorney's fees.

Get any other parents you can find to support you, and seek support in the community. Use the media, carefully. Write a reasoned, restrained letter to the editor of your newspaper. Don't make it a personality clash, stick to the issue of separation of church and state, and the possible negative effects on children of other religions.

If nothing else works, have your lawyer go to court.

This is one of many religion questions that may come up. If you feel your school has gone too far with a religious program or policy, you should:

- Find out what policy, if any, your district has concerning the particular problem. This is almost always a helpful first question and may lead to a quick resolution of the problem. You may also consult a lawyer familiar with education law in your state.

- Discuss the problem with the principal to see if it can be resolved at that level.

- Contact your state department of education, if the principal can't help.

- As a last resort, if the problem remains unresolved, you may consider legal action.

There's considerable public sentiment for more prayer in public schools, in part because many people fear their children aren't being inculcated with proper values. There have been proposals over the years for a constitutional amendment to allow prayer in public schools. Obviously, if you support that notion, you can write your congressman or join with like-minded parents. But many schools across the country have found a constitutionally acceptable alternative to teaching values, and that is the character education movement. Several states, including Mississippi, New Jersey, and New Hampshire, and many cities, including St. Louis, Seattle, Chicago and San Antonio, have embraced the movement, and more schools are looking into it every day. The goal is to teach children right from wrong, to teach them basic values and moral reasoning.

In schools that have adopted the idea, teachers either teach separate classes on values, or, more commonly, incorporate instruction on values into the entire curriculum. Here's how it usually happens, said Professor Thomas Lickona of the State University of New York at Cortland, who many consider the national leader of the character education movement:

The faculty at a school will study character education either in summer programs, at faculty seminars, or through courses at nearby colleges. They'll learn how to incorporate lessons in such values as honesty, responsibility, respect, and fairness. They will design ways to put these lessons to use. For example, Lickona said, a school might designate a value of the month. If honesty is the value for October, students could write essays about honesty, discuss the benefits of honesty, or look for examples of honesty throughout history. The idea is to not to teach religion, but core values. Your parents group could initiate your school's involvement in the movement by bringing it up in informal discussions with the principal or at meetings with faculty members.

Character education is a complex issue. As with sex education, it raises the question of what role parents should play, and what role schools should play. Clearly, the parent should be the primary teacher of moral values, the principal architect of a child's character. In thinking about character education, schools must emphasize and reinforce the role of the parent.

◆ SELECTED QUESTIONS ◆

Can religious materials be posted in classrooms or handed out in schools?

No and no. The Supreme Court shot down a Kentucky law requiring that the Ten Commandments be posted in classrooms.[17] In a more recent case, a federal appeals court upheld a ban against distribution of bibles by the Gideon Society to a fifth grade class.[18] Where this becomes iffy is when religious groups pass out announcements of upcoming events. If, for example, members of a certain religion pass out announcements of a march or demonstration, do those announcements constitute "religious materials"? If you are faced with this situation, first find out what school policy is. If there is no policy, urge your principal or school board to clarify the issue by creating a policy.

Is it legal to give tax credits to the parents of parochial school students?

The courts initially shot down such plans. But a Minnesota tax credit plan was upheld, in large measure because it offered tax credits for educational expenses to all parents.[19] In other words, you could deduct the money you spent for your child's education from your income taxes. The Supreme Court upheld this scheme even though, because public schools were free, the benefits went overwhelmingly to the parents who were paying to keep their children in private schools, which were mostly parochial schools. This may be a harbinger of things to come with regard to vouchers.

Would public vouchers to private or parochial schools be unconstitutional?

Many political leaders favor offering vouchers to students to use at any school, public or private. They claim vouchers would create competition, which would improve public schools, and they say the public's responsibility is to provide education, not support an educational system. Opponents say this idea will ruin the public schools and further divide the haves and have-nots.

Two decades ago, the Supreme Court likely would have found vouchers to parochial schools a violation of the First Amendment. But as education law expert Thomas B. Mooney says, the landscape is changing today, and it's hard to tell if voucher opponents can rely on constitutional prohibitions. Proponents may prevail with the argument that the benefit goes to the parents, not the school. Mooney says the voucher question may have to be debated strictly on its merits, on whether or not it works.

Can students stay out of school on religious holidays without penalty?

Yes, that is the custom in nearly all of the country, at least with major holidays of major religions. Others have to be negotiated with school officials.

Is it legal to create a public school for members of a particular religion?

No. In 1994 the Supreme Court heard a case about a school district created in the village of Kiryas Joel in New York, a village of Hasidic

Jews. The district was to educate 13 special education students. The children had been educated in annexes to the local yeshiva schools by public school teachers. But when earlier court decisions such as Grand Rapids said public teachers couldn't go into private schools, the village created the special school district. The court found the arrangement unconstitutional, saying that creating a public school district to benefit the members of only one religion was a violation of the establishment clause. The court suggested Grand Rapids and similar decisions that caused the problem be reconsidered and possibly overturned.[20] So it's possible public school teachers will again be allowed back in private schools, under some circumstances.

If prayer isn't allowed in schools, is it also illegal to teach religion in schools?

Note this distinction. It is illegal to pray in school or to proselytize a particular religion. But it is not illegal to teach about religion. Professor Thomas Lickona said there is increasing dialogue from across the political spectrum that there is a place for the discussion of religion in public schools. Lickona said every major social movement in the country had its origins in religious beliefs. Not to understand this is not to understand the origin and nuances of our culture, he said.

FOR FURTHER INFORMATION

Center for the 4th and 5th Rs (Respect and Responsibility)
Education Department SUNY-Cortland
Cortland, NY 13045
607–753–2455

Josephson Institute of Ethics
4640 Admiralty Way, Suite 1001
Marina Del Rey, CA 90292
310–306–1868

Center for the Advancement of Ethics and Character
Boston University
605 Commonwealth Avenue
Boston, MA 02215
617–353–2000

American Civil Liberties Union
132 W.43rd Street
New York, NY 10036
212–944–9800

Council for American Private Education
1726 M Street NW, Suite 1102
Washington, DC 20006
202–488–7000

American Association of Christian Schools
P.O. Box 1088
Fairfax, VA 22030
703–818–7150

National Catholic Education Association
1077 30th Street NW, Suite 100
Washington, DC 20007
202–337–6232

People for the American Way
2000 M Street NW, Suite 400
Washington, DC 20036
202–467–4999

NOTES

1. See Justice Douglas's concurrence in *Lemon* v. *Kurtzman,* 403 U.S. 602, 91 S. Ct. 2105 (1971).

2. *Everson* v. *Board of Education,* 330 U.S. 1 (1947).

3. *Board of Education* v. *Allen,* 392 U.S. 236, 243 (1968).

4. *Lemon* v. *Kurtzman,* 403 U.S. 602 (1971).

5. *Wolman* v. *Walter,* 433 U.S. 229 (1977).

6. *Grand Rapids School District* v. *Ball,* 105 S. Ct. 3216 (1985).

7. *Aguilar* v. *Felton,* 105 S. Ct. 3232 (1985). See also *McCollum* v. *Board of Education,* 333 U.S. 204 (1948), in which the court disallowed a program where Protestant, Catholic, and Jewish clergymen came into the school during "released time" to teach religion. But the court upheld a New York program that allowed youngsters on released time to leave school and go to religion classes: See *Zorach* v. *Clauson,* 343 U.S. 306 (1952).

8. *Zobrest* v. *Catlina Foothills School District,* 113 S. Ct. 2462 (1993).

9. *Engel* v. *Vitale,* 370 U.S. 421 (1962).

10. *Abington School District* v. *Schempp*, 374 U.S. 203 (1963).

11. *Duffy* v. *Las Cruces Public Schools*, 557 F. Supp. 1013 (D.N.M. 1983).

12. *Lee* v. *Weisman*, 908 F. 2d. 1090, 111 S. Ct. 1305 (1991).

13. *Jones* v. *Clear Creek Independent School District*, 977 F. 2d 963 (5th Circ. 1992, cert. denied, 1993) and *Harris* v. *Joint School District No. 241*, 821 F. Supp. 638 (D. Idaho 1993).

14. *Widmar* v. *Vincent*, 102 S. Ct. 269 (1982) and *Lubbock Civil Liberties Union* v. *Lubbock Independent School District*, 669 F. 2d 1038 (5th Cir. 1982).

15. *Board of Education of the Westside Community Schools* v. *Mergens*, 110 S. Ct. 2356 (1990).

16. *Lamb's Chapel* et al. v. *Center Moriches School District*, slip opinion 91: 2024 (1993).

17. *Stone* v. *Graham*, 449 U.S. 39, 101 S. Ct. 192 (1980).

18. *Berger* v. *Rensselaer Central School Corporation*, 982 F. 2d 1160 (7th Cir. 1993).

19. *Mueller* v. *Allen*, 433 U.S. 388 (1983).

20. *Village of Kiryas Joel* v. *Grumet*, 62 U.S.L.W. 4665 (1994).

RACIAL
QUESTIONS
IN SCHOOLS

◆ INTRODUCTION ◆

In the 1960s Dr. Martin Luther King, Jr., had a dream that the children of slaves and the children of slave owners would one day sit at the same table. King fervently hoped black and white youngsters would go to school together and live together in an integrated America.

King was killed in 1968 before his dream was realized. Since then, many schools have been named after him. Sadly, as Jonathan Kozol has noted, most of these schools are in urban centers and are racially segregated. King's dream still eludes millions of American youngsters, black and white. America still struggles with the challenge of making the pot's ingredients melt together, of becoming a multicultural democracy.

Because the fight goes on, parents still face questions connected to race. This chapter looks at the history of court-ordered desegregation and also considers:

- *Have desegregation programs worked?*

- *Where do integration efforts stand now?*

- *Do integrated schools improve educational opportunities for white and minority youngsters?*
- *What discriminatory practices are illegal?*

◆ DISCUSSION ◆

Race relations have been characterized as the American dilemma. Clearly, learning to live together has been our greatest challenge as a society and schools have been a focal point of this challenge. Although slavery was abolished during the Civil War, racial prejudice was not. In the South and in some of the rest of the country, African Americans were forced to attend separate schools. This arrangement was given official approval by the U.S. Supreme Court in the infamous 1896 decision *Plessy* v. *Ferguson.* Under the doctrine of "separate but equal," the court said equality of treatment is reached when substantially equal facilities are provided, even when they are separate.[1]

One of the many fundamental problems with this theory was that the facilities were almost never equal. Blacks always got the worst schools, books, and facilities. However, by the 1940s and 50s, the NAACP's Legal Defense Fund, headed by Thurgood Marshall, began to fight back. The first few cases they brought and won involved black, public graduate schools that were patently inferior to their white counterparts.[2]

Some school officials in the South started to sense which way the wind was blowing and began building spanking new brick schools for blacks. It was too late for the separate but equal doctrine. In 1954 cases from four states were joined and heard by the U.S. Supreme Court. The decision is known by the name of the case from Topeka, Kansas, *Brown* v. *Board of Education,* and is one of the best known Supreme Court decisions. Chief Justice Earl Warren said segregated schools are "inherently unequal," and that when laws create such schools, those laws are unconstitutional and must be struck down. Students in segregated schools are "denied equal protection of the laws." Warren said that in the field of public education, "the doctrine of 'separate but equal' has no place."[3]

The strong definitive language of Brown suggested it might sweep away school desegregation immediately, but it didn't. Actually, for more than a decade, not much happened. For one thing, it wasn't immediately clear if the court was just saying segregation was unconstitutional, or was going a step further and ordering states to integrate their schools. A year later, a federal judge ruled that states didn't have to integrate as such, all they had to do was not deny anyone entrance to any school.[4] For several years, schools that didn't want to integrate weren't required to.

Some Southern officials did everything they could to stop integration. Federal troops had to be called out to escort black children in Little Rock, Arkansas. Some districts closed all public schools and gave students vouchers to attend private schools. This practice was finally shot down by the Supreme Court in 1964.[5] In the mid-1950s, jurists thought racial desegregation would happen "with all deliberate speed." A decade later, it was clear this wasn't happening.

SIX YEARS OF PROGRESS

The courts began getting help in the school integration battle from other branches of government. Federal civil rights legislation, and the threat of withholding federal funds, helped local school officials to see the light. But it became clear that more court action would be necessary.

The first major case came in 1968. Some schools across the South had tried to comply with judicial demands for integration by establishing "freedom of choice" or "free transfer" programs, in which black or white parents could choose to send their children to any school in the district. The problem in many districts was that black parents weren't choosing to send their children to white schools, and vice-versa. In other words, choice wasn't working as a tool for integration.

Such was the case in rural New Kent County, Virginia. There were two schools there, one black and one white, and children were actually bused to segregated schools. The county put in a choice program, and no white students opted for the black school, and no black children chose the white school.

Black parents challenged this arrangement. The case went the Supreme Court, which held that if a school district's plan for integration wasn't working, it had to come up with a plan that would work.⁶ In this important case, the court held that the district had to "effectuate a change" toward a "unitary, nonracial" school system. The next year the court went even further. It ordered the 17 Southern and border states that continued to operate dual school systems to immediately stop this unconstitutional practice and begin operating "unitary schools."⁷

In many rural parts of the South, where there was no housing segregation, schools could be integrated by simply assigning the students to their nearest school. A different question was posed in large cities. What if there was segregated housing? How could you then integrate schools?

The court faced this dilemma in a case from the city of Charlotte, North Carolina, and surrounding Mecklenburg County.⁸ The county school system was the 43rd largest in the country, with 84,000 students. It had maintained segregated schools. In deciding which of several plans to adopt, the court made several important decisions about school desegregation:

- The court for the first time sanctioned forced busing as a tool to bring about integration.
- The court allowed one-race schools to continue to exist, but said they would be closely scrutinized to make sure they weren't caused by state-sponsored segregation.
- The court allowed the district to alter school attendance zones to effectuate integration.
- While giving federal judges wide latitude, the court allowed limited use of racial quotas to help remedy past segregation.

Thus far, most cases had involved legal, or "de jure," segregation in the South. What about the North and West? Those parts of the country didn't have de jure segregation. Or did they? A case from Denver answered that question in the affirmative. The court found that by site selection and pupil assignment—in this case, in the Park Hill section of Denver—a school can violate the constitutional rights of minority children.⁹

The case opened the door to citywide busing in the North and West. It said practices such as locating a segregated school in the middle of a minority neighborhood, or not sending minority children in an overcrowded school to a nearby white school with room, were forms of state-sponsored segregation and were unconstitutional. Another notable result of the Denver case was the order that Latino children be integrated with Anglo children.

After the Charlotte and Denver cases, the floodgates opened. Hundreds of desegregation cases and busing orders were filed in cities around the country. Many of these orders were initially met with violence and vituperation, but most were followed. Some even worked.

As Harvard University school desegregation expert Gary Orfield points out in his excellent book, *Must We Bus?* (Brookings Institution, Washington, D.C., 1978), this rapid array of court orders were all over the legal lot. Some demanded immediate desegregation and proportional enrollment in every school. Other judges ordered gradual, and sometimes only partial, desegregation. In districts where black students predominated, decisions were "perplexingly diverse," Orfield says. In some cases, schools desegregated by placing a minority of white students in each school. In other districts, courts did nothing at all.

But in most cases, something was done. Busing was a volatile political issue in many cities. Nonetheless, civil rights advocates thought they saw a new day dawning. It looked like a generation of American children might finally go to integrated schools. But a case in 1974 stopped much of that momentum, cold.

DETROIT CITY LIMITS

As desegregation cases began reaching the courts in large numbers, an obvious question presented itself. If a city was unconstitutionally segregated, and the city was largely minority, could the courts reach across the district lines to remedy the situation? Could the court order that youngsters be taken out of the inner-city minority schools and be placed in mostly white suburban schools?

After failing to agree on a case from Richmond, Virginia, in 1973, the court faced the question again in 1974 with a case from Detroit. Because the city schools were then almost 70 percent minority, a lower court had reasoned that the only way to integrate them was to allow city students to attend schools in 59 surrounding suburban districts.

In a tense political atmosphere, a divided court overturned the lower-court decision and ruled 5–4 against interdistrict desegregation, unless it could be shown that the state or suburban districts helped cause the segregation in the city schools. The court could find no evidence of this in the Detroit case.[10]

Civil rights advocates were stunned. They had argued that the Detroit school system couldn't be integrated by itself. Justice Thurgood Marshall, who had argued so eloquently for Topeka's children in the *Brown* case, wrote in his angry dissent that the court had provided Detroit's children with "no remedy at all." Thus ended the most active period in U.S. school desegregation.

Whether a child gets an integrated education now is often a factor of where he or she was born, a city or county school system. In a county system such as Charlotte-Mecklenburg, children are being bused throughout the system for integration. In Richmond, an area with about the same number of students but with a city district and several suburban school districts, the story is different. Youngsters in the mostly minority city district stay there, as do the kids in the mostly white suburban districts. With few exceptions, they don't get an integrated education.

The Detroit case still stands, more than two decades later. Many believe it greatly increased white flight from most of our large cities and their school systems, leaving them overwhelmingly full of poor, minority children. The Council of the Great City Schools, representing 47 of the largest districts in the country, report their districts now average 75 percent minority children.

WHERE WE STAND NOW

It's not fair to say that all school integration stopped after the Detroit case. In some cases, courts were able to reach out across district lines. In St. Louis, for example, a court settlement gave inner-city children the right to attend suburban schools. Now, about 13,500 St. Louis youngsters are bused out of the city, and about 1,000 suburban youngsters are bused into magnet school programs in the city.

Some argue, persuasively, that this isn't a perfect solution. They say that better students are chosen for choice programs or magnet schools, which only makes things worse for the kids left behind. Indeed, there is considerable sentiment in St. Louis to drop the program. Nonetheless, if an integrated society, a melting pot, is the goal, then the choice programs and magnet programs are something. At least they get kids of different races into the same schools.

Also, hundreds of thousands of minorities have reached the middle class and moved to the suburbs in the past 30 years. However, this suburbanization hasn't always caused a dramatic change in desegregation numbers, because minority housing patterns in the suburbs are often segregated, just as they were in the cities.

Nonetheless, in scores of small and middle-sized communities, school desegregation programs have worked. In Charlotte, for example, 9,000 of 82,000 students are still bused for integration purposes. The schools are integrated, and getting good results. Whites didn't flee the city. In retrospect, officials praise the court decision.

"It was a great decision," former Charlotte school superintendent Dr. Peter Relic said in an interview. "The judge (James McMillan) stated a great confidence in the community to do it, and that was the driving force to do it right. One key was that resources were added to schools receiving students for integration, so the students wanted to go to them."

"Nobody was crazy about it," said school board spokesman David Hains, "but most people kind of agreed it was necessary, and we had strong community leaders who made it happen . . . One of the best things is that it's done, and we've been able to spend our energy on other things we needed: an airport, an auditorium, a football team, a basketball team . . . "

Desegregation plans have also achieved reasonable degrees of success in Louisville, Kentucky; Tampa, Florida; Wilmington, Delaware; Nashville, Tennessee; and Greensboro, North Carolina.

TODAY

But despite these successes, the overall national picture on integration hasn't improved much since the mid-1970s. According to a 1988 study by the National School Boards Association, affirmed with a 1992 study, there's been no progress in integration of black students since the 70s, and the segregation of Hispanic students has gotten significantly worse.[11]

In recent cases, cities have been looking to dismantle desegregation plans, and courts have been willing to let them, if the city appears to have made a reasonable effort to integrate. Oklahoma City once had segregated schools and segregated housing. In 1972, after a decade of litigation, a federal court ordered the city to integrate. The order was extremely strict; each school had to reflect the racial balance of the entire city. After two decades, local officials went back to court to say they had done the job and asked the court to lift the order.

The case reached the Supreme Court, which sent it to a federal district court to determine if the order should be terminated. The judge agreed to lift the order.[12] The segregation order came despite the fact that the city still has schools that are heavily identifiable by race. According to the *Daily Oklahoman*, nine schools in the northeast part of town are about 90 percent minority, while five schools in other parts of the city are 80 percent white.[13]

Nonetheless, the court held that the city had made a good-faith effort to eradicate the "vestiges of a dual system." Blacks, the court said, once could only live in one part of town, but now lived in every school district. If there was residential segregation left, it was a matter of private choice, of such factors as economic status and housing availability, and not the old de jure segregation, the court said. At most, black and white preferences and income disparities may be caused by "general societal discrimination," but that, the court said, cannot be laid at the feet of the Oklahoma City school board.

The court said the board had eliminated school segregation "to the extent practicable," although it's a little unclear what "practicable" means. The court also said it is "impracticable" to keep busing forever and a neighborhood school policy is not unconstitutional, even if a racially identifiable school is the result. A neighborhood school could lead to more parental and community involvement, the court said.

Finally, the court said the city had a free transfer program, which meant a minority student could choose to transfer to a predominantly majority school, theoretically opening all schools in the city to all prospective minority students. An appeal of the decision was turned down by the 10th Circuit Court of Appeals in the fall of 1993. While local civil rights advocates condemned the decision, supporters said the city was in fact much better integrated than it was two or three decades ago.

In another case, the high court allowed a court-supervised desegregation order in De Kalb County, Georgia, to be dismantled in stages, saying the county had reached some of its goals. The court also held that a school district was under no obligation to remedy segregation "caused by demographic factors."[14]

While neither of these cases appears to resolve the school segregation issue, they clearly represent a stepping back from *Brown* and the years of judicial activism for integration. After Oklahoma City and De Kalb, other cities under desegregation orders presumably have an out. They can claim that today's segregated schools and housing are the results of "demographics," and get their court orders lifted. This means, as one lawyer put it, there's no *Brown* remedy left in federal court to stop school segregation.

Some proponents of court-ordered integration are trying a new tack, filing cases in state courts, basing their claims on state constitutional provisions calling for equal education. Such cases have been filed in Minneapolis, Minnesota, and in Hartford, Connecticut. Both claim urban youngsters aren't getting an equal education because of the heavy concentration of poverty in the respective cities, and both claim their systems are underfunded. If integrationists won both cases, we might see another flurry of desegregation cases across the country. Time will tell. At this writing, the plaintiffs in Connecticut lost at the trial level and are awaiting judgment on appeal, while the Minnesota case has yet to be heard. The "concentration of poverty" argument raises a complicating question in these cases: Do urban students suffer from racial or economic segregation? Often, the poorest families in a region live in its inner city. Poverty is connected to several major pathologies—crime, drugs, gangs, teen pregnancy—that lead to family breakdown. This, sadly, translates to children who aren't ready to start school or who are disruptive in school. Too many of these children in one class "tips" the class, as some teachers say, making it very difficult to teach. This is the core problem with many schools, yet it is becoming increasingly difficult to solve it with lawsuits about racial segregation.

When busing orders were first put in place, most people thought they wouldn't last. They thought cities would integrate and the busing orders would be needed no longer. It's happened in some places, and it hasn't happened in many others, despite a lot of effort. In many of our large cities, the rhetoric now is about "quality schools" rather than "quality integrated schools." While this may be the only hope at the moment, it isn't encouraging. Making a minority urban school as good as a white suburban school sounds a lot like "separate but equal," the catch phrase from *Plessy* v. *Ferguson* a century ago.

WHY ARE WE DOING THIS?

Many people believe the neighborhood school ought to be the national model for a public school, regardless of the demographic status of the school. There are indeed many good arguments for neighborhood schools: They encourage more parental and community involvement, they require kids to spend less time in transit, they make after-school programs easier to arrange. But do students miss something if they are in a single-race school?

Some research indicates that minority students do better academically in integrated schools, while white students do no worse. This is one of the arguments in favor of regional desegregation plans. But other researchers such as Dr. Mary Kennedy of Michigan State University say these conclusions are far from certain. She said it isn't clear that dispersing minority children from a poor urban neighborhood to a white, wealthy, suburban neighborhood is in the best interest of the city youngsters. "It may take away the support systems they have. There are a lot of subtleties to this that we don't fully understand," she said.

Other factors such as available funding, well-trained teachers and parental involvement can be more important in determining how well a minority student will do in school than who his classmates are.

While integration may or may not improve the education of students, many experts are convinced integration does improve the socialization of children. Majority and minority children who go to school together learn to live together. An extensive study by Dr. James McPartland of the Center for the Social Organization of Schools at Johns Hopkins University and two other experts on desegregation, Dr. Robert L. Crain and Dr. Jomills Henry Braddock, shows that both black and white children educated in an integrated environment are more likely to live successfully in a multiracial work and residential environment.

The study, "A Long-Term View of School Desegregation: Some Recent Studies of Graduates as Adults," found that blacks and whites from desegregated schools are more likely to be working in multiracial firms and companies, have multi-racial social contacts and live in integrated neighborhoods. Also, the study found, employers gave preference to blacks from desegregated schools. Because the vast majority of employers are white, blacks from segregated schools are at an obvious disadvantage.

So, it would seem, the integrated society Martin Luther King dreamed of should be a national goal. What can a parent do?

◆ ACTION STEPS ◆

The early remedies for segregated schools were redistricting and voluntary or involuntary busing across district lines. As we have seen, courts today are backing away from ordering students to be bused to achieve desegregation. Court decisions have also greatly limited redistricting as an option. It isn't likely that many school districts will see new busing or redistricting orders. Where does this leave parents who want to send their child to school in a multiracial environment? You can:

- Move to a different neighborhood or town. It's a little extreme, and probably out of the question for most parents, but some have done it.

- Send your child to a private school. As we suggested earlier, those who have the money have school choice. More than a few parents have sent their children to private schools because the private school had more of a multicultural student body than the local public school.

- Send your child to an interdistrict magnet school. Magnet schools are probably the most popular desegregation remedy today. Just make sure the magnet school wasn't set up too hastily and can offer thematic continuity. For example, if you have the chance to send your child to an elementary magnet where the theme is, say, Latin and Greek, but there is no high school program in Latin and Greek, then think twice.

As a member of your parent-teacher group, you can also:

- Urge your school to take part in voluntary programs that bring students of other races to your school as students, perhaps from nearby urban areas.

- Create a partnership arrangement with a school where most students are members of a different race or ethnic group. This could involve pen pal programs, classroom visits, jointly sponsored programs, music events, sports programs, simultaneous televised programs, and other projects. To work, these programs must involve frequent contact, says Professor David Reuman of Trinity College in Hartford, Connecticut. He said frequent contact allows students to get to know each other as individuals. Otherwise, brief contact might simply reinforce stereotypes.

- Urge your school to use a multicultural curriculum. There are curriculums teachers can use to teach students about multiculturalism. One of the best known is "A World of Difference" from the Anti-Defamation League. The Nation Conference, formerly the National Conference of Christians and Jews, offers a curriculum called "Actions Speak Louder" for Brotherhood/Sisterhood Week in February. One unique aspect of this program is a segment in which students create a "label junkyard," in which each child writes down a label he or she would never like to hear again, and all get thrown into the junkyard. Parents groups can review these curriculums by contacting the sponsoring organizations (end of chapter).

- Parents' groups can use widely publicized events such as the Rodney King beating or the O. J. Simpson trial to invite persons of other races to participate in school discussions of matters related to race and multiculturalism.

DISCRIMINATION IS STILL WRONG

While racial desegregation has stalled in many parts of the country in the past 25 years, we've made some progress is a related area, racial discrimination. It is against the law for a school or school board to discriminate against students or faculty on account of race. To see how a school district that on paper appeared integrated could practice massive racial discrimination, consider a federal magistrate's report about the Rockford, Illinois, school system.[15]

In Rockford, minority and white children went to the same schools. But that was about the extent of integration. In many of the schools:

- Blacks and whites were educated in separate classrooms.
- Blacks and whites ate at different lunch times and entered through different doors.
- Black and whites used separate bathrooms in separate corridors.
- Latino students going to white neighborhoods for bilingual classes had to wait on the bus until school started, while Anglo students got to play in the playground.
- Minority students were "tracked" into slow learning or remedial classes, while whites went into college prep and honors tracks. Some of the minority students placed in slow classes had tested in the 90th percentile. As we noted in Chapter Six, this has been a problem for decades.

Magistrate P. Michael Mahoney said the school district "practiced such open acts of discrimination as to be cruel." A federal court order is being prepared to remedy the situation.

Rockford isn't alone. Richmond, Virginia, parents recently complained that white students were being "clustered" in certain schools. Under threat of federal intervention, the school district took action to resolve the problem.[16] Yonkers, New York, had the inverse of this problem: minority students being clustered.[17] In Cicero, Illinois, according to Professor Orfield of Harvard, a principal drove a black student to Chicago rather than allow him into a local school. He changed his mind when faced with a court action.

◆ Action Steps ◆

As we said earlier, courts have held that discriminatory testing and placement, as well as discriminatory tracking, is illegal. Also, several suits have challenged disproportionate disciplining and suspension of minority children.[18] These cases stand for the proposition that racial or ethnic discrimination in school discipline is illegal. Courts have also held on many occasions that school faculties and staffs must be integrated as well as student bodies.[19]

If you suspect that your school is practicing racial or ethnic discrimination, you can:

- Bring the matter to the attention of school officials and school board members. Ask for a meeting to discuss the matter quietly. This should be an informational meeting; bring as much information as you can, ask as many questions as you can.

- If the meeting fails to resolve the problem, there is a state agency you can appeal to. It may be called the Civil Rights Commission, the Commission Against Discrimination, Human Rights and Opportunities Commission, or something like this. There may also be a city commission or agency handling such complaints first.

- Call your local chapter of the Urban League, NAACP, or American Civil Liberties Union and discuss the matter. They may be able to suggest the name of an experienced civil rights lawyer in your area with whom to discuss the matter.

- If the matter isn't settled to your satisfaction, you may file a complaint with the U.S. Department of Education's Office for Civil Rights, which is located at 400 Maryland Avenue, SW, Washington, D.C. In addition to enforcing Title IX's prohibition against sex discrimination, the civil rights division also enforces federal laws that bar discrimination based on race, age and disability.

- If minorities are underrepresented on your faculty and staff, look into it. Before taking the matter to your superintendent, study the union contract. Some union contracts have provisions meant to encourage racially balanced faculties at schools. If your contract has such a provision, it should help get the matter straightened out. Take it to the school board and superintendent. Recruit community leaders to help. Find out what's been going on. If what you believe is true, insist that it be changed.

◆ SELECTED QUESTIONS ◆

Our school district is considering establishing an Afrocentric curriculum. What is an Afrocentric curriculum?

The short answer is that the terms "Afrocentric curriculum" or "African-centered education" refer to a variety of efforts in mostly large cities across the country to recognize the contributions of Africa and African Americans to the worlds of culture and learning. However, critics say some of these curriculums go too far, and are racist and unscholarly.

In several major cities, including Baltimore, Detroit, Milwaukee, and Portland, schools with Afrocentric curriculums have been started in the last couple of years. These schools stress the achievements of African Americans and use some African materials to teach basic subjects and, proponents say, build self-esteem among students. At Malcolm X Academy in Detroit, students wear uniforms and discipline is strict. Cleotha Jordan, who directs the Detroit program, said 15 of the city's 250 schools now use an Afrocentric curriculum, and said a school with a Native-American curriculum is due to open soon. She said the idea behind the Afrocentric curriculum is to let children see what people who look like them accomplished, in order to build self-respect, self worth and a sense of community.

However, critics charge some Afrocentric curriculums go way too far. In some, for example, there is a huge emphasis on Ancient Egypt, with claims that these Africans really started most of the mathematical and philosophical principles usually credited to the Greeks. Many scholars, including many African-American scholars, say this just isn't so. Many Afrocentric materials "offer shoddy scholarship and some even promote intolerance and racism," said Linda Chavez, director of the Manhattan Institute's Center for the New American Community. For a critique of Afrocentrism, see "Alternatives to Afrocentrism" a series of essays published by the Manhattan Institute, 1745 N Street NW, Washington, DC 20036 (202–466–7300).

Some criticize Afrocentric schools because they go against the grain of integrated public schools. Defenders liken them to the traditional black colleges, where blacks have gone for an education, then joined the larger society. Perhaps the argument was given perspective by a teacher at one of the schools, who said the Afrocentric schools that make it will be those with decent resources, strong parental involvement and smaller classes.

When is a school considered desegregated?

From a strictly legal point of view, a school is considered desegregated if at least one minority student attends. A school is considered integrated, or racially balanced, if the percentage of minority students reasonably reflects the percentage of minority students in the whole system. Of course, it doesn't mean much if a school district is one percent minority, and a school has a one percent minority student body.

Our district has a 12 percent minority student body, but 35 percent of the children in special education classes are members of minority groups. Is there something wrong with this picture?

Yes. Over-placement of minority children in special education classes has been a problem in many districts around the country. In some cases, teachers used special education as an escape valve when they couldn't cope with cultural diversity. It isn't fair to the children. Set up a meeting with the principal. Get the problem on the table. Present the numbers. Get case-by-case information on why so many minority students were referred to special ed. Ask for a reappraisal. If the administration won't respond, talk to your state education officials.

FOR FURTHER INFORMATION

Anti-Defamation League Training Division
World of Difference Institute
823 U.N. Plaza
New York, NY 10017
212–490–2525

National Conference
71 Fifth Avenue
New York, NY 10003
1–800–352–6225

Center for the Social Organization of Schools
The Johns Hopkins University
3505 N. Charles Street
Baltimore, MD 212128
410–516–8800

Council of Urban Boards of Education
National School Boards Association
1680 Duke Street
Alexandria, VA 22314
703–838–6722

Educational Equity Project
Institute for Public Policy Studies
Vanderbilt University
Peabody College
Box 516
Nashville, TN 37203
615–322–8104

NOTES

1. *Plessy* v. *Ferguson,* 163 U.S. 537 (1896).

2. *Sweatt* v. *Painter,* 70 S. Ct. 848 (1950).

3. *Brown* v. *Board of Education,* 347 U.S. 483 (1954).

4. *Briggs* v. *Elliot,* 132 F. Supp. 776 (E.D.S.C. 1955).

5. *Griffin* v. *County School Board of Prince Edward County,* 84 S. Ct. 1226 (1964).

6. *Green* v. *County School Board,* 391 U.S. 430 (1968).

7. *Alexander* v. *Holmes,* 396 U.S. 19, 90 S. Ct. 29 (1969).

8. *Swann* v. *Charlotte-Mecklenberg Board of Education,* 402 U.S. 1, 91 S. Ct. 1267 (1971).

9. *Keyes* v. *School District No. 1,* 413 U.S. 139, 93 S. Ct. 2686 (1973).

10. *Milliken* v. *Bradley,* 418 U.S. 717, 94 S. Ct. 3112 (1974).

11. Orfield, Gary; Monfort, Franklin; Aaron, Melissa, "Status of School Desegregation," (1989), National School Boards Association, Alexandria, Va.

12. *Dowell* v. *Board of Education of the Oklahoma City Public Schools,* 778 F. Supp. 1144 (1991, 1992).

13. Sanger, Lillie-Beth, and Boczkiewicz, Robert, "Court Closes Book on Forced Desegregation," *Daily Oklahoman,* Nov. 5, 1993.

14. *Freeman* v. *Pitts,* 112 S. Ct. 1430, 118 L. Ed. 2d 108 (1992).

15. Pasternak, Judy, "Illinois City Accused of Racial Shell Game," *The Los Angeles Times,* Nov. 8, 1993.

16. Chira, Susan, "Housing and Fear Upend Integration," *The New York Times,* Feb. 14, 1993.

17. "Yonkers: The Price of Desgregation," *The New York Times* editorial, July 3, 1993.

18. *Ross* v. *Saltmarsh,* 500 F. Supp. 935 (E.D.N.Y. 1980).

19. *Morgan* v. *Kerrigan,* 509 F. 2d 580 (2d Cir. 1974).

INDEX

Injuries, 162–77
　action steps, 168–69
　information sources, 176–77
　negligence and, 163–64
　school gym rentals and, 174–75
　school's level of duty and, 164–68
　sports and, 169–74
Institute for Responsive Education (Boston),
　21
Insubordination, 74
Integration. *See* Desegregation
Intentional torts, 163
IQ test, 106, 112, 115
Irving Independent School District v. *Tatro*,
　130–31

Jacob K. Javits Gifted and Talented Students
　Act, 111
Jefferson, Thomas, 2, 252
Joplin Plan, 109
Josephson Institute of Ethics (Marina Del
　Rey, CA), 262

Kentucky, 222–23
Kindergarten, 10–13, 19–20
King, Martin Luther, Jr., 265
Kirby, Douglas, 185–87
Kiryas Joel, NY, 261–62
Kolbe, Lloyd, 179, 180, 181, 183
Korn, George, 41–42
Kozol, Jonathan, 219, 223

Labeling, 87
Language, bilingualism and, 60–63
Learning disabilities, 120. *See also* Special
　education
Lemon Test, 253–54, 258
Lemon v. *Kurtzman*, 253
Lewd and indecent speech, 141–42
Liberty, deprivation of, 154–55
Lickona, Thomas, 259, 262
Lim, Jeanette, 247–48
Lincoln, Abraham, 228
Little Alternative Public Schools, 8
Local education funds, 227–28
Locker searches, 153
Los Angeles City Elementary School Music
　Association, 65
Los Angeles Education Partnership, 227
Loshbough, Bill, 30
Lowell High School (San Francisco), 243
Lowering grades, 157–58
Low-income parents, assistance available to,
　19, 195
Lunch programs, 194–96

Magnet schools, 8, 270, 271, 276
Mainstreaming, 128–30
Maintenance of building facilities, 228–32,
　233
Malcolm X Academy (Detroit, MI), 279

Malpractice, educational, 87–88
Mann, Horace, 2, 3, 64, 252
Marijuana, 208
Married students, expulsion of, 248
Marshall, Thurgood, 266, 270
Massachusetts, 55, 109–10, 222
Memphis Parent Training program, vii
Mentor programs, 83, 201, 242
Merit pay plans, teacher, 87
METCO (Boston), 7
Michigan, 212–13
Minnesota, 56, 245
Minority children. *See also* Desegregation
　corporal punishment and, 146
　language education and, 60–61
　special education and, 134, 277, 280–81
　testing of, 92–93
　tracking and, 105–7, 277
Moment of silence statutes, 256
Monitor programs, for buses, 32–34
"Monkey Trial," 51
Mooney, Thomas B., 151, 261
Morningstar, Mary, 129–30
Multiculturalism, 54, 276
Music education, 63–67
Muther, Connie, 49–50, 59

NAACP's Legal Defense Fund, 266
Nardelli, Steven, 32, 33
National Assessment of Educational
　Progress, 102, 103
National Association for Gifted Children,
　118
National Association for the Education of
　Young Children, 12, 20
National Association of Elementary School
　Principals, 21
National Association of State Boards of
　Education, 209
National Association of State Directors of
　Special Education, 138
National Catholic Education Association,
　263
National Center for Health Education, 210
National Center For Home Education, 16,
　21
National Center for Research on Teacher
　Learning, 88
National Center for Science Education, 60
National Center for the Study of Corporal
　Punishment and Alternatives, 145,
　160
National Coalition for Music Education, 69
National Coalition of Advocates for
　Students, 160, 209
National Coalition of Education Activists,
　88
National Commission on Excellence in
　Education, 45–46
National Committee for Citizens in
　Education (NCCE), vi, x